Historical Empathy and Perspective Taking in the Social Studies

Historical Empathy and Perspective Taking in the Social Studies

Edited by O. L. Davis Jr., Elizabeth Anne Yeager, and Stuart J. Foster

ROWMAN & LITTLEFIELD PUBLISHERS, INC.
Lanham • Boulder • New York • Oxford

ROWMAN & LITTLEFIELD PUBLISHERS, INC.

Published in the United States of America
by Rowman & Littlefield Publishers, Inc.
4720 Boston Way, Lanham, Maryland 20706
www.rowmanlittlefield.com

12 Hid's Copse Road, Cumnor Hill, Oxford OX2 9JJ, England

Copyright © 2001 by Rowman & Littlefield Publishers, Inc.

British Library Cataloguing in Publication Information Available

Library of Congress Cataloging-in-Publication Data

Historical empathy and perspective taking in the social studies /edited by O.L. Davis Jr., Elizabeth Anne Yeager, and Stuart J. Foster.
   p. cm
   Includes index.
   ISBN 0-8476-9812-2 (alk. paper) — ISBN 0-8476-9813-0 (pbk. : alk. paper)
   1. Social sciences and history. 2. Empathy—social aspects. 3. Social sciences—Methodology. 4. Social psychology. 5. History—Study and teaching. I. Davis, O.L. (Ozro Luke), 1928- II. Yeager, Elizabeth Anne, 1960- III. Foster, Stuart J., 1960-

D16.166 .H56 2001
907—dc21

00-066466

Printed in the United States of America

⊖™ The paper used in this publication meets the minimum requirements of American National Standard for Information Sciences—Permanence of Paper for Printed Library Materials, ANSI/NISO Z39.48-1992.

To Joanie, Meredith, and Oz
—*O. L. D.*

To Jamie and Benjamin
—*E. A. Y.*

To Sean
—*S. J. F.*

The thoughts and resultant actions of (say) a Polish-German day laborer working near Auschwitz in 1944, a person who sees the full trains come and the empty trains go, might be appreciably different from the conclusions about the Holocaust reached by an outraged American teenager sitting in an unthreatened high school classroom fifty years later. It will help the teenager to absorb the complexity if he can reflect from the shoes of the laborer, not necessarily to agree but to empathize, to understand.

—Theodore R. Sizer and Nancy Faust Sizer,
The Students Are Watching: Schools and the Moral Contract

Contents

Chapter 1

In Pursuit of Historical Empathy

O. L. Davis Jr.

The end-of-chapter exercise in my eighth grade class's American history textbook instantly captured my attention. It was unlike any previously included exercise. Although I cannot remember its precise phrasing, it went something like

> You and your family departed Pittsburgh a week ago on your flatboat trip down the Ohio River. You will not reach your destination, at an unknown town in southern Illinois, for several more weeks. Write a letter to a friend back home in which you tell about your experiences and your feelings on the trip.

The class had nearly completed its study of a unit that focused on the opening of the Northwest Territory and Kentucky to settlement. I thought that the textbook exercise held rich possibilities for students to put themselves into both the period and a particular situation, so I assigned the task. A day or so later, I collected the "letters." I remember that I was stunned and very disappointed as I read them.

The thirteen- and fourteen-year-olds in my class dutifully had written letters, most of them short, one-page messages. All mentioned in their letters significant key words of the exercise, e.g., the flatboat journey, the river, and Pittsburgh. However, most of the students only minimally invested themselves in thinking with the facts they had learned about the historical period, the rigors of the voyage, the landscape and people they "might have encountered," uncertainties about the prospects of life in their new home, and concerns about previous circumstances. As I remember, almost all wrote in the present tense, not in some historic "present," but in their own present.

After I read the "letters," I talked with the class members about the assignment. Students, by and large, realized that they wrote their "friends" about what they thought the persons would like to know: mainly that the trip was boring and that the letter writers desperately missed their friends back home. In most cases, "boring" camouflaged either their lack of information or their lack of interest. They realized that they were not involved in the requirements of the exercise. Thinking with and about history simply was a casualty of the moment.

I have thought a number of times about this failed pedagogical encounter across the past forty years. In my professional journey, I have found a word, "empathy," that names the concept that denotes this type of exercise and which I found to be at once so very provocative and vexing. I have thought about the type of involvement expected by such exercises. On occasion, I've written similar, or intentionally better, exercises intended to evoke empathy and perspective taking. I have also thought about the roles of teachers who would attempt to engage students in thinking about historical circumstances and interactions. Without question, I have wondered about how students, young and older, attempt and fail, as well as attempt and succeed, in their efforts "to put themselves into a past time" or to think about an historical circumstance with different perspectives. I have also encouraged and conducted research about historical thinking. Without question, I continue to pursue an increasingly robust understanding of empathy as well as varied means by which individual students may think in context with the history that they study and learn. Importantly, other teachers and other scholars have been similarly interested. This pursuit is not only personal; it is part and parcel of recent efforts to reform history teaching.[1]

National standards published during recent years, not only in the United States, but in other countries as well, generally recognize empathy as an important goal of teaching history. History teachers and textbooks, however, are not ready for this kind of emphasis. Additionally, some historians and a scattering of pundits have objected sharply to this focus and have advocated that teachers ignore this potential focus and increase attention to prominent official narratives. After the draft of the national history curriculum standards for England and Wales was published, some commentators mocked the inclusion of empathy as a concern in school history.[2] One especially ridiculed example, as I remember it, called for children to think of themselves as Roman legionnaires manning Hadrian's Wall and to relate some recent experiences in a letter to their families living in Rome. Not unlike my experience with the Ohio River exercise, this sample exercise is as simplistic as it possibly is provocative.

Pedagogic time spent on such an exercise certainly may be trivial. It need not be, however. It signifies the importance of students' thinking seriously and contextually about particulars of their history studies. Increased development of empathy seems vital to their continuing effort to understand history. Still, assertions of possibility may be only statements of an empty faith. Much more than assertions is needed.

Empathy, Some Dimensions of Its Meaning, and Ideas about Its Development by Students

Too commonly, people misunderstand historical "empathy" as sympathy or a kind of appreciative sentiment. To develop empathy, according to this unfortunate notion, is to develop a positive attitude or feeling toward an individual, event, or situation. Such meanings wreak violence not only against empathy, but, also, against the entire sense of history. In no small part because empathy carries a heavy burden of misuse and misunderstanding, another term, "perspective taking," offers a fruitful assist to meaning. In this book, we do not abandon the term "empathy"; it is too valuable. At the same time, we frequently employ the term "perspective taking" as a means to extend understanding.

Empathy characterizes historical thinking that yields enriched understanding within context.[3] For the most part, it is intellectual in nature, but certainly it may include emotional dimensions. It arises or develops from the active engagement in thinking about particular people, events, and situations in their context, and from wonderment about reasonable and possible meanings within, in a time that no one can really know. It adheres to sensitively crafted narratives, and it may be identified in research and thinking and in the writing or telling of stories and accounts. Frequently, empathy springs from considerations of more than one, even several different, points of view or perspectives. It is robust, tough, and insightful even as it is imaginative, and it is always based upon available evidence.

Historical empathy also represents an end-in-view rather than fulfillment of a destination. It is not a once-and-forever matter. Simply, therefore, individual historians and history students can reach or develop empathy only approximately and always in comparison with the achievement of others. This caveat in no way diminishes the sterling historical thinking of able and sensitive historians, even those whose peers acknowledge them as masters of their craft. Similarly, it also does not permit depreciation of the efforts of younger students. Most scholars, indeed, humbly admit that inquirers who will follow them and who will use the same evidence that they have employed likely will think differently than they have and also may write more richly interpretative portrayals than they have. Major qualitative differences in empathy, nevertheless, surely will exist always in the thinking and writing of individuals who study history. This observation surely is as true for experienced historians as it is for younger students. Improved thinking, more competent interpretations, and more carefully developed ideas represent serious and reasonably ambitious goals for sustained historical inquiry.

Especially, then, teachers and others should accord respect to the thinking and empathic understandings evidenced by students in their engagements with history.[4] Respect, here, acknowledges achievement within the constraints of instructional possibility. It must be informed by the knowledge available to students, by teachers' knowledge both of history and of teaching, by available sources of evidence (e.g., documents, books, and other materials), and by students' progress in the development of their historical thinking, as well as the level of their familiarity with the tasks of thinking with historical evidence. This respect certainly should not dismiss error, ignore implausibility, or honor untenable interpretation. Clearly, the development of empathy in school history is not a whimsical pursuit. Always, it is imagination restrained by evidence.

Perhaps an untoward example is helpful here. Several years ago during my visit to an elementary school, a very pleased fourth-grade teacher called my attention to her students' work on a giant mural across a wall in the school's foyer. The number of children actively at work impressed me. They were enjoying the experience; most were having fun. Many painted figures of individuals. Some drew horses. Others, I noticed, painted cannons firing, solid shot in the air, and bursts of explosives in the sky. I asked the girl who was beginning to write the caption what the mural depicted. It portrayed, she reported, Confederate soldiers fighting German settlers who were unionist sympathizers near the frontier settlement of Fredericksburg, Texas, during the American civil war. The teacher added that the children chose this subject because it appealed to them more than did any other topic that they recently had studied in their Texas history unit. I stood for too long a time to gawk at the scene. A very few elements comported with authentic evidence; most were fictive, translated by unrestrained imagination from televised or filmed images of Civil War battles.

This school scene remains vividly in my memory. It illustrates serious inattention to meanings developed by children who read and talked about an historical incident. The students and the teacher did read historical sources, although they did so superficially; furthermore, they demonstrated incorrect and inadequate understandings of fact and distortions of context and of interpretations. I continue to wonder how and with whom, if anyone, they sought to verify accounts, to consider context, and to think about the meanings of words that they read. One of the special tragedies of the civil war in Texas was the unprovoked raid by confederate irregulars on the German frontier settlement at Fredericksburg. Not only did they terrorize the settlers, the confederates chased them for miles and brutally killed men, women, and children. These German-Texans had remained Unionist sympathizers following the Texas secession. The fourth graders' errors and misshaped thoughts included, for example, cannon and flags that were not actually used in this episode and the absence of terrified women and children who were present. Their painted scene appeared more like a cartoon of a major battle, perhaps like that of Gettysburg, than what actually transpired. The student muralists, I believe, did not intend to misportray; they undoubtedly drew upon what they knew and added a dash of their unrestrained imagination to how they understood combat during the Civil War.

That these students only learned partial and superficial knowledge in their study is serious. Of special, perhaps even of greater concern, is that they did not learn that their knowledge was filled with errors. Their study, to be sure, had not been a consideration of the story, for example, that emphasized different and conflicting perspectives about the war and personal political decisions of conscience, that elaborated context, and that searched for motivations of participants. Skeptics might question whether fourth graders can engage in such thinking. My response is unhesitant: of course they could have. They could have engaged such questions at their own developmental level and with the knowledge that they held. Abundant research in our field, particularly by Levstik and Barton demonstrates that improvement of history teaching cannot rest easily on either doubts or confidence. Clearly, it needs more and more substantial research, increased consideration about children's development of historical meanings, and additional efforts to task children to think and wonder and imagine with knowledge and evidence.

Empathy, Knowledge, and Teaching for the Development of Empathy

Empathy almost never is discounted as a necessary ingredient of proper historical inquiry. Many educational critics and practicing teachers, as well as a number of historians, however, question its emphasis in school history instruction. Two central issues figure in these dissents about the efficacy of the development of empathy by students in school history. Both raise important issues, but neither necessarily is a proscription against empathy nor an unreasonable caution to practice.

In essence, many of the objections to empathy in school history rest upon claims about prior knowledge, in the first instance, and, subsequently, about instructional sequence. These concerns, of course, are intimately related.

Students must possess knowledge in order that they may engage empathy in historical thinking. On that central point, no dispute occurs. In some instances, students must know much information in order that they adequately may think with new evidence; in others situations, they need to possess less knowledge for such tasks. To stress historical empathy in school history courses, a general assumption appears to hold. Students become increasingly able to engage empathy better as they have more historical knowledge with which to think and gain increased experience in taking various historical perspectives or, simply, as they know more history. Still, students' possession of knowledge does not guarantee their ability to think with it. With their knowledge, much or scant, students may hold steadfastly to unsubstantiated or inadequate generalizations. The point remains that students must know, rather more than fewer, historical facts, concepts, and interpretations as they continue their engagements in historical thinking.

However, this substantial position does not argue against empathic instructional tasks in several instructional conditions. For example, young students can engage in some of these tasks; they need not wait until they are enrolled in higher-grade levels and/or take more advanced courses. Similarly, students at different ages and at various stages of their study of history productively can engage such tasks before they know as much, reasonably, as they should or as they later will come to know. Certainly, students can learn from such tasks that they need to know much more. These claims, however, are not guarantees.

Consider a group of fifth graders who were studying the American Civil War. After they read their textbook, they were presented with copies of five letters written by Confederate soldier sons to their families in Georgia. They read and talked about these letters in both large and small group settings. They manifested considerable difficulty in making sense of the contents of the letters and, even after considerable interaction with their teacher, most of the children held only personal and presentist positions. Especially, they relied on their textbook narrative as the authoritative source of interpretation even when evidence in the letters conflicted with the information in the textbook. These students, for example, mainly understood the textbook's narrative of General Sherman's march to the sea to mean that Union troops burned all homes in Georgia. Further, most of these students, all good readers, comprehended statements as literal descriptions of events. Almost unanimously, for example, they accepted as actual evidence one son's exaggerated comments about the smoke of campfires being so acrid that he surely would lose his sight. They did not connect this sentence with the previous one that begged the father to write more frequently. Similarly, they found difficult any but the most obvious inferences about the individuals who wrote and read the letters. For example, all the letters were addressed, "Dear Father." Most students refused to seriously consider multiple explanations of this fact, e.g., the formality of the period, the possibility that the mother was unable to read. In particular, girls in the class expressed concern that the mother seemed at the margins of consideration by her sons.

An understanding of this classroom exercise admits that these fifth graders unsuccessfully engaged much of the analysis of historical evidence and the employment of differing perspectives to the evidence. Such a conclusion, however reasonable, probably overstates the case.

These students' engagement with primary source documents was their first, not just the first time in the fifth grade, but their first time ever to consider such evidence. Clearly, they did not know how to read these documents; they read them as if they were textual narratives and they were not. They studied versions of the letters that were transcribed from the original copies, none edited for unconventional grammatical constructions and misspellings. They had to confront and attempt to understand, consequently, an unfamiliar type of text, very dissimilar to narratives in their reading and social studies textbooks. They also encountered new words utterly unknown to them. These words, of course, were not defined either in context or by note.[5] Without doubt, in such an unfamiliar and difficult situation, they held fast to understandings that they gained from their textbook, ordinarily an unquestioned source of pedagogic authority, and discredited the strange and, in some respects, discrepant evidence in the letters. They advanced interpretations that were neither warranted nor credible; clearly, their prior knowledge was insufficient and they needed more knowledge. Their historical perspective was severely limited.

Moreover, that these students had difficulty in their first serious exercise in the use of primary sources and failed to demonstrate any but a slight beginning of historical perspective taking seems insufficient grounds on which to base a decision not to use such an exercise with pupils of their age. Certainly, the evidence revealed that the children made a beginning in their struggle with unfamiliar evidence and, especially, with pedagogic expectations quite dissimilar to normal instructional routine. In their previous social studies, they had been readers only, mainly casual and distant if not disinterested observers. This exercise called for them to become searchers for possibilities, to admit alternative views based on different perspectives, and, in a sense, to be companions to the writers and readers of the letters. That they began, even as late as fifth grade, and achieved as little as they did constitutes achievement, even if it was modest.

These children not only began to engage in historical thinking, most of them recognized two critically important understandings about historical knowledge. They and their teacher discovered that they did not know enough to engage the instructional task and this awareness frustrated them. Additionally, they and their teacher realized that some of their knowledge interfered with their interpretations. These children and their teacher knew that they wanted more knowledge. Moreover, they looked forward to another such exercise.

Of course, students' prior knowledge is important. Also important is the awareness that students can gain increased knowledge as they engage exercises in historical thinking. Essential to heightened consideration of this point is that incorrect and incomplete historical knowledge is, nevertheless, a kind of knowledge. Historians respect this reality and seek more complete, more accurate renderings. Likewise, many if not most students in school history courses can develop, to some degree, a similar kind of sensitivity. They can, however, only if their history curriculum and teaching emphasize these proper aspects of knowledge. Considerations of prior knowledge and new knowledge are both necessary. This optimism is not vapid and spineless, but, rather, robust and vigorous.

Another case further illuminates these interpretations. A twelfth grade teacher of economics sought to help her students more fully grasp human dimensions of life during the Great Depression in the United States. She organized a series of lessons in which she and her students first talked about their current understandings of that period. As she expected of these adolescents, most of them reached into the memory of their previous year's American History course to craft their remarks. They noted that most American adults of the time were unemployed, that both work and food were scarce, and that people's lives were characterized as dull, empty, and hopeless. The teacher then assigned students to read selected portions of Studs Terkel's *Hard Times*.[6] Previously, none of these students had used original sources in their historical studies. Over several days, students discussed the recollections of Terkel's interviewees who had lived during the Depression. Students also wrote several response papers on various topics. Subsequently, they learned about the conduct of oral history, prepared individual interview guides, and conducted oral histories with individuals in the community who had lived during the Depression era.[7] Students presented oral reports about their interview findings and also wrote short essays to highlight their interviewees' remembered experiences about the Depression.

For the most part, these students' oral history interviews focused on individuals' personal and family finances. Their course was Economics, after all. To students' surprise, most interviewees told them that their families had not been ruined financially, that they had access to very little money, less than they had before the economic "bust," to be sure, but they continued to enjoy full lives— with entertainment and socialization—in line with the period. They remembered richly and responded fully to interview questions. Students took seriously and sensitively their informants' recollections. Details of the interviews varied, but no interviewee remembered being involved in an exodus like that depicted in *The Grapes of Wrath* nor had they or members of their families stood in lines for food. On the other hand, some interviewees reported their personal witness to the economic ravages on adults and children of unemployment and lack of food, clothing, and housing.

Students' problems in this short instructional unit occurred as they worked to make intellectual sense of the information that they earlier had learned and the new knowledge that they had gathered. They recognized quickly that their initial perceptions were superficial and even misinformed. In small groups and as an entire class, students worked to express particularity without overgeneralization. Through their reading of Terkel's accounts and their consideration of their own and their classmates' oral history interviews, they recognized variety and individual experience in these points of view. They recognized, as they considered the Depression era from different perspectives, that it did not have standard effects on Americans and, further, that they found difficult their personal reconciliation of the abundant discrepant evidence. Students, as they proceeded in this study, became increasingly cautious as they discussed and wrote generalizations and interpretations.

Without doubt, the twelfth graders participated in their historical thinking and empathy exercise more fully than did the fifth graders. Certainly, the older students engaged more actively with and thought more carefully about issues from different perspectives on issues than did the younger children. High school seniors, of course, reasonably should be more experienced students and should accomplish more than can 11- and 12-year-old children. On the other hand, this scant evidence is insufficient to argue for the postponement of empathy exercises until late adolescence. Both groups experienced problems related to their prior knowledge. Both groups gained additional knowledge and progressed in their appreciation of different perspectives through their engagement with primary source documents. Moreover, both groups were handicapped in their engagement because of the novelty of the task; these occasions were the first times for both groups to be tasked to think away from the official knowledge of textbooks, with discrepant historical evidence, and with the consideration of different perspectives.

This analysis and related examples raise once again major elements of the central question about curriculum practice.[8] Special attention is accorded to what levels of empathy or perspective taking should be offered (and expected) in which sequence to which students. These concerns can be sidestepped only at serious risk. More likely than not, these questions can productively be confronted and deliberated by teachers in local school settings, especially in department and classroom milieus. Bureaucratic curriculum standards and administrative directions probably cannot assure adequate responses to these and related curriculum questions. Suggestions for and illustrations of pedagogic practice based on results of sound research as well as on pedagogic wisdom, on the other hand, can and should be included in these and other guides to improved curriculum and teaching.[9]

Teachers are key figures in all suggestions for students' development of empathy. Not only will they choose tasks and allocate instructional time, they are the adults who will guide students as they analyze, puzzle, and wonder in their historical thinking. They will offer questions and suggest options. They will offer assistance of additional evidence and sources. They will encourage students to develop alternative perspectives rather than seizing only one as sufficiently explanatory. On the other hand, teachers may decide to stick closely with the textbook and curriculum guide and to ignore historical thinking tasks. Indeed, most American social studies teachers engage in such conventional classroom practices. Teachers change their practices, but almost never will they change whimsically.[10]

Most practicing school history teachers as well as recently prepared teachers have little personal and direct experience with serious historical thinking tasks.

Although the evidence is thin, some teachers have reported that they never engaged in such tasks with historical sources in any of their undergraduate history courses. Consequently, their efforts to think historically are likely to be weak. In order for them to stimulate and guide students' historical thinking, obviously, teachers must personally be able to think historically and possess reasonable experience in such thought. Some restructuring of history courses as well as courses in history pedagogy in teacher preparation programs, therefore, appears to be an important action item.

Advocacy of changed teaching practice ordinarily is insufficient to influence actual change.[11] Teachers may understand encouragement to teach about historical perspective taking as another whimsical innovation like others about which they hear almost yearly. In essence, these advocacies, even those that initially attract attention, have a short life. Teachers know that most advocacies are as cheap as they are popular and, thus, these teachers continue to teach the best way they know how to teach. In most cases, teachers comment about new advocacies as being "impractical." Teachers ordinarily evaluate the practicality of teaching practices on a simple criterion, i.e., what works for them in the classroom. Consequently, they seem not at all resistant to changing their teaching practices under conditions of personal practicality. These criteria include their recognition that the reform is personally valid, that it is consistent with their preferred teaching style, and that it does not require excessive costs in either time or money or both. Especially for practicing teachers, these criteria can frame in-service education programming that offers opportunities for teachers to gain personal experience in thinking with historical evidence, in their tough-minded consideration of perspective taking, and in actual teaching with an emphasis upon the development of empathy.[12]

Only a few dimensions of teaching for the development of historical empathy were discussed here. Many others will be identified and explicated in the next few years. This further development surely will follow increased attention to empathy and perspective taking by teachers and researchers.

An Invitation to Invent and to Research

This book constitutes a next step in the extension of the scholarly pursuit of historical empathy. Quite a number of individuals, including the contributors to this volume, are now engaged in this activity.[13] We confess that we do not know enough even about the concept of empathy, but we are continuing to learn. We are increasing what we know about individuals' (students' and teachers') historical thinking, some of which yields empathy or perspective. The continued pursuit promises to yield much, much more knowledge. Already, many children and youth in school history courses are benefiting from the insights that have emerged from recently undertaken research inquiries. Scholarly interest in historical thinking, almost absent a decade ago, increases every year. All of us researchers and teachers, in our own ways, have been frustrated and excited, as well as dulled and thrilled, by our efforts to involve children and youth in rich, textured, meaningful thinking about history. We seek to convert findings into mindful inventions of curriculum opportunities and instructional tasks. We invite other teachers and other educational researchers to join in that pursuit.[14]

Notes

1. S. J. Foster, J. W. Morris, and O. L. Davis Jr., "Prospects for Teaching Historical Analysis and Interpretation: National Curriculum Standards for History Meet High School History Textbooks," *Journal of Curriculum and Supervision* 11 (Summer 1996): 367-385.

2. See, for example, S. J. Foster, "Politics, Parallels and Perennial Curriculum Questions: The Battle Over School History in England and the United States," *The Curriculum Journal* 9 (Summer 1998): 153-164; F. H. Doppen and E. A. Yeager, "National versus State Curriculum Standards for History in the United States: Where Will the Debate Lead Us?" *The Curriculum Journal* 9 (Summer 1998): 165-175.

3. S. Pate, "Elementary School Children Thinking about History: Use of Sources and Empathy" (doctoral dissertation, The University of Texas at Austin, 1999).

4. O. L. Davis Jr., "Inquiring about the American Experience," in *Teaching American History: The Quest for Relevancy* ed. A. O. Kownslar (Washington, D.C.: National Council for the Social Studies, 1974), 41-55.

5. See, particularly, *Language and Concepts in Education,* ed. B. O. Smith and R. H. Ennis (Chicago: Rand McNally and Co., 1962); also, G. Ryle, *The Concept of Mind* (London: Hutchinson, 1949).

6. S. Terkel, *Hard Times: An Oral History of the Great Depression* (New York: Pantheon Books, 1970).

7. C. L. Klagas, "Secondary Social Studies Students' Engagement with Historical Thinking and Historical Empathy as They Use Oral History Interviews" (doctoral dissertation, The University of Texas at Austin, 1999).

8. A. W. Foshay, "The Curriculum Matrix: Transcendence and Mathematics," *Journal of Curriculum and Supervision* 6 (Summer 1991): 277-293.

9. W. A. Reid, *Curriculum as Institution and Practice* (Mahwah, N.J.: Lawrence Erlbaum Associates, 1993).

10. A. W. Foshay, *The Curriculum: Purpose, Substance, Practice* (New York: Teachers College Press, 2000).

11. O. L. Davis Jr., "Beyond 'Best Practices' Toward Wise Practices," *Journal of Curriculum and Supervision* 13 (Fall 1997): 1-5; also, O. L. Davis Jr., "Thinking in the School Subjects: Toward Improved Teaching and Learning," *Journal of Curriculum and Supervision* 13 (Spring 1998): 205-209.

12. See, for example, J. P. Shaver, O. L. Davis Jr., and S. W. Helburn, "The Status of Social Studies Education: Impressions from Three NSF Studies," *Social Education* 43 (February 1979): 150-153.

13. See, for example, E. A. Yeager and O. L. Davis Jr., "Understanding the 'Knowing How' of History: Elementary Student Teachers' Thinking about Historical Texts," *The*

Journal of Social Studies Research 18 (Fall 1994): 2-9; E. A. Yeager and O. L. Davis Jr., "Between Campus and Classroom: Secondary Student-Teachers' Thinking about Historical Texts," *Journal of Research and Development in Education* 29 (Fall 1995): 1-8; E. A.Yeager and O. L. Davis Jr., "Classroom Teachers'Thinking about Historical Texts: An Exploratory Study," *Theory and Research in Social Education* 24 (Spring 1996): 146-166; C. H. Bohan and O. L. Davis Jr., "Historical Constructions: How Social Studies Student Teachers' Historical Thinking is Reflected in Their Writing of History," *Theory and Research in Social Education* 26 (Spring 1998): 173-197.

14. W. Doyle and G. Ponder, "The Practicality Ethic in Teacher Decision Making," *Interchange* 8 (1977): 1-12.

Chapter 2

The Role of Empathy in the Development of Historical Understanding

Elizabeth Anne Yeager and Stuart J. Foster

A substantial body of research has focused on students' understandings of history, taking into account important aspects of historical thinking: the power of narrative and storytelling, historical imagination, the context and authorship of historical sources, detection of bias, the nature of conflicting accounts and interpretations, and the tentative and ambiguous nature of historical conclusions.[1] In particular, this research emphasizes the importance of students' understanding that historical interpretation is a process of finding meaning through a variety of actors on the historical stage.[2]

The perspectival nature of historical inquiry necessarily highlights the role of empathy as yet another powerful tool for understanding history. Empathy merits specific attention because historians must bring it to their inquiry in order to analyze the events, actions, and words of key figures in the historical record. As Berlin explained, good history offers a window on human character, motivation, and principles.[3] In the construction of historical meaning, empathy for participants in historical events is central.

This chapter addresses the notion of historical empathy by discussing theories and meanings of historical empathy, drawing from previous research.[4] We assert that historical empathy should not be based simply on exercises in imagination (e.g.,"Imagine you are an Apache warrior"), overidentification (e.g., asking students to identify with Adolf Hitler), or sympathy (e.g., encouraging students to sympathize with victims of slavery). Rather, we attempt to show that the development of historical empathy in students is a considered and active process, embedded in the historical method, involving four interrelated phases: the introduction of an historical event necessitating the analysis of human action, the understanding of historical context and chronology, the analysis of a variety of historical evidence and interpretations, and the construction of a narrative framework through which historical conclusions are reached.

Clearly, a fundamental characteristic of the idea of empathy concerns the use of hindsight as a way of understanding and interpreting the past in a meaningful way. The appropriate application of historical empathy in understanding the past is a central element of the discipline of history. If the task of the historian—or the history student—is to reconstruct, understand, and make sense of the past, then historical empathy has a significant role to play. Shemilt argues that "empathic construction of action and meaning amounts to the reduction of a puzzle, to the rendering of the strange and unintelligible down to the recognizable and comprehensible."[5] In other words, if the task of the historian is to make sense of a past of which only partial knowledge exists, then the use of empathy may be crucial to the process of understanding.

Historical Empathy: Possible Meanings

The central aim of the historian is to understand and interpret past events. The historian is, however, hindered by the fact that the past is an incomplete entity and thus, he or she must use the best available evidence to construct a reasonably accurate portrayal; a complete array of perspectives and facts is largely out of the question. For example, when trying to understand the position of President Harry Truman in his decision to use the atomic bomb on Japan, it is necessary to draw together materials that help explain the context in which Truman was operating. What were the sociopolitical pressures on him? Did public opinion play a role? What were the customs, values, and conventions of the era? What information did Truman have access to when making his decision? What strategic considerations were at play, etc.? Other questions and answers may exist that are unavailable to the historian. But having established context as best they can, historians may then draw on the knowledge gleaned from hindsight—a precious tool because it enables them to see the consequences of a particular set of actions.

Between the two elements of context and consequence (as viewed with the benefit of hindsight) lies the nebulous, indeterminate area of action. Essentially, this is the "why" of history: Why did an individual or group of people, given a set of circumstances, act in a certain way? Here, historical empathy is of fundamental importance because it plays a role in the process of adductive, inferential thinking that allows the historian to make sense of past actions. Historical empathy applied to the available evidence helps the historian bridge the gaps in what is known; that is to say, it involves some ability to infer from given knowledge an explanation of certain actions. Historical imagination also comes into play, not as a fanciful notion but, as Rogers asserts, as an intelligent re-creation of a situation given an understanding of its context, outcomes, and evidence.[6] Ultimately, therefore, historical empathy combines the adductive and logical thinking associated with the use of evidence and the inferential and appropriately creative skills that seek to bridge the gap between what is known and what may be inferred from history.

Interestingly, Downey's study uses the term "perspective taking" instead of empathy to describe an activity that is, in Boddington's view, not primarily creative but rational, intellectual, and "concerned with explaining actions, attitudes, and concepts which are alien to our own."[7] To engage in historical perspective taking, Downey argues, is to try to understand an historical character's frame of reference without trying to identify or sympathize with his or her feelings. Downey emphasizes that historical perspectives are not waiting to be discovered, like photographs; rather, they are constructed on the basis of facts and evidence. Perspective "construction" is one of the most difficult tasks of historical thinking, he states, because it involves trying to escape one's own attitudes and world views in order to understand those of the past.

Downey's main point is that this task is especially problematic for young students, who do not have access to the same skills, knowledge, and experience that historians possess. "Expert" and "novice" historical thinking are, he argues, differences of kind rather than degree. Thus, the development of criteria for evaluating historical perspective taking must be done prudently and with reasonable expectations.

Whether historical empathy is an outcome or a process has not been well established in the literature on historical thinking. In fact, such an argument may be unnecessary, and we argue that historical empathy is both a process and an outcome. Meanings of historical empathy articulated by, for example, Downey, Portal, and Ashby and Lee, contain elements of both the outcome and process points of view.[8] Ashby and Lee assert that empathy in history is

> where we get to when we have successfully reconstructed other peoples' beliefs, values, goals, and attendant feelings. . . . To say that a student has empathized is to say that he or she is in a position to entertain a set of beliefs and values which are not necessarily his or her own.[9]

Portal says that it is necessary to establish "what people thought was going on and how they saw their own range of options before any explanation of their motives has a chance of success."[10] Generally, Ashby and Lee argue, empathy in history rests on reasoned evidential reconstruction that is also "broadly inferential."[11] Portal argues that empathy is achievable through a balance of "imaginative speculation" and "methodical investigation" in historical inquiry.[12]

With regard to the teaching and learning of history in schools, Portal states that empathy ought not to be a discrete section of a history course syllabus, but a "characteristic dimension of each of the other historical skills."[13] Thus, instead of having "empathy exercises" as such, the importance of empathy would appear in the method used for the "presentation and teaching of evidence work, explanation, etc. . . . by introducing into all such work the circumstances and points of view of particular people."[14] He emphasizes that the first step in the development of historical empathy among students is that they be able to project their own ideas and feelings into an historical situation.[15] Second, he emphasizes the importance of the "element of paradox at some point where our scheme of things does not account for the behavior of the past," so that students can distinguish the period they are studying from their own.[16] Third, he states that students must be able to employ a collection of reference materials and contemporary sources appropriate to the topic at hand.[17] Fourth, the development of empathy requires the "presentation of a particular person or situation in terms that extend beyond the merely typical to encompass the unique circumstances of the case."[18] Finally, Portal recommends the use of the two-sided narrative "where the inadequately empathic relationship between the historical participants leads to misunderstanding, conflict, (or) tragedy."[19] Taking such viewpoints into account, students may be able to develop general principles for understanding opposing viewpoints and for the study of successive, related events.

Portal and others cited in the introduction to this chapter have argued that students' exposure to particular historical sources and to appropriate "empathic questions" are important starting points in their inquiry. A few researchers have specifically studied how exposure to these sources and questions might stimulate empathic responses among students. Downey's study of historical perspective taking included a writing assignment.[20] His fifth-grade participants were asked to write a narrative that explained events between the end of the French and Indian War and the Declaration of Independence, that examined the roles of individuals in these events, that presented the perspectives of the actors involved, and that made connections between events when appropriate. The students were not given a model for systematically approaching this task; they were asked simply to answer the questions after their exposure to a variety of excerpts and quotations from primary and secondary historical sources and their involvement in class discussion and research. Downey concluded that the narrative-writing task was a more successful perspective-taking exercise than other tasks in his study (role playing and letter writing) because students had sufficient information and time to account for the perspectives they took and to construct explanations rather than merely describe historical points of view. Also, students were able to shift from one perspective to another with relative ease in order to explain causal relationships. In addition, Cooper, in his study of primary school children's historical understanding, concluded that the experimental group with access to a wide variety of historical sources was better able to "make a range of valid suppositions about sources" in order to "try and understand how people in the past may have felt and thought" and to begin to "try to explain attitudes and values different from their own."[21]

Downey also has several recommendations for evaluating evidence of successful historical perspective taking.[22] First, students must indicate that they realize the past is different from the present and that some historical outcomes are specific to time and place. Second, perspective taking must be measured in terms of the students' ability to distinguish between past perspectives and to shift from one to another from a relatively detached point of view. Third, students should be able to explain the perspectives they take and their consequences for the historical participants involved. Fourth, the perspectives students take must be grounded in historical evidence and be factually accurate.

Conclusions on Historical Empathy

Ashby and Lee, Cooper, Booth, Rogers, Portal, and others suggest that the teaching of historical thinking can emphasize the necessary awareness for the development of historical empathy. Ashby and Lee conclude from their research among English pupils that the acquisition of a disposition to empathize and to understand why empathy matters is perhaps the most important task in the teaching of history. Students who understand this and who can achieve empathy have not only taken a step forward in their study of history, but they also may be more likely "to be able to cope with the present world" and can better discern how what they do affects other people.[23] The possibility thus exists that certain dispositions and strategies learned in history lessons may have an immediate importance outside history; history is not "inert and arid, but affects the whole way in which we see the world—past, present, and future."[24] Portal states that an understanding of the importance of empathy

> as a dimension of every historical topic and situation would do a great deal to underline the humane quality of history, as a subject concerned primarily with the intentions and actions of human beings and the ways in which these purposes interact and influence each other.[25]

Although empathy does not constitute the entire existential domain of history, he argues, to provide for its development may be viewed as an important heuristic that nurtures the imaginative aspects of history.

This chapter provides a glimpse of the possibility that historical empathy may allow the subject of history to come alive in the minds of students. Nurtured in a teaching environment that offers considerable depth of inquiry and discourse, historical empathy has the potential to engage students in the process of historical inquiry and interpretation and to encourage them to think critically about the past.

Historical empathy need not be jettisoned from the curriculum because some of its applications are shallow and capricious. Neither should it be abandoned because of the difficulty of pinning down a precise meaning of the concept. Historical empathy has an important function in the understanding of the past and an essential role in the nature of historical inquiry. Although engagement in historical empathy renders no absolute truths, it is still a worthwhile practice that ultimately may give students a richer understanding of the past. Hopefully, the research in this book will lead to new understandings of the development of students' historical empathy, given their use of particular sources and questions, upon which teachers can build in their own classrooms.

Notes

1. M. T. Downey, "Perspective Taking and Historical Thinking: Doing History in a Fifth-Grade Classroom" (paper presented at the annual meeting of the American Educational Research Association, San Francisco, Calif., 1995); M. S. Gabella, "Beyond the Looking Glass: Bringing Students into the Conversation of Historical Inquiry," *Theory and Research in Social Education* 22 (1994): 340-63; P. Seixas, "Students' Understanding of Historical Significance," *Theory and Research in Social Education* 22 (1994): 281-304; M. Booth, "Students' Historical Thinking and the National History Curriculum in England," *Theory and Research in Social Education* 21 (1993), 105-27; B. VanSledright and J. Brophy, "Storytelling, Imagination, and Fanciful Elaboration in Children's Historical Reconstructions," *American Educational Research Journal* 23 (1992): 837-53; S. S. Wineburg, "On the Reading of Historical Texts: Notes on the Breach Between School and Academy," *American Educational Research Journal* 28 (1991): 435-513; M. T. Downey and L. S. Levstik, "Teaching and Learning in History," in J. P. Shaver, ed., *Handbook of Research on Social Studies Teaching and Learning* (New York: Macmillan, 1991), 400-410; S. J. Thornton and R. Vukelich, "Effects of Children's Understanding of Time Concepts on Historical Understanding," *Theory and Research in Social Education* 15 (1988): 63-82; L. S. Levstik and C. C. Pappas, "Exploring the Development of Historical Understanding," *Journal of Research and Development in Education* 87 (1987): 1-15; W. J. Friedman, "Introduction," in W. J. Friedman, ed., *The Developmental Psychology of Time* (New York: Academic Press, 1982), 1-11; M. Booth, "A Modern World History Course and the Thinking of Adolescent Pupils," *Educational Review* 32 (1980): 245-57.

2. M. S. Gabella, "Beyond the Looking Glass: Bringing Students into the Conversation of Historical Inquiry," *Theory and Research in Social Education* 22 (1994): 340-63.

3. I. Berlin, "The Concept of Scientific History," in W. H. Dray, ed., *Philosophical Analysis and History* (New York: Harper and Row, 1966), 5-53.

4. M. T. Downey, "Perspective Taking and Historical Thinking: Doing History in a Fifth-Grade Classroom"; P. Seixas, "Students' Understanding of Historical Significance"; M. Booth, "Students' Historical Thinking and the National History Curriculum in England"; B. VanSledright and J. Brophy, "Storytelling, Imagination, and Fanciful Elaboration in Children's Historical Reconstructions"; P. Lee, "Historical Knowledge and the National Curriculum," in R. Aldrich, ed., *History in the National Curriculum* (London: Kogan

Page, 1991), 33-65; S. S. Wineburg, "On the Reading of Historical Texts: Notes on the Breach Between School and Academy"; P. Knight, "Empathy: Concept, Confusion, and Consequences in a National Curriculum," *Oxford Review of Education* 15 (1989): 41-53; S. S. Wineburg and S. Wilson, "Models of Wisdom in the Teaching of History," *Phi Delta Kappan* (September 1988): 50-58; R. Ashby and P. Lee, "Children's Concepts of Empathy and Understanding in History," in C. Portal, ed., *The History Curriculum for Teachers* (London: Falmer Press, 1987), 62-88; C. Portal, "Empathy as an Objective for History Teaching," in C. Portal, ed., *The History Curriculum for Teachers* (London: Falmer Press, 1987), 83-33; A. Dickinson, P. Lee and P. J. Rogers, *Learning History* (London: Heinemann, 1984); D. Shemilt, *Schools Council History* 13-16 *Project: Evaluation Study* (Edinburgh: Holmes, McDougall, 1980).

5. D. Shemilt, "Adolescent Ideas about Evidence and Methodology in History," in C. Portal, ed., *The History Curriculum for Teachers* 44.

6. P. J. Rogers, "History: Why, What and How?" in *Teaching of History Series*, Number 60 (London: Historical Association, 1990).

7. T. Boddington, "Empathy and the Teaching of History," *British Journal of Educational Studies* 28 (1980): 18.

8. M. T. Downey, "Perspective Taking and Historical Thinking: Doing History in a Fifth-Grade Classroom"; C. Portal, "Empathy as an Objective for History Teaching"; R. Ashby and P. Lee, "Children's Concepts of Empathy and Understanding in History."

9. R. Ashby and P. Lee, "Children's Concepts of Empathy and Understanding in History," 63.

10. C. Portal, "Empathy as an Objective for History Teaching," 89.

11. R. Ashby and P. Lee, "Children's Concepts of Empathy and Understanding in History," 63.

12. C. Portal, "Empathy as an Objective for History Teaching," 34.

13. C. Portal, "Empathy as an Objective for History Teaching," 34.

14. C. Portal, "Empathy as an Objective for History Teaching," 34.

15. C. Portal, "Empathy as an Objective for History Teaching," 95.

16. C. Portal, "Empathy as an Objective for History Teaching," 95.

17. C. Portal, "Empathy as an Objective for History Teaching," 96.

18. C. Portal, "Empathy as an Objective for History Teaching," 96.

19. C. Portal, "Empathy as an Objective for History Teaching," 97.

20. M. T. Downey, "Perspective Taking and Historical Thinking: Doing History in a Fifth-Grade Classroom."

21. H. Cooper, "Children's Learning, Key Stage 2: Recent Findings," in M. Booth, H. Moniot, and K. Pellens, eds., *Communications of the International Society for History Didactics* 16 (1995): 55.

22. M. T. Downey, "Perspective Taking and Historical Thinking: Doing History in a Fifth-Grade Classroom."

23. R. Ashby and P. Lee, "Children's Concepts of Empathy and Understanding in History," 64.

24. R. Ashby and P. Lee, "Children's Concepts of Empathy and Understanding in History," 65.

25. C. Portal, "Empathy as an Objective for History Teaching," 98.

Chapter 3

Empathy, Perspective Taking, and Rational Understanding

Peter Lee and Rosalyn Ashby

The Conceptual Issues

Historians need to understand the way in which people in the past saw their world, at various times and places. They also need to understand why people took the actions they did. These two assertions do not seem particularly adventurous, even though they beg some important questions. It might therefore not be too outrageous to conclude that children learning history might also need to understand these things, even though they are likely to understand them less well than professional historians.

In the UK, understandings of this kind acquired the label "empathy," largely because other words were even more problematic. One possible alternative, "rational understanding" seemed too cumbersome, and confused people about the kind of claims being made about human rationality.[1] On the other hand, "understanding" on its own covered too many other ideas. "Perspective taking" was also cumbersome, and arguably too wide in scope. An advantage of "empathy" was that it was short, and as an imported term, could to some extent be *given* an English meaning. Once "empathy" was adopted by the Schools History Project (SHP), it stuck.[2]

The problem with "empathy" was that it encouraged a wide range of interpretations, some of which ran into serious conceptual difficulties. In particular it encouraged the misleading idea that students were being asked to share the feelings of people in the past. An entertaining side effect of this idea was an ill-informed public debate in which some right-wing education-watchers became alarmed that school students were being asked to "empathize" with (for example) Cuban supporters of President Castro; the confusion of "empathy" and "sympathy" was confounded and enhanced by selective examples of "empathy" with the "wrong" people.[3] More serious was the confusion that arose among some teachers and educationists. By the late 1980s considerable progress had been made in sorting out this confusion (at least in schools working with the Schools History Project), but just as some of the sillier notions were beginning to disappear from the schools, a spate of articles purporting to attack "empathy" began to appear in the press and in journals like *Teaching History*. Much (but by no means all) of this criticism was from writers close to the Thatcher government. It was therefore not surprising that the new National Curriculum made no reference to "empathy," "although it smuggled the central ideas back into school under an attainment target entitled "Knowledge and Understanding."

As a preface to attempting to salvage something from the muddles, we will comment briefly on two different kinds of confusion involved in the debates, exemplified in two contributions to a single issue of the British Historical Association's journal *Teaching History*. Both papers share a pre-emptive strategy of defining empathy in such a way as to make it absurd.

The first kind of confusion arises from attempts to settle substantive issues by appeal to the dictionary. Ann Low-Beer makes use of dictionary definitions and etymology to define "empathy" in terms of "feeling," without regard to the actual usage of Schools History Project teachers or examiners, and then claims that "empathy" cannot be assessed.[4] As a result, her discussion falls into serious confusion. Low-Beer is right to assume that some teachers behaved (and continue to behave) as if empathy were a feeling and a skill. She is also right to say that "feelings are not skills and cannot be treated as if they were. . . . Feelings cannot be practiced." This kind of failure to distinguish between teaching students key concepts and giving them skills has caused problems in many areas beyond "empathy."[5] But Low-Beer is in no doubt that empathy is a feeling. She opens her discussion with an unequivocal assertion: "The concept belongs within the affective rather than the cognitive domain of knowledge." Later she adds, "Vast ranges of feelings, including empathy, are intrinsic to the human condition, developing throughout life as we respond to situations and reflect on our reactions."[6] Despite selective unattributed quotation of examination questions, she fails to explore the detailed assessment processes evolved by SHP, which might have warned her that "feelings" were not, after all, what were at issue.[7] Nor does she mention the work of project personnel giving very different (more sophisticated and wide-ranging) analyses than her own paper.[8] The argument that empathy is necessarily about feelings, and therefore cannot be assessed, clearly fails if "empathy" is used to refer to something quite different. Low-Beer is entitled to complain that the word is inappropriately used, but the rest of her argument collapses into misleading irrelevance.[9]

The dictionary cannot settle substantive matters about what is involved in historical understanding. It is not the definition of the word "empathy" that is the issue here, but a clarification of what is involved in understanding actions and institutions in the past (in terms of reasons, beliefs, and values). Empathy can then be treated as the most common word employed by teachers and examiners to stand for a certain kind of historical understanding, in the absence of a "native" word that did the job.[10] The task of sorting out what is and is not part of such understanding remains.

The second kind of confusion is more interesting, and arises when empathy is defined as something unachievable. In the same issue of *Teaching History* Keith Jenkins and Peter Brickley launch a mildly polemical postmodern critique of empathy, at the same time claiming to explain how it came to be accepted in British schools.[11] The basic position seems to be that "the past is never empathetically retrievable: it cannot come back. Nor can you think yourself straight into the past; beam back unmediated by the historian." It should hardly be necessary to point out that the first two phrases are not equivalent, and that any serious discussion of understanding people in the past is precisely about the mediating role of historians. Jenkins and Brickley's arguments do not demonstrate the impossibility of empathy, they simply define it away. However, the authors clearly do not believe their own arguments, since (1) they think that they can know enough of J. S. Mill's mind to explain what is "central to [his] idea of freedom," and (2) they elucidate the process of historical mediation in terms which assume that teachers understand historians, students understand teachers, and moderators understand students. And at the end of their paper they admit that "if we want to close empathy down because its aims are strictly unrealizable, then we had better abandon history too, failing as it does, in any rigorous way, to achieve its general intention of explaining what, how and why things happened in the past. But this we don't wish to do" (p. 22.). So the argument has no consequences. "Strictly" turns out to mean "pointlessly misdefined."[12]

What can be sensibly asserted about the group of ideas usually associated with the labels "empathy," "perspective taking," or "rational understanding"? The central concepts here are of meaning, reasons, and understanding. If history is to be possible, historians must understand past meanings, whether of documents or artifacts. (Is this find a cup or a cult object? Is this document a minute or a report? Does it make a threat or a promise?) If they cannot do this, then there can be no historical evidence. Historians must also be able to give sense to actions and to social practices and institutions in terms of people's reasons for doing or believing what they did. To complain that these tasks can only be inferential (because we have no direct access to the past) is merely to give, in the guise of a strange lament, the reason why we have the academic discipline of history. The particular (and further) problem of access to other minds is an interesting and important one, but not special to history, unless we wish to insist that other minds can be understood only in face-to-face relationships. Claims to understand past documents, artifacts, actions or institutions are not claims to certain knowledge, but that does not mean that no knowledge is possible. As with almost all interesting or important knowledge claims, we often have better reasons for accepting one story than another.

In order to understand actions and institutions in terms of reasons, beliefs and values, we must be able to see how something could be a reason for action or belief. This is not merely to make a general point to the effect that historical knowledge should not be inert, but to argue that empathy or rational understanding means being able to see and entertain as conditionally appropriate (not necessarily to accept or share) *connections* between intentions, circumstances, and actions. It is not merely knowing that certain historical agents or groups had a particular perspective on their world, but being able to see how that perspective would actually have affected actions in particular circumstances. This requires hard thinking on the basis of evidence, but it is not a special kind of mental process. It is not any kind of *process* at all, let alone a special *faculty*, but where we get to when we know what past agents thought, what goals they may have been seeking, and how they saw their situation, and can connect all this with what they did. Historical empathy and rational understanding, in this sense, are different names for an *achievement*.[13]

What has this to do with feelings, projection, and other elements of a dictionary definition of empathy? Understood as a shorthand for historical understanding, empathy involves feelings only in the etiolated way indicated by Collingwood, and later elucidated by Mink.[14] In the first place, historical understanding is not itself a feeling at all. It is emphatically not "a" (special kind of) feeling, although it may involve recognizing that people had feelings. These would have to be characterized for what they were, which would mean distinguishing, say, anger and jealousy. It is precisely because feelings and emotions carry cognitive loads that we are able to make such distinctions. If we are angry, as opposed to jealous, this is because we see the world differently: we think actions have taken place that count as having insulted us, rather than thinking that a loved one has switched affections to someone else. Our emotions cannot be adequately characterized in terms of sensations in our stomachs or other bodily signs: their knowledge components are central.

For this reason *shared* feelings cannot be part of historical understanding or "empathy." We cannot, for example, share the hopes or fears of people when we know those hopes or fears came to nothing. We cannot ourselves feel past participants' sense of pride in (say) a political or military victory, when we no longer hold the values of those who won it, values that made their sense of pride what it was. Nor can we share the participants' exaltation, based on their expectations about the significance of their achievement, when we know that those expectations were wrong. This is not merely a problem of access, or of evidence. There are logical limits here, imposed by the cognitive element in emotions.

It is possible to *entertain* purposes and beliefs held by people in the past without *accepting* them. They can still function in a kind of calculus of practical reasoning, even if we know that what was believed to be true was mistaken, and do not share the purposes; moreover, in entertaining the beliefs, we can know what feelings they would have carried with them. But our historical understanding comes from knowing how people saw things, knowing what they tried to do, and knowing *that* they felt the appropriate feelings, not from feeling those things ourselves. This does not rule out sympathy, and it certainly depends on knowing what it is to have feelings. But historical understanding is not sympathy, and it cannot depend on sharing feelings, for that would make it impossible.

Empathy, as historical understanding, demands hard thinking on the basis of evidence. It requires students to know some history, and to be able to *use* that knowledge in order to explain actions and institutions. If it is to be given any sensible meaning in history, empathy is where you get when you have done the hard thinking, and produced an explanation based on the evidence you can find. It means entertaining complex ideas and seeing how they shape views of historical circumstances and goals, even when such ideas and goals may be very different from (and perhaps opposed to) our own.

All this indicates that historical empathy is going to be difficult for youngsters. But learning history at school is not becoming a historian. Progress is not all or nothing. We try to give students more powerful ideas than the ones they start out with. Teaching historical understanding is in part an exercise in giving students a different intellectual apparatus, different assumptions and strategies. Research suggests that some of these ideas are likely to be counter-intuitive: that is, that the assumptions students derive from the everyday world conflict with the ideas they need if they are to make sense of history (both the discipline and the past it constructs). This seems to be true of a range of different ideas commonly employed by students to make sense of history, but it is particularly evident in the area of empathy and rational understanding of action.[15]

The Research Context

There is a growing volume of research in Europe and North America bearing on students' ideas about historical understanding, whether characterized as "empathy," "understanding" or "perspective taking."[16] Some of the work has been specifically designed to explore the ways in which students make sense of past actions, practices, or institutions. No attempt can be made here to summarize this work, but it is noteworthy that sometimes research primarily concerned with other ideas has illuminated aspects of students' understanding of people in the past. What is striking is that such research has uncovered, almost in passing, ideas consistently reported from the earliest days of the investigations targeted on "empathy." The recent work of Keith Barton serves as a particularly interesting example.

Barton's "Narrative Simplifications in Elementary Students' Historical Thinking" discusses children's comments on change, and in doing so provides insight into the assumptions with which children approach the past.[17] Because he is asking about change, not seeking ideas about empathy, the remarks of the children he talks to are all the more instructive. The ideas he reports are instantly recognizable to British researchers, and Barton's comments elegantly interrelate the basic ideas of change as rectification of a deficit past state, rational understanding of change as action, and the ignorance and inferior ability of those in the past, so familiar from "empathy" studies.

First, changes in everyday appliances, in fashion, in ideas about race, and even in names, were all seen as ultimately deriving from overcoming deficits. People in the past gradually learned to do things better, where "better" means more like us. The past is not just a foreign country, but a rather ignorant one, where things were as they were because that was all people could manage. This can even be applied to changes in names. Barton quotes Tonya, "People have all changed, and when other things change, people like to change too, so their names get better along with all the other things that get better." The use of "better" here was glossed by another student, "You don't want a really beautiful girl, and her name is Flossie, or a really cute boy, and his name is Oliver."

Barton warns that students' ideas about rational improvement from deficit states are in uneasy tension with awareness of causal factors not so susceptible to the assumption of past inferiority, and illustrates this tension with the comment of one student that if bell-bottoms come back into fashion, "they won't be as lame as they were back then . . . because there's like more threads and stuff that they can use now than they could probably use back then, and they can make it like better fashions."

American children seem to work with the same apparatus as British children. People were less smart in the past; nowadays we've "figured things out." People didn't know how to do things then. The notion of being more or less "smart" seems to oscillate (as with British children) between capacity for intelligence and degree of knowledge.

Second, Barton shows that, for many children, to understand *is* to give reasons, and this is so strong an imperative that if necessary reasons must be made up. This extends to people discovering at particular moments in time that they had got things wrong. Laura claimed that people do not believe in witches now because "some people proved that they could not be witches, and they thought whoever could float was like a witch, cause they thought their specter was holding them up, and it's not true, cause why would your specter really want to hold you up?" Kenny simply said that at a specific trial witchcraft had been proved wrong. A similar set of assumptions lay behind the students' explanations of how racism had come to be seen as an evil.

Put together, these common-sense ideas are a powerful obstacle to historical understanding. They are often coupled with irritation and condescension in the face of what can seem to children almost wanton stupidity or moral weakness in the behavior of people in the past. Sam Wineburg points out that "'presentism'— the act of viewing the past through the lens of the present—is not some bad habit we've fallen into, but is instead our psychological condition at rest, a way of thinking that requires little effort and comes naturally."[18] And of course, thought of in this way, presentism covers the whole range of repertoires we have for explaining human actions and behavior, including the templates we use for "standard" sets of circumstances and conditions.[19] Wineburg quotes Primo Levi on the Holocaust, questioned by a fifth grader on why he did not escape, and given a plan of action to follow should he ever find himself in a similar position.[20] It was a simple matter: cut the sentinel's throat, put on his clothes, shut off the electricity and climb the fence. Levi's experience fits the responses children make to problems of historical explanation: Jellicoe at Jutland and Chamberlain at Munich simply failed to make obvious moves, the sort of thing any half-intelligent person could see was required. History is a story of feeble-minded people blundering from one self-evidently mistaken course of action to another.[21]

Recent research in England has found ideas very similar to those found by earlier UK work, and, more interestingly, bearing a strong resemblance to some of the thinking Keith Barton found among American students.

The CHATA Research

Project CHATA (Concepts of History and Teaching Approaches 7-14, funded by the Economic and Social Research Council) explored students' ideas about understanding past actions and institutions, building on earlier small-scale work carried out between the mid-1970s and mid-1980s.[22] Three written task sets using different content but similar questions were completed by 320 students aged between 7 and 14, and all seven- and eight-year-olds were interviewed. (For older students the task sets were administered over a period of three weekly sessions, but for the second graders the gaps were longer.) The students were drawn from nine rural, suburban, and urban schools. Subsequent phases explored progression over a period of two terms with a separate sample of 92 students from a further seven schools, and followed the second graders from the second sample through to fourth grade (with an unfunded extension to fifth grade and the end of their primary schooling). Discussion here is confined to the larger, first phase, sample, and we will pay particular attention to the youngest group, the seven- and eight-year-olds.

The first task set asked about a particular action, initiated by one agent: why had Claudius decided to invade Britain in A.D. 43? The responses to this have been discussed elsewhere, so we will concentrate here on the second and third task sets, which dealt more with institutions than with actions.[23] Task set 2 gave students materials about the Roman Empire, and on slavery in Roman society, and then told the story of the murder of Pedanius by one of his slaves, and the subsequent crucifixion of all 400 slaves in his household. Students were first asked why the Romans had a law saying that if a master was murdered by a slave, all the slaves in the household should be killed, and, second, why the law had been carried out on this occasion.

Task set 3 described the Anglo-Saxon institution of trial by oath helping and the ordeal, and asked why the Anglo-Saxons used the ordeal to find out if someone was guilty of a crime. The materials provided took the students through the proceedings in a series of cartoons, and further illustrated the procedure with a story of a particular trial. They also gave details of the social organization of Anglo-Saxon England, of religious beliefs, and the punishments employed.

In both task sets responses were initially analyzed inductively, picking out recognizable ideas that (given the nature of the data) could not be broken down into combinations of simpler ideas. These were then grouped into broader categories, and responses coded by two raters. Agreement between raters was 93 percent for the second task set using 25 categories. In the third task set four groups of categories were employed: deficit (16 categories), beliefs (23 categories), purposes (11 categories), and situation (5 categories), and agreement was better than 92 percent. There is space here to give illustrations only of some frequently used ideas from the broader categories.

Common ideas used to explain the Roman law demanding the execution of the slaves (the Pedanius task) included, for example, appeal to notions of deterrence and prevention of further offences. Explanations suggesting that the Romans were trying to prevent other slaves from the same household (who might have been complicit in the murder) from repeating the offence, were coded under the category "Prevention." Responses suggesting that the law would deter potential offenders, either with the assumption that even if the perpetrator remained unidentified he or she would still not escape, or with no indication as to how deterrence might work, were coded under "Deterrence." If a mechanism were suggested that worked by making potential murderers feel guilty about what would happen to their comrades, the response was coded in the category "Moral deterrence." Responses suggesting that deterrence might be designed to operate through ensuring that slaves reported any threat to their masters, rather than being dependent on deterring the potentially dangerous individuals themselves, were coded under "Prudential deterrence."

Some explanations referred to Roman views about slavery. Examples of ideas grouped in this category (ideas about the status of slaves) were the notion that slaves "were not proper human beings," or were regarded "as property." Where students' ideas went beyond Roman views about slaves to consider the social situation created by such views, responses were allocated to the categories "System of slavery" or "Slave-related situation." Examples of the "system" category were the idea that (given the status of slaves) masters were vulnerable because of the sheer numbers of slaves, or that Pedanius's importance in such a social system demanded symbolic action in response to his murder.

In making sense of the Anglo-Saxon trial by ordeal (the Saxon law task), some students tried to explain the mechanisms involved in trial by ordeal. The category "God helps" included the idea that "God would do it" (make the accused sink or float), and that "God would help" the accused. The category "God sign" included ideas of "a message from God," "a sign from God," and "consulting God." Ideas that appealed to the nature of God in the eyes of the Anglo-Saxons were categorized under "God nature," and included notions like that of an all-seeing God, or an interventionist, miracle-working God. Explanatory references to particular features of the process of the ordeal—for example, the importance of the priest, or the use of holy water—were allocated to the category "Specifics." As in the Pedanius task, the idea of deterrence was frequently invoked. Separate categories were used for ideas that stopped at general and unspecific deterrence, reference to deterrence from crime through the threat of suffering, and ideas that saw the ordeal as aimed at deterring people from making spurious claims to innocence, or as a way of stopping frivolous appeals.

How did students approach the problem of making sense of strange past institutions, and what can we say about their conceptions of historical understanding or empathy on the basis of their responses? In the remainder of this paper we will briefly set out some broad patterns of differences in ideas between younger and older students, and then look in more detail at the ideas of the seven- and eight year-olds.

Some Broad Patterns in the CHATA Responses

There is not space here to examine fully the complex and varied ideas in students' responses, so this section will refer to some indicative patterns, characteristic either of a wide range of responses, or revealing major differences between younger and older students.

In the case of both the Roman law demanding the execution of the slaves (the Pedanius task) and the Anglo Saxon trial by ordeal (Saxon law task), many students, but especially younger ones, explained the paradoxical behavior in terms of a deficit. Deficit explanations were those in which institutions were explained in terms of what the Romans or Saxons did not have or did not know. They had no practical or scientific knowledge, they were morally ignorant, or more generally lacked understanding.

Hence people in the past had no other way of dealing with the problem they faced, or knew no better. A common claim was that the Romans did not know who Pedanius's killer was, or that they did not know any way of finding the culprit (and wanted an easy solution), or that they did not know what to do with the rest of the slaves. Some younger students were inclined to explain in terms of moral deficit, maintaining that the Romans did not know about God and Jesus (see figure 2.1).

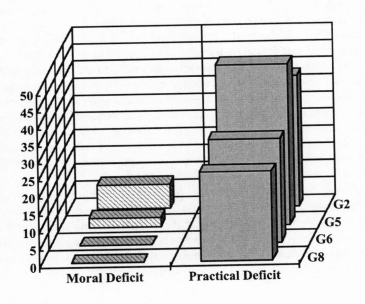

Figure 2.1 Pedanius Task
Deficit explanations, by grade

Similarly, the Saxons had no other way of finding out who was guilty, did not know about police or courts, or did not know about human healing and medicine, or about the practical physics of floating and sinking (see figure 2.2). Deficit explanations were more frequent among younger students, who were also more

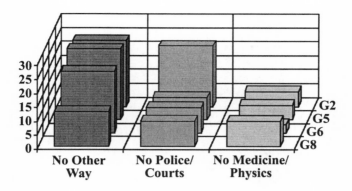

Figure 2.2 Saxon law task
Deficit explanations, by grade

likely than older students to say that the people concerned were not clever. In the Saxon law task older students tended to complain that the practice would not work, rather than that the people were stupid, but, perhaps surprisingly, were also more likely than younger students to claim that everyone would die, or—depending on the student's assumptions—be found guilty or innocent. There was a tendency to assume that the Saxons did not know about very simple practical matters, and could not, for example, have observed how and when people floated or sank, or rates of healing.

An error in the cartoon allowed us to press very hard on students' ideas about this latter point. The cartoon showing the examination of the accused person's hand after trial by hot water carried the text "It hasn't healed properly! You are guilty!" Before they began the task, students were asked to turn to this cartoon, and were told that a very serious mistake had been made in the wording. Instead of "hasn't healed," it should read "isn't healing." The students were then instructed to alter the wording to correct the error. This did not stop large numbers of students complaining that it was stupid to expect a scald to heal in three days (see figure 2.3).

Fewer students commented directly on the stupidity of the Romans (although deficit explanations were very common, as figure 2.1 indicates). This may be because of substantive ideas about the Romans (who may have acquired a certain grudging respect), but might also be a consequence of differences in the tasks. In the Saxon law task the purpose is built into the practice, but does not seem to make any sense, whereas in the Pedanius task it is the purpose of the law that is the problem. The Saxon law task thus demands an explanation beyond the (given) purpose, in effect directly demanding how the institution could conceivably be understood as meeting its purpose: it is perhaps not surprising that some students

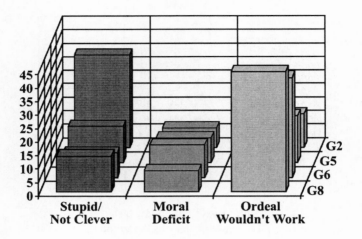

Figure 2.3 Saxon law task
Ineptitude, by grade

were driven to express contempt for what they saw as Saxon stupidity (see the discussion of "purposes" immediately following, and of "fixed human beliefs" in the second grade in part 5 below).

The purposes students offered for the institutions in question showed a shift (with age) from everyday present conceptions to responses that took account of the beliefs and values of the time. Younger students in both the Pedanius and the Saxon law tasks tended to convert the institution itself into something different, allowing it to be made intelligible in modern terms. Hence the Saxon ordeal was converted from a trial into the punishment (or torture) of someone already known to have been guilty, and the Pedanius law was construed as being designed for cases where the killer was not known (see part 3 for second-grade examples).

Many students (in all grades, but more in grades 6 and 8) used the notion of deterrence, usually thinking in present terms: avoidance of personal suffering in the Saxon law task, avoidance of bringing suffering upon other slaves—moral deterrence—in the Pedanius task (see figures 2.4 to 2.6).

A few older students tied deterrence to the beliefs of the time, in the case of Roman law, to the idea that deterrence would work through the need to keep masters informed of any plots, and also to the necessity of maintaining the existing social order. In the Saxon ordeal, very small numbers of students attributed the deterrent effect of the ordeal to belief in God. More sophisticated recognition of the role of beliefs about God were coded under "religion" and "mechanism" (see figures 2.7 and 2.8).

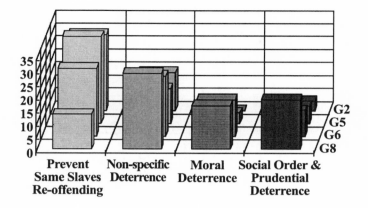

Figure 2.4 Pedanius task

Purposes of law, by grade (most frequent response categories)

Attempts to unpack the beliefs and values that might lie behind the institutions, and to use them in explanations, were more frequent with older students, but where younger students adopted this approach, there was often still a stereotypical element in their suggestions. In the Pedanius task relatively small numbers of responses explained the law by reference to ideas: most students who did so either explained in general terms that the Romans did not care about their slaves, or, more attentive to specific Roman values, pointed out that to the Romans slaves were "res," "things" (see figure 2.9). On the Saxon task, where the purpose of the ordeal was already given, there were more attempts to fit it into a

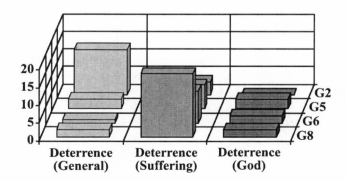

Figure 2.5 Saxon law task

Deterrence, by grade

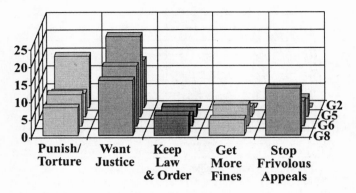

Figure 2.6 Saxon law task
Purposes (other than deterrence), by grade

pattern of beliefs and values (see figure 2.7). Students from all grades recognized that Anglo-Saxon religion played a part, but the younger students who mentioned this tended to explain that "it was just their religion." A large group of responses from all grades (but with few from second graders) explained that the Saxons had a "strong belief" in God. The small number of students who pointed out how the *kind* of God the Saxons believed in explains why the ordeal would make sense mostly came from grades seven and eight. This latter group cited, among other things, Saxon belief in God's omniscience, and the fact that he worked miracles on a daily basis.

By grade six considerable numbers of students were postulating a *mechanism* for the ordeal, ranging from simply saying that God would "help," through the

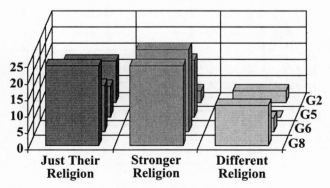

Figure 2.7 Saxon law task
Anglo-Saxon religion, by grade

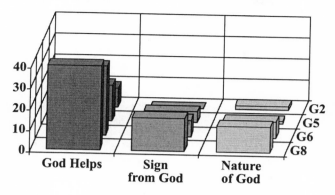

Figure 2.8 Saxon law task
Mechanism for ordeal, by grade

more specific claim that the ordeal amounted to a "sign" from or "consultation" of God, to pointing out how an interventionist and all-seeing God would explain the workings of the ordeal (sometimes with reference to the use of holy water and the role of the priest) (see figure 2.8).

Very few of the younger students (none from the second grade) appealed to the wider situational context to explain the institution in question. In the Pedanius task, the majority of references to the situation were made in atemporal or present terms (often mentioning the problem of selling "tainted" slaves). A few students

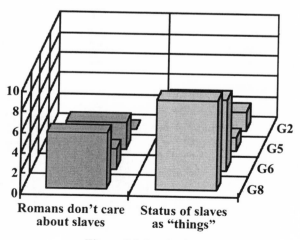

Figure 2.9 Pendanius task
Ideas about slaves, by grade

P. Lee and R. Ashby

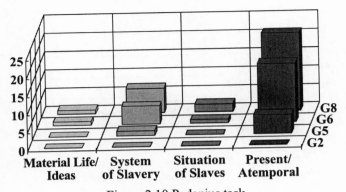

Figure 2.10 Pedanius task
Reference to situation by grade
(Note that both the grade order and shift in complexity in ideas
are reversed in this figure to allow clearer display.)

referred to issues arising from slavery as a system (for example, the vulnerability of the masters, or the symbolic importance of a man of Pedanius's stature). Some referred to the origins of slaves, and two students, one in grade six and one in grade eight, appealed to wider issues of culture (the strict norms of the Empire) and material life (see figure 2.10).

References to the situation were also absent from the second grade in responses to the Saxon law task, and only one fifth grade student mentioned the wider context. A small number of sixth and eighth grade students, however, used elements of the situation to explain the ordeal, mentioning, for example, the importance of the Church and the hierarchical social structure (see figure 2.11). All these contextual matters were highly visible in the materials, but only a few students chose to employ them to explain the problematic institutions.

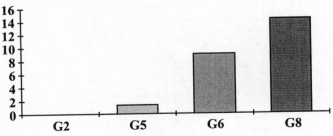

Figure 2.11 Saxon law task
Numbers of reference to situation by grade

The Responses of Second Graders

We should stress right at the outset that there was a very wide range in the responses of students in grade two. Some second graders responded in a way more characteristic of eighth grade students. They behaved as if they believed that even puzzling institutions like the ones in the tasks could be made intelligible by understanding how people saw their world. They recognized (if sometimes tentatively) that people in the past would not necessarily see the world as we see it. As a consequence they did not assume that the past could be simply explained by appeal to what it did not have or did not know, let alone by resort to the assumption that people in the past were stupid. The number of second graders thinking like this was small—three or four out of 55—but the importance of these students is that they indicate how mistaken it would be for teachers to have low expectations of young children.

On the Pedanius task, having already talked in terms of preventing further killing by the slaves of Pedanius's household, and deterring other slaves, Katie explained the law by saying that slaves "had to look after their master, not kill him." The interviewer (looking for a mechanism) asked why the law might have stopped slaves killing their masters. Katie replied, "'Cos he, one of the slaves, might have told someone that he was going to kill the master and the other slave could try to stop him." Katie may have hit on this mechanism by chance, but her claim that the Romans were "probably cleverer than us in different ways," although tied to concrete matters like armor, indicates a readiness to take the Romans seriously in their own right. Her response on the Saxon law task indicates that this was not merely respect for the Romans.

Katie:	God might not forgive him about what he did, so he'll get caught by it, by putting his hand in water or something.
Interviewer:	So it had something to do with God, did it?
Katie:	Yeah.
Interviewer:	Why do you think the Anglo-Saxons had an idea that it had something to do with God?
Katie:	'Cos he could make it heal and things like that.

Once again Katie was able to give a mechanism, allowing her to cash the information she had picked out about Saxon ideas of God. Even many older students did not do this, and (as suggested by figures 2.1 to 2.3) were content to ascribe the ordeal to Saxon ignorance and stupidity. [24]

Although Katie was sure that the Saxons were technologically inferior—"they lived in a different time when things weren't invented"—she chose the statement, "They were just as clever as we are, but they had a different idea of

what God would do than we have," as the best explanation. She was very clear
that the Saxons had different ideas from us, although she found it hard to explain,
and, under strong pressure from the interviewer, resorted to concrete items to
exemplify her stance.

Interviewer: But apart from, like, *things*, do you think their *ideas* were different
               to ours?
Katie: Yes.
Interviewer: Not their ideas about *things*, but their ideas.
Katie: Yeah.
Interviewer: What, what made them different to ours, what makes them, what
               makes their ideas different to our ideas?
Katie: 'Cos. . . . Don't know.
Interviewer: You said they believed in God.
Katie: Yeah.
Interviewer   Yeah. And that was, helped explain why they had the ordeal.
               Don't you think we believe in God?
Katie: Yeah.
Interviewer   Why don't we have the ordeal then?
Katie: Because we have other ways to find out if someone has taken
               something or not.
Interviewer   Right, so why didn't they have other ways?
Katie: 'Cos electrical things wasn't invented. . . .
Interviewer   Mm hmm.
Katie: . . . and things like that.
Interviewer: So how does that help understand when somebody's committed
               a crime or not?
Katie: Don't know. [25]

Tom also unpacked the ideas behind the ordeal. He wrote, "Because they
would think God was seeing it went right. The Anglo-Saxons must have thought
it was one of God's miracles." He explained to the interviewer:

Tom: 'Cos like, if they thought God could do miracles, they would do
               that, and if they were innocent it would make, like [inaudible]
               people, if they were guilty, because of what happened to the
               guilty people.
Interviewer: Right. . . .
Tom: I thought it was that.
Interviewer: . . . right, so what were they asking God to do, really?
Tom: Er, not look after the one that's guilty, so [inaudible].
Interviewer: Right, not look after the one that's guilty. Right, and . . .
Tom: . . . and, and the cold water one, don't look after the innocent one,
               'cos that one sinks.

Tom chose the same summary explanation statement as Katie, confirming his confidence in the abilities of the Saxons.

Rhys took a similar line.

Interviewer:	Why do you think they did that [used the ordeal], Rhys?
Rhys:	Erm, God might, make it heal if, they're not guilty and he might leave it if they were guilty.
Interviewer:	Mm, so it had something to do with God, did it?
Rhys:	Yeah.

He expanded on this later in the interview.

Rhys:	'Cos they were clever as much as us, but they knew other things. And their idea of God for the ordeal was, that they would make, if they done the hot iron, and it never healed, they would know that God never made it, made it heal, so he was guilty.
Interviewer:	Right.
Rhys:	God saw him do it.

Asked whether it is hard to understand people in the past, Rhys said it is, and explained, "Because we never knew what things happened in their time, so we wouldn't know what they are talking about." This is possibly less profound than it may seem, because most students who say things like this are referring simply to problems of access to the past, sometimes expressed in the phrase "No one was there in those days." Nevertheless, Rhys did not locate the problem in the ignorance and technological ineptitude of the past, but with our knowledge. This idea would be impressive even were it found in a much older student.

Much more typical of second graders was the "deficit" approach to explanation offered by Stephen.

Interviewer:	What do you think about these ordeals?
Stephen:	I think it's stupid.
Interviewer:	Tell me more.
Stephen:	Because nice people might have been found guilty, because if it was that bad to hold it might not have healed in three days—it might not have healed for a month if they're not careful, and they could have been injured a long time.
Interviewer:	So why do you think the Anglo-Saxons used this way of trying to find out whether someone was guilty or innocent?
Stephen:	Because they might not have known another way to do it. So they just made up some to see if they floated or not.

There were signs elsewhere in Stephen's interview that he recognized that the Saxons might not have agreed with him, but at the end of the task he chose as the best summary explanation the sentence, "They were backward and stupid. It is ridiculous to throw people in the water or make them carry hot iron. You can't expect people living so long ago to know any better." A stronger case still was put by Michael: "Because, erm, they didn't know as much as us. And they couldn't execute people, 'cos they didn't have enough stuff to execute people."

Terry, considering the law that demanded the execution of all four hundred of Pedanius's slaves, wrote "Because it was the only punishment they could think of." The Romans carried out the punishment because "They didn't know about God and Jesus." Louise, having assimilated the case to the more intelligible situation in which the killer was not known ("they did not know which one killed Pedanius") explained "if they didn't know what to do they'd probably kill them all." Michael's view of the Romans indicated that the deficit was a moral one: they had the law "Because they were cruel." Alex said, "They were just being horrible."

Many youngsters explained the problematic institutions by direct reference to modern institutions or technologies that the Saxons or Romans did not have. Gemma explained the Saxon ordeal in this way.

Interviewer: Why do you think they used it [the ordeal]?
Gemma: Because they didn't sort of have a court at that time.
Interviewer: Mm.
Gemma: And they didn't know what, sort of, to say in the court, so they just sort of tried, erm, these ordeals.
Interviewer: Why do you think they did it like this though? Why have the ordeal? You're right, they didn't have the same sort of trial as we've got today, but why did they do it like this?
Gemma: Because they didn't know any other way of how to do it, did they?
Interviewer: Mm.
Gemma: This, sort of man, probably thought it up.

Gemma's explanation of the ordeal in terms of its origins appears to mirror some of the responses found by Keith Barton: the default explanation for the origin of a social institution is that an individual made it up (see also Stephen's response, quoted above). Thomas came even closer to Barton's respondents, postulating that the ordeal must have been tested.

Interviewer: Why did they do this?
Thomas: Because if they didn't do it they wouldn't know if they were guilty or not.

Interviewer:	So it's their way of finding out whether somebody was guilty or not? Why do you think they chose this way of doing it?
Thomas:	Because if they had a different way, it wouldn't really work. But this way they tested it with someone very brave, and someone was right and someone was wrong, they test it—but they have to be very brave first—and then it just worked.

Michelle also argued that the Saxons must have tested the ordeal.

Interviewer:	Why do you think they used the ordeal?
Michelle:	Erm, because they might not have any other way to test it and it might not have been right.
Interviewer:	All right, well why do you think they had it this way?
Michelle:	Because someone, erm, actually said they were guilty and they, erm, did the test, they did a test, the ordeal anyway and it actually worked.

This does not stop Michelle from thinking the Saxons have failed to notice some basic practical features of human behavior in water.

Interviewer:	So do you think it always worked? And they always got the right answer, you know, innocent or guilty?
Michelle:	No, because, somebody, erm, you know when you're in the swimming pool and you take a deep breath and you float, that's what could have happened. . . .
Interviewer:	Mm.
Michelle:	. . . to somebody who was actually innocent.
Interviewer:	Right, so what's the, do you think the ordeal was very reliable?
Michelle:	No.
Interviewer:	So why do you think they used it? Why did they have this really complicated system that wasn't even very reliable anyway?
Michelle:	Because there probably wasn't, there wasn't another one that was as good as that.
Interviewer:	So this was the best they could come up with. . . .
Michelle:	Yes.
Interviewer:	. . . was it?
Michelle:	They weren't very clever.

It was very common for students of all ages, but especially the younger ones, to assume that people in the past did not grasp simple practical features of the world. Earlier small-scale video recording of students revealed that some even assumed that the Saxons did not understand that people are unable to breathe under water, and similar kinds of response occur throughout the larger CHATA sample. Michelle's ideas exemplify this sort of assumption. Even allowing for the interviewer's introduction of the phrase "the best they could come up with" (which was intended as a disconfirmation check), it is clear that Michelle is operating with a deficit explanation here. Nevertheless, there are some signs that she might be ready to concede that the Saxons were rational enough at least to make the best of what they had.

Another major feature of many of the second graders' responses was the assumption of fixed human values. This was often powerful enough to persuade the students that the institutions *must* have been something that they were not. If the ordeal is to be intelligible, it *must* have been a punishment, not a trial. To make sense of the Roman law about the slaves, it *must* have been the case that the Romans couldn't find out who had carried out the murder of Pedanius. Hence Michelle felt able to explain the law, until the interviewer brought her up against her assumption.

Interviewer:	So why do you think the Romans had this law for killing everybody?
Michelle:	'Cos they didn't really know, um, which slave killed Pedanius.
Interviewer:	Ah, but that's not the law. The law said even if they did know, they'd still kill all 400. Why would they have a law like that?
Michelle:	[Pause.] You've got me thinking now. [Pause.] Because, maybe, they didn't think it was fair on the person who killed him, or something like that.

Joanne's thinking was similar. Having complained that it was unfair to kill all the slaves, she explained "Because, erm, the person who done it, erm, didn't own up and then, and they decided to kill all of them." Hannah went further. Under pressure from the interviewer about the facts of the case, she advanced a conspiracy account, which allowed her to preserve her value assumptions.

Interviewer:	So why did they have a law like this then?
Hannah:	Don't know. Perhaps because they didn't know who killed the, Pedanius. So, er, they killed all of them.
Interviewer:	Right. I think they might have known who did it, and they still crucified them all.
Hannah:	Yes.
Interviewer:	And I think the law was that it didn't matter. . . .
Hannah:	Yes.
Interviewer:	. . . who did it.
Hannah:	Yes, but . . .
Interviewer:	They all had to . . .
Hannah:	. . . yes, 'cos they might have, 'cos they might have poisoned them, and then they, and then they looked at the poison, and then they looked at the hand marks.

Interviewer: I see, OK. You said you think they had it, because if somebody killed somebody else they would not know who killed the person.

Hannah: Mm.

Interviewer: But they had the rule, and they had to do that even if they *did* know.

Hannah: Yes.

Interviewer: So why?

Hannah: Because they, because all of them could have got together as a gang, and then they all could have done it.

Much the same assumptions were apparent in the Saxon case. Victoria explained that the ordeal was "So they would make the right person suffer"; the ordeal was in effect a punishment. Alexandra simply assumed the guilt of the accused, writing "because they steal other people's property." Amanda thought of the whole business as putting people under duress to force the truth out of them: "Otherwise they wouldn't tell the truth if they'd done it." Tommy explained, "Because if they murdered someone they could, erm, get them back." He glossed this further, "'Cos so they were punished."

Ideas of this kind were very common among students in the second grade. People in the past *must* have been doing what we would have done, which means they couldn't be doing what the materials said they were doing. Only our values (fixed in time) could make the institutions intelligible. It seems likely that it is the assumption of fixed human values that provokes students into postulating implausible deficits in past knowledge even of the everyday practical world, or extreme technological deprivation. The Saxons *can't* have known the simple facts about floating, sinking, and scalding or have had axes to execute people in the "normal" way, because there is no other way to explain their breach of basic values.

Conclusions

The importance of recent work (and particularly Keith Barton's) is that it suggests ways in which different strands of students' ideas may be related (the researcher's decision to treat certain ideas as distinct concepts may not, of course, be one that a student would accept in the first place). Deficit explanations fit well with the assumptions about change picked out by Barton, which in turn ring true in the light of classroom experience. Students seem to work with a set of assumptions that reinforce one another, are congruent with ideas that serve well in daily life, and also fit what seem to be widespread beliefs about progress. A picture is emerging of a set of "default" assumptions that students employ to make sense of a historical world that does not always conform to their expectations. Components of this set might include the following:

- *Rational action, understood in terms of shared conventions.*
  Explanation in terms of reasons is the basic way in which humans deal with everyday life; but once the shared conventions cannot be relied upon, either there must be something wrong with the people (they are stupid, ignorant, or morally defective), or else the institution must be assimilated to something that fits the conventions.

- *Technological progress.*
  It is apparent from everyday experience, and from what our parents and grandparents say ("We didn't have those in our day"), that technology in its broadest sense is improving all the time. It follows that the past was defective, technologically speaking.

- *Increasing knowledge and understanding.*
  History is progress in knowledge: we know more than our ancestors, and we understand more. This is apparent in every aspect of life, but follows above all from the previous assumption.

- *Rational change.*
  Change, being progressive, is also likely to be rational. People decide to make changes, because they will improve things.

- *"Event change," in particular "knowledge events."*
  Change, the development of institutions (and indeed any process in history) actually happens as discrete events. This "quantum" idea of change is linked to the notion that change is equivalent to events, a finding of work on the Schools History Project. [26] It may be that the idea derives from the previous assumption about rational decisions.

If we combine these ideas (by now rather well attested in the research), we can perhaps begin to see how they produce the kinds of explanations reported in this paper.

- Change takes place when people suddenly realize (by experiment or on the basis of someone's insight or wisdom) that they have got things wrong, or when technological advances allow obviously "better" ways of behaving.
- So if no rationale (practical inference) can be constructed in our terms to make sense of an action or institution, it was probably benighted in some way, generally as a result of ignorance or poor technology.

Researchers are in the process of establishing a picture of students' ideas about understanding past actions, institutions, and social practices (in terms of past values and beliefs about the world) that seems to fit student behavior in both the United Kingdom and the United States. So long as we are clear what is meant, the issue of whether we categorize such ideas as empathy, rational understanding, or perspective taking is not of central importance. If over the next few years we can relate ideas of this kind to notions of progress and change, an important step will have been made to understanding how everyday conceptual frameworks and assumptions affect students' conceptions of history. More work across different cultures may help to shed further light on the currency of similar sets of ideas, and on their stability in different educational and social environments. [27]

The implications of the research on empathy for teaching are considerable. There is not space to discuss these systematically here, and many of the main issues have been discussed elsewhere, so we will confine ourselves to one central matter. [28] Our comments are based on what has happened in the United Kingdom, but it is clear that the ways of thinking described in what follows are likely to be widespread, and to have similar effects elsewhere.

The National Curriculum in England lays down target understandings for young students, not just lists of content. This is one potentially valuable feature of such a centralized institution, but in practice it has had unfortunate consequences. The National Curriculum for history has been set out by unaccountable bureaucratic institutions, which have paid little attention to research, or to the very considerable experience of teachers and examiners involved in the process of curriculum innovation that underpinned the developments in history teaching over the past three decades. Many teachers and textbook writers seem to construe the target understandings in mechanical ways that can cause serious problems. This may be a predictable problem facing centralized systems, but if there is no mechanism for dealing with it, students may learn lower level ideas than they start out with.

In the area of empathy the culprit has been the idea—on the face of it a very sensible one—that young children should learn about similarities and differences between the ways of life of people now and in the past. Unfortunately, textbook writers and teachers set on meeting the targets without thinking what is involved, or understanding where such work is intended to lead, may end up reinforcing the very ideas that research suggests stand in the way of children's understanding. In the absence of any model of progression, the algorithmic collection of similarities and differences may proceed apace, at the expense of the wider issues at stake.

Take the following passages from a textbook about life in the 1920s, designed for first graders:

> Ada worked at home, looking after the children.
> There were no washing machines, so Ada scrubbed
>   the clothes with a bar of soap on a washboard.
> Then she put them through a mangle to squeeze the water out.
> Ada had to put her iron on the range to make it hot.
> There were no electric irons.

Or, later:

> Jean could not watch television.
> There were no televisions when Jean was a little girl.

These passages represent a very natural way to talk to youngsters about the past, and the book is filled with similar examples. Indeed, almost every aspect of life in the 1920s is characterized by the absence of something that we now have: they had no bathrooms or central heating, the radio was sometimes very difficult to hear, and they did not have our medicines. It is important that students learn about past ways of life, and sensible to indicate differences between our lives and theirs. Where it all goes wrong is in the unnoticed assumptions that slip in, and the failure to think about what the underlying message might be, or what the point of all this "then and now" work might be.

The most serious mistake is the causal language. "There were no washing machines, so Ada scrubbed the clothes with a bar of soap on a washboard." But if technological explanations are at stake, Ada's use of a washboard and soap is not explained by the condescending claim *"because she did not have a washing machine,"* but by the more appropriate statement *"because in the 1920s people had equipment that allowed them to wash clothes at home,"* not by rubbing them with stones at the riverside.

Young children exposed to texts or teaching of this kind are likely to have their everyday ideas reinforced. They are already exposed to this kind of thinking in many aspects of their culture, from parents and grandparents on the one hand, to advertisements for new technology on the other, not to mention a host of more subtle reaffirmations of progress. If it becomes the basis of their history, instead of moving on to a different—historical—way of looking at the past, they will learn that the past was an unfortunate and benighted world, and their assumptions will stand in the way of their understanding.

CHATA evidence suggests that a few very young children already work with ideas more closely approximating historical assumptions about the past and how we may understand it. There seems good reason to think that with suitable teaching, many more of them might be encouraged to think in this way. Some key ideas in history may be counter-intuitive, but they are not insuperably difficult, and if we recognize that an important part of learning history is to help students gradually build more powerful ideas, teaching becomes a more purposeful and exciting activity.

Learning history is learning about particular passages of the past, but it is also acquiring historical ways of making sense of what is learned. Students have ideas about how the world works, including the past world, and teachers must know what kinds of ideas their students are working with, if they are to have any chance of changing them. Such changes in ideas are at the heart of history teaching. In this sense, history should be thought of as a progressive, not merely aggregative, subject. An education in history is not just the accumulation of discrete items of knowledge, but the acquisition and development of historical understandings.

Notes

1. For accounts of historical understanding that elucidate the sense and degree of rationality required, see R. G. Collingwood, *The Idea of History* (Oxford: Oxford University Press, 1946); W. H. Dray, *Laws and Explanation in History* (London: Oxford University Press, 1964); and G. H. von Wright, *Explanation and Understanding* (London: Routledge & Kegan Paul, 1971).

2. The Schools History Project (originally the Schools Council Project History 13-16) developed an examination course designed to introduce students to history as a form of knowledge—its key methodological ideas as well as its accounts of passages of the past. By the late 1980s, well over one third of 16-year-olds studying history in the UK were following the course.

3. S. Deuchar, *History—and GCSE History* (London: Centre for Policy Studies, 1987).

4. A. Low-Beer, "Empathy and History," *Teaching History* 55 (April 1989): 8-12. Our comments here recognize the enormous importance of the Schools History Project (SHP) in this area, but our position does not mean that we accept all the practices of SHP. In any case, "the Project" likely never had a monolithic position on many major issues. This suspicion becomes a near certainty if "SHP" is understood to include its teachers.

5. Warnings about "skills" were evident in the 1970s. See, for example, A. Gard and P. J. Lee, "Educational Objectives for the Study of History," in *History Teaching and Historical Understanding*, ed. A. K. Dickinson and P. J. Lee (London: Heinemann Educational Books, 1978), 21-38. Still, confusion continues. The worst muddles occur in the assimilation of complex multi-track cognitive abilities to single track skills improved by practice (Low-Beer is spot on target here) and in the confusion of specific historical conceptual understanding with acquisition of generic "skills" like "analysis" or "synthesis."

6. Low-Beer's position here is obscure. Unclear is whether or not she wants to deny that feelings *should* be or that they *could* be developed in school. If feelings develop, why could they not be helped to develop in school, even though worries may attend such efforts in the context of history?

7. Low-Beer also seems to think that if research findings are cautious and qualified, then they can be ignored. See, for example, A. Low-Beer, "Empathy and History," *Teaching History* 55 (April 1989): 8. Presumably, on this basis, one is then free to assert what one pleases without having to deal with inconvenient evidence.

8. D. Shemilt, "Beauty and the Philosopher: Empathy in History and Classroom," in *Learning History*, ed. A. K. Dickinson, P. J. Lee, and P. J. Rogers (London: Heinemann Educational Books, 1984), 39-84.

9. Low-Beer eventually gets around to mentioning more germane uses of the notion of empathy, but fails to distinguish different senses of "looking at events and issues from several points of view." Also, she never manages to get beyond the vague idea of making "human" sense of historical information, which she claims is unhelpfully "contrasted with rote-learned, dry-as-dust facts." See A. Low-Beer, "Empathy and History," *Teaching History* 55 (April 1989): 10-11. Some sympathy for her position might be garnered if anyone had actually argued the case she attacks, but, apparently, she simply has confused at least three different ideas: general nostrums about "making sense of information." Margaret Donaldson's highly specific use of "human sense," and the idea that historical explanation in terms of reasons for action requires knowledge to be harnessed to understanding how something could be a reason. See, also, M. Donaldson, *Children's Minds* (London: Fontana, 1978).

10. This treatment is congruent with the historical record of history education in general in Britain, and the Schools History Project in particular. Low-Beer's article curiously fails to take into account the developing patterns of usage in the late eighties.

11. See K. Jenkins and P. Brickley, "Reflections on the Empathy Debate," *Teaching History* 55 (April 1989): 18-23.

12. Jenkins and Brickley operate from a concealed empiricist base: either we know things directly, or we do not know them. Hence, they deny that truth is an appropriate term for historians to use. Furthermore, they appear to get into a weird muddle when they argue "clearly we cannot empathize *directly* with Cromwell because we have only reached him [sic] *indirectly*, i.e., via Elton *et al.* So actually we are not empathizing with Cromwell at all, with his mind, but Elton's." See K. Jenkins and P. Brickley, "Reflections on the Empathy Debate," *Teaching History* 55 (April 1989): 22. (Presumably, Elton's mind is accessible and Cromwell's would have been, if only Elton were not in his way. However, if Cromwell's mind is inaccessible in principle, so is Elton's, and with it, in the same way, Jenkins' and Brickley's.) Jenkins and Brickley jump out of their empiricism to pour scorn on it, but back into their stance in order to justify their claims that the past is unknowable and that understanding other people is impossible. For an expansion of Jenkins' position, see his *Rethinking History* (London: Routledge, 1991), in which the Jekyll and Hyde empiricism is even more pronounced.

13. This necessarily brief, perhaps tendentious, account omits the important notion of empathy as a *disposition*, which is arguably central to history. For a more detailed discussion, see P. J. Lee, "Historical Imagination," in *Learning History*, ed. A. K. Dickinson, P. J. Lee, and P. J. Rogers (London: Heinemann Educational Books, 1984), 85-116.

14. See R. G. Collingwood, *The Idea of History* (Oxford: Oxford University Press, 1946); L. O. Mink, "Collingwood's Dialectic of History," *History and Theory* 7 (1969):

3-37; and L. O. Mink, *Mind History and Dialectic* (Bloomington: Indiana University Press, 1969).

15. Recent work on students' ideas about historical accounts suggests a similar relation between everyday ideas and those required for history. One important way in which children learn the notions of truth and falsity is in learning to "tell the truth" about past events. Notions of "truth" and "story" are closely linked, and telling the truth is judged by whether the told story represents the known story. In this sense, the story is a known, fixed pattern of actions and events (picked out by common assumptions about what is at stake—e.g., torn clothes or arrival late for a meal—in a shared way of life) that acts as a touchstone for truth. In history, no fixed, known story exists to serve as a touchstone and the assumptions of the actors in the story cannot be assumed to fit shared conventions. Everyday concepts of story and truth, therefore, mean that the relevant historical concepts are counter-intuitive.

16. See R. Ashby and P. J. Lee, "Children's Concepts of Empathy and Understanding in History," in *The History Curriculum for Teachers*, ed. C. Portal (Lewes: Falmer Press, 1987), 62-88; K. Barton, "Narrative Simplifications in Elementary Students' Historical Thinking," in *Advances in Research on Teaching Vol. 6: Teaching and Learning History*, ed. J. Brophy (Greenwich: JAI Press, 1996), 51-83; P. J. Lee, "Explanation and Understanding in History," in *History Teaching and Historical Understanding*, ed. A. K. Dickinson and P. J. Lee (London: Heinemann Educational Books, 1978), 72-93; A. K. Dickinson and P. J. Lee, "Understanding and Research," in *History Teaching and Historical Understanding*, ed. A. K. Dickinson and P. J. Lee (London: Heinemann Educational Books, 1978), 94-120; A. K. Dickinson and P. J. Lee, "Making Sense of History," in *Learning History*, ed. A. K. Dickinson, P. J. Lee, and P. J. Rogers (London: Heinemann Educational Books, 1984), 117-153; M. Downey, "Perspective Taking in Historical Thinking: Doing History in a Fifth-Grade Classroom" (paper presented at AERA Annual Meeting, San Francisco); L. Jacott, A. Lopez-Manjon, and M. Carretero, "Generating Explanations in History," in *Learning and Reasoning in History*, ed. J. E. Voss and M. Carretero (London: Woburn Press, 1998), 294-306; P. Knight, "A Study of Teaching and Children's Understanding of People in the Past," *Research in Education* 44 (November 1990): 39-53; P. J. Lee, A. K. Dickinson, and R. Ashby, "Just Another Emperor: Understanding Action in the Past," in *International Journal of Educational Research* 27 (1997): 233-244; C. Portal, "Empathy as an Objective for History Teaching," in *The History Curriculum for Teachers*, ed. C. Portal (Lewes: Falmer Press, 1987), 89-99; and D. Shemilt, "Beauty and the Philosopher: Empathy in History," in *Learning History*, ed. A. K. Dickinson, P. J. Lee, and P. J. Rogers (London: Heinemann Educational Books, 1984), 39-84.

17. K. Barton, "Narrative Simplifications in Elementary Students' Historical Thinking," in *Advances in Research on Teaching Vol. 6: Teaching and Learning History*, ed. J. Brophy (Greenwich: JAI Press, 1996).

18. S. Wineburg, "Historical Thinking and Other Unnatural Acts," *Phi Delta Kappan* 80 (March 1998): 488-499.

19. The work of Peter Seixas on students' reading of films provides evidence from a slightly different starting point for this component of their ideas. Seixas found that for some students one criterion of *plausibility* (and possibly even *authenticity*) was the degree to which past moral attitudes and concerns depicted in the films resemble ours. If the

present provides a touchstone for plausibility, then the working assumption is that people in the past were fundamentally like us in values and beliefs. Students believing this are likely to find it difficult to make sense of past ideas and practices. See, for example, P. Seixas, "Confronting The Moral Frames of Popular Film: Young People Respond to Historical Revisionism," *American Journal of Education* 102 (May 1994): 261-285.

20. Quoted in S. Wineburg, "Historical Thinking and Other Unnatural Acts," *Phi Delta Kappan* 80 (March 1998): 498.

21. See P. J. Lee, "Explanation and Understanding in History," in *History Teaching and Historical Understanding*, ed. A. K. Dickinson and P. J. Lee (London: Heinemann Educational Books, 1978), 72-93; and A. K. Dickinson and P. J. Lee, "Understanding and Research," in *History Teaching and Historical Understanding*, ed. A. K. Dickinson and P. J. Lee (London: Heinemann Educational Books, 1978), 94-120.

22. R. Ashby and P. J. Lee, "Children's Concepts of Empathy and Understanding in History," in *The History Curriculum for Teachers*, ed. C. Portal (Lewes: Falmer Press, 1987), 62-88; and A. K. Dickinson and P. J. Lee, "Making Sense of History," in *Learning History*, ed. A. K. Dickinson, P. J. Lee, and P. J. Rogers (London: Heinemann Educational Books, 1984), 117-153.

23. P. J. Lee, A. K. Dickinson, and R. Ashby, "Just Another Emperor: Understanding Action in the Past," *International Journal of Educational Research* 27 (1997): 233-244.

24. Figures 2.1-2.3 show proportions of students who included deficit ideas in their responses. Many of these students will have had further, more powerful ideas, too. These figures should *not* be taken to indicate that all these students stuck at deficit explanations.

25. This interview was the last of Katie's three interviews. Therefore, the interviewer felt free to push harder than she would have done earlier; the interviewer faced no danger of influencing later responses.

26. D. Shemilt, *History 13-16 Evaluation Study* (Edinburgh: Holmes McDougall, 1980).

27. Taiwanese researchers are beginning to research in this field and work recently completed in Portugal and nearing completion in Spain and England will provide a wider base for our understanding. See I. Barca, "Adolescent Students' Ideas About Provisional Historical Explanation" (unpublished doctoral dissertation, University of London, 1997), and L. Cercadillo, "Significance in History: Students' Ideas in England and Spain" (doctoral dissertation in progress, University of London, forthcoming).

28. R. Ashby and P. J. Lee, "Children's Concepts of Empathy and Understanding in History," in *The History Curriculum for Teachers*, ed. C. Portal (Lewes: Falmer Press, 1987), 62-88; A. K. Dickinson and P. J. Lee, "Understanding and Research," in *History Teaching and Historical Understanding*, ed. A. K. Dickinson and P. J. Lee (London: Heinemann Educational Books, 1978), 94-120; A. K. Dickinson and P. J. Lee, "Making Sense of History," in *Learning History*, ed. A. K. Dickinson, P. J. Lee, and P. J. Rogers (London: Heinemann Educational Books, 1984), 117-153; C. Portal, "Empathy as an Objective for History Teaching," in *The History Curriculum for Teachers*, ed. C. Portal (Lewes: Falmer Press, 1987), 89-99; D. Shemilt, *History 13-16 Evaluation Study* (Edinburgh: Holmes McDougall, 1980); and D. Shemilt, "Beauty and the Philosopher: Empathy in History and Classroom," in *Learning History*, ed. A. K. Dickinson, P. J. Lee, and P. J. Rogers (London: Heinemann Educational Books, 1984), 39-84.

Chapter 4

From Empathic Regard to Self-Understanding: Im/Positionality, Empathy, and Historical Contextualization

Bruce A. VanSledright

By 1830, the Cherokee people of the North American southeast confronted a set of laws imposed on them by Andrew Jackson and the United States government that threatened their inhabitancy of a large area in present-day Georgia and Mississippi, a place they had called home for generations. Brought together to discuss their fate, the Cherokee spoke of many things. However, they were most concerned with their potential removal from their homeland. One Cherokee leader remarked:

> We are aware that some persons suppose it will be for our advantage to remove beyond the Mississippi. We think otherwise. Our people universally think otherwise...We wish to remain on the land of our fathers. We have a perfect and original right to remain without interruption or molestation. The treaties with us, and laws of the United States made in pursuance of treaties, guarantee our residence and our privileges, and secure us against intruders. Our only request is, that these treaties may be fulfilled, and these laws executed.[1]

This passage appears in Howard Zinn's *A People's History of the United States* in a chapter in which he describes in rather vivid detail the events surrounding the southeast Indians' forcible dispossession of their lands in the course of U.S. "expansion."[2]

An articulate, white, middle-class prospective elementary teacher, Lynn, who was reading this Zinn chapter and thinking aloud about what she read, reacted to the Cherokee leader's remarks with this vocalization:

> So, they are trying to—they are pleading for the government it seems—they are trying to make an effort to gain support from the U.S. government. But I guess the U.S. government keeps turning them back. This makes me, ah, this makes me just hate Europeans, and you know, I keep saying "we" like, because I guess it is my ancestors and most everybody's ancestors that live in this country—well, I guess a lot I should say—but it just makes me hate my heritage almost, you know. I guess it is a different time, a different place, and different attitudes but, it really frustrates me and it definitely gives me a different perspective on my feelings today, and understanding how things are today, and why they are today. It really gives me new insight to have a better perspective on things right now. (protocol transcript p. 42)

Here, Lynn appears to experience a form of collective guilt. Reluctantly identifying with her white European ancestors, she attempts to distance herself from them by locating the policies and practices of Indian dispossession in another era, one with different customs, attitudes, and values. She seems to use this "distancing" maneuver as a method of reducing her sense of guilt, but she cannot quite bring herself to escape it. Noting that she now has gained a different sense of her white Anglo legacy, she remains plagued by a feeling of collective historical responsibility for that legacy. She evaluates her European ancestors and finds them morally suspect. Despite her efforts to locate their legacy in a different era, characterized generally by values and attitudes at odds with her own, she still feels that she cannot escape the ethical taint of their actions because she traces her ancestry to these same Anglo-Americans, and back through their origins to Europe.

This passage appears to help reconfigure Lynn's understanding, to make her more sensitive to the responsibilities of a legacy she is convinced she shares. The passage simultaneously provokes an attempt at catharsis as Lynn seeks a release from a feeling of collective guilt by locating what she reads to be revolting actions in another historical era. This move is only partially successful, largely because details about what might make the Jackson-era policies more historically comprehensible and potentially less aberrant and morally dubious are not made available to her in Zinn's narrative.[3]

* * * * *

Is Lynn engaged in a historically empathic act here, one registered in her expressions of contempt for her ancestors and their treatment of the Cherokee? Does she genuinely feel what the Cherokee must have experienced as they attempted to ward off what many of them must have worried was inevitable?

Is she inside their world, their heads, their hearts, looking out at a strange power intent on moving them—despite promises and treaties to the contrary—off a land they have only known to be home. Or is she simply presentizing her understanding, imposing her own moral sentiments on events, and maneuvering to distance herself from historical moral culpability. Does she understand Andrew Jackson, Manifest Destiny, and the historical context of events that were perpetrated by agents who lived during a period where our present-day sensibilities were not shared?

These are tough questions to answer. Most likely, Lynn is in some sense empathically engaged here (but not necessarily in an historical way). She seems to feel for the Cherokee. As she reads the way Zinn amasses the evidence in his narrative account, she can look out from where the Cherokee sit and see what portends for them. The sight is one of dispossession and misery. Her ethical disposition is offended by the actions of those who seem so callously ruthless toward what seem like civilized, peaceful people, who are pursuing a last ditch effort to find a way to save their native land and their way of life. She also seems aware that, by virtue of blood, she is closer to the perpetrators than to the victims. This makes her angry, because pangs of collective guilt well up inside her.

Prior to reading Zinn's account of Jackson's forced dispossession of the southeast Native American tribes, Lynn reported that her memory of this portion of American history was characterized by thoughts of Jackson the war hero, the rugged frontiersman, the people's democrat. She noted that she knew the Native Americans were gradually but systematically herded onto reservations, on which many of the rights Americans often assume as entitlements were denied and/or suspended. However, she knew few of the details, particularly of events during Jackson's administration. Zinn's story put flesh and bones on these events, as it turned what to her had been only an abstraction called the "Trail of Tears" into an unforgettable human tragedy.

On the other hand, as Lynn reads, she also realizes that this period in question occurred more than 160 years ago. She understands that circumstances then were not as today. Indeed, she remarks, ". . . it [was] a different time, a different place, and [people had] different attitudes. . . ." In this phrase, she appears to engage in a bit of historical contextualization in an attempt to make sense of the period on its own terms, rather than by assessing it against her own present standards. However, she has difficulty pushing this notion very far. She does not speak in detail about how things were different. She simply makes note of the situation and then uses it as a method to rationalize why she need not feel too collectively guilty after all. She does not appear to understand Jackson and his desire to move "un-Americanizable" Indians off land that held, from his perspective, the key to U.S. economic and democratic expansion. She has difficulty seeing the world from Jackson's perspective. Zinn's account propels her to see only the damage Jackson causes, his racist removal policies, and his apparent self-righteousness.

In fairness, Zinn appears to be a relative master at portraying events in a way that may well dispose many readers to react as Lynn does. Zinn has little interest in encouraging sympathetic, much less empathic, responses towards Jackson and his policies. If anything, by the way he structures this account, one cannot help but see Jackson as duplicitous, cruel, and unforgivable. Zinn's sentiments lie with the Cherokee, and the Choctaw, and Seminole—those dispossessed and marched to the Oklahoma Territory on the infamous "Trail of Tears." This chapter in Zinn's text is difficult to read and not be moved to identify with the plight of the Natives. Still, as historian David Harlan notes, powerful history books make us respond in just this way, as though the historian's own caring about those with whom he/she chooses to show affinity is transferred to the reader.[4]

Zinn's book is an unapologetic historical treatise on turning the consensus, military-economic-political celebration scholarship of the 1950s upside down. He makes clear that his intention in the 600-page *People's History* is to tell an American story from the vantage point of those typically marginalized and/or ignored by the consensus histories of the 1950s. In much of the book, he adopts the role of social historian, one in which "the common people" such as African slaves, women, day laborers, Native Americans, and various ethnic groups are characterized as perhaps more to be credited for the making of the "mighty" United States of America than are the long-celebrated Anglos who have tried to dominate the military, the economic system, and the political process. Zinn argues throughout that Anglo success is dependent on the efforts and energies of these "common folk"; their blood and sweat have made America great.

Empathic Regard

So then, what sort of reaction to Zinn's account is Lynn's? Is it the sort of empathy that historians use when they attempt to understand the worlds of people they inquire about? Is it the type that comes with the process of historically contextualizing the past, setting it into its own historical milieu so that it can be comprehended on its own terms? Is Lynn's reaction to the passage an effort to get inside the heads and hearts of the historical agents in question, so as to better make sense of why they did what they did? Or is her reaction of a different sort of empathy, one that represents a more common emotional response to a tragedy almost too difficult to bear? Is she reacting as someone might who was observing the closing scenes of the latest incarnation of Shakespeare's centuries-old *Romeo And Juliet*?

From what we can tell, her response is most likely more the latter rather than the former. However, it contains elements of both: (1) a form of emotional empathy that people experience with tragic Shakespearean characters because their actions often can be interpreted and understood in present-day terms and judged by contemporary standards, and (2) a form of historical empathy that is different than emotional regard because it recognizes that identification with the circumstances in question needs to be qualified by the passage of time, that time has altered the landscape in ways that make comprehending historical agents and their actions more arduous. Lynn demonstrates each here, but in a way that makes teasing them apart difficult and perplexing.

Ashby and Lee contend that, when applied to understanding the past, empathy does not take the form of a simple and temporary propensity "to feel like" or "walk in the shoes of" those who lived before us "as though they were us." Rather, historical empathy is—although a mysterious accomplishment—one that demands considerable thoughtful effort. They argue:

> Entertaining the beliefs, goals, and values of other people or—insofar as one can talk in this way—of other societies, is a difficult intellectual achievement. It is difficult because it means holding in mind whole structures of ideas that are not one's own, and with which one may profoundly disagree. And not just holding them in mind as inert knowledge, but being able to work with them in order to explain and understand what people did in the past. All of this is hard because it requires a high level of thinking.[5]

Borrowing from the "empathic stages" work of Shemilt,[6] Ashby and Lee re-characterized historical empathy along a range of five "levels," from a very primitive form (the past as virtually incomprehensible) to an extensive "achievement" (historical agents are understood and their actions explained in full historical context). Three levels concern us here, from the middle range to the upper end (i.e., levels 3, 4, and 5). Ashby and Lee call the middle-range "everyday empathy" largely because it is relatively easily achieved. It is that which involves understanding historical circumstances in terms of their import for us in our present-day contexts and judging agents and actions by our standards. As Lynn empathizes with the plight of the dispossessed Native Americans (with help from Zinn), she turns to express collective guilt about her Anglo legacy and the role she believes it played in Indian removal policies. These expressions, however, are largely borne of contemporary standards about the ways in which such minorities are to be treated by and protected under present law. Because in this portion of her reaction Lynn does not historically contextualize the actions of Andrew Jackson, she appears to lack a sense of the attitudes, values, and early-nineteenth-century sensibilities that drove what to her current perspective simply seem like inexcusably brutish Indian-removal tactics. This notion is everyday empathy by Ashby and Lee's lights.

However, in much the same breath, Lynn acknowledges that these were times long past, ones in which people did the things they did because they operated on different assumptions and held different values. In Ashby and Lee's characterization, this understanding is "restricted historical empathy" (level 4).

It is considered "restricted" because no effort is made to explain agents' actions with regard to the nature of the period in question, a time in which the policies and practices of individuals such as Andrew Jackson must be located in order for them to be more fully understood. The notation that the time was different from our own and that this acknowledgment meant values, attitudes, beliefs were foreign to our current sensibilities is registered, but it is not pursued as an explanatory device. Therefore, according to Ashby and Lee, historical empathy is incomplete. It does not reach the final achievement (level 5) of "contextualized historical empathy," wherein "there is a clear differentiation between position and point of view of the historical agent, and that of the historian; between what the agent knew and what we know; between the beliefs, values, goals and habits enshrined in the past institution or social practice, and those which are prevalent in our own society."[7]

Now, my point here is not to use Lynn's reaction to suggest that she is slow or dull because she falls one step short on a scale of "degrees of empathy." After all, she receives considerable assistance from Zinn in understanding the desperate fate of the Cherokee and their personal and collective reactions to it without similar explications of Andrew Jackson and the sources of his policies and actions. By Zinn's pen, the Native Americans become tragic heroes in technicolor detail, while Jackson is excoriated for his complicity in the tragedy his Indian-removal policies wrought. Zinn offers no similarly detailed account of the 1830s policy culture in the nation's capital to explain the source of Jackson's apparent ruthlessness.

Furthermore, my purpose here is not to use Lynn's response to reify Ashby and Lee's empathic levels. To the contrary, close analysis of Lynn's reaction to the text that she read indicates that she is at two empathic levels simultaneously. This realization suggests to me that "levels" is probably as conceptually problematic as were Shemilt's earlier Piagetian-influenced "stages" of historical empathy which Ashby and Lee here take some pains to reconceptualize.[8]

While both are important, the preceding issue and this latter one take us onto the plane of a somewhat different discussion than I wish to pursue here. Rather, I want to focus on several questions. I want to ask why it is that, like many of the adolescents studied by Ashby and Lee (and most of those studied by Shemilt), Lynn did not achieve the highest and most complex form of empathy?[9] Zinn's rhetorical machinations aside for the moment, why for Lynn is fully contextualized historical empathy such a difficult achievement? Why must it be? I explore these questions, and note along the way some of the problems associated with the notion of historical empathy. Then, I examine a bit of the terrain that these problems leave for us.

The Problem of Historical Empathy

In its more complex manifestations, historical empathy is a genuinely significant and highly prized accomplishment. Some consider it one of the weightiest feats to which historical understanding can aspire.[10] Its achievement promises to allow us to assemble accounts of the past that get us as close as we might ever get to what life might have been like "back then." It makes possible the reconstructions of past events in a way that helps us appreciate the significant differences between the present world and the world being described, while simultaneously bringing that world, theoretically at least, much closer to us. In the ideal, this tempers and textures our understanding of our ancestors and what makes them seem so odd at first glance. It makes us less quick to judge them as short-sighted dimwits with idiotic beliefs and stupid customs. By extension we therefore would be less quick then to judge those in our contemporary world who do not share our sentiments and sensibilities. In this idealized form, one could say that historical empathy is essential to the health of pluralistic democracies. Understanding of the type succored by richly empathic considerations and brought forth by contextualized historical inquiry offers a compelling rationale for the importance of the study of the past.

Having admitted these prospects, authentic, contextualized historical empathy may well be impossible to achieve. Why might this be? Cognitive psychologists have made convincing arguments about the situated nature of the way we think.[11] And those who have researched empathy in the domain of history have reported some initially impressive data concerning how this situated thinking influences historical understanding.[12] With regard to thought about the past, I have described the manifest forms of situated cognition as rooted in and a function of the thinker's historical "positionality."[13] By this notion of positionality, I mean the current, socioculturally permeated deportment or stance any historical thinker brings to the task of making sense of the past. An often implicit theory functions as a set of sometimes immovable, other times resilient, temporal bearings that hinge on pivotal ontological (what's my world view), existential (who am I), and epistemological (how do I know) questions. Because the theory is thoroughly saturated with ontological, existential, and epistemological assumptions, it cannot help but also be deeply imbued with sociocultural, racial, ethnic, class, and gendered components.

In approaching the past of Andrew Jackson and the Seminole, Choctaw, and Cherokee, Lynn confronts Zinn's depiction using her own historical positionality—her current socioculturally permeated assumptions and anchors—to make sense of what she reads. In other words, what we witness in her response is the way in which she "imposes" these assumptions and anchors on the past conveyed by Zinn. What the think-aloud protocol elicits is an impositional response, where her present temporal bearings—her positionality—impinge on, invade, and configure what she reads. This process is inescapable. To access the past, to make sense of it, requires impositionality, in which the historical thinker can only construct meaning and pursue understanding through the presently situated assumptions and mediations they possess. History is never accessible on its own terms, shorn of some perspective or stance assumed by those who attempt to make sense of it. Positionality is the lens through which and impositionality is the vehicle by which understanding is possible in the first place.

Zinn's own positionality also plays a role. To make his text accessible at all to readers like Lynn, he must write it in a way that shows some respect for his or her current temporal bearings and invites their imposition. If his account does not somehow mesh, for example, with what Lynn brings to the text by way of beliefs, assumptions, and sociocultural anchors, she cannot construct meaning from it. Its power to influence her temporal bearings is lost. Yet, lost on Lynn it was not, as her final several phrases indicate. What makes Zinn's text "work" in facilitating something approaching empathic regard involves the way in which Zinn's positionality overlaps that of Lynn's.

The overlap of Lynn's positionality with that of Zinn's enables empathy, but it does so in a particular way. Because it does, it also serves to constrain her empathic regard in other ways. Lynn's cursory prior knowledge of Jackson is limited to a general apprehension of him as the military hero, the people's democrat, the frontiersman. She possesses equally slender knowledge about the specifics of Jackson's Indian-removal policies, their consequences among the southeast Native American tribes, and the tribes' reactions. In short, Lynn's understanding of Jackson is stereotypical and her knowledge about the Native Americans affected by Jackson's policies is generalized. Zinn knows much more about both, but he is not content to convey his knowledge regarding each to assist Lynn in fully contextualizing this period (assuming that were possible). His sympathetic regard lies with the Cherokee and other tribes and he stakes out this position early and clearly, hoping that, as he imposes it on his depictions of events, it will overlap just enough with Lynn's that a connection will be made and she will continue reading, intrigued by the unfolding drama. The rhetoric of his argument will do the rest to reconstruct Lynn's understanding such that, with some luck, it aligns with his own.

Zinn's account of the period cannot help but reflect his im/positionality, just as the consensus histories of the generation of scholars before him did, those im/positionalities of the past that, ironically, he seeks to overturn. As a result, both histories—the consensus celebratory one and Zinn's revisionist version—permit, at best, variations on Ashby and Lee's notion of restricted historical empathy. In Zinn's case, because his text intentionally errs on the side of the

Native Americans' experience, he offers what can inspire empathic regard for the southeast Native Americans, but little that will help readers such as Lynn to understand Jackson on his own terms in the context of the period in which he lived. In the 1950s consensus histories, the direction of that regard generally was reversed, pointing toward Andrew Jackson, the military, economic, and political hero.

* * * * *

For the reader—Lynn, in this case—the idea that the sort of highly prized empathic response that is contextualized and takes pains to avoid presentism (Ashby and Lee's level 5) seems to require at barest minimum (1) a rather well developed self-consciousness about one's historical positionality and how it is imposed on the past; (2) a process in which one then brackets out his or her positionality as inquiry into the past proceeds; and (3) a critical sensitivity to the positionalities embedded in historical source material as expressed by authors and agents (e.g., Zinn's text, the primary source material he cites). For the author, Zinn, the same minimum requirements seem to be in order (adjusted to reflect a focus primarily on the task of writing rather than reading). However, distinct problems exist in coming to terms with these requirements.

The first matter that makes this sort of empathy such a difficult accomplishment is that it demands a Herculean level of self-examination concerning our assumptions and experience- and knowledge-based theories of the world, about the past, and about a possible future. These assumptions are often so commonly taken for granted that we frequently lack the right sorts of questions with which we could undertake this thorough self-examination.

Second, some literary critics and historians have noted that, although empathy and contextualization require close investigations of and critical sensitivities to the positionalities of the authors of historical texts/artifacts—the latter arguably being the *sine qua non* of historical understanding and empathy—we lack the well-honed tools and sufficiently unbroken evidence chains to accomplish this feat with the degree of rigor necessary to promote the highest level of empathy. Even when we sharpen our tools to razor's edge (to the extent that this is possible), the nature and availability of the evidence can otherwise thwart our best use of those tools. Imagination turns out to be the inquirer's best but perhaps least trustworthy ally.[14]

Moreover, if this situation were not enough, achieving the level of authentic, contextualized empathy appears to demand that, as we read, respond to, and write the past, we engage in the inexplicable act of corralling our positionalities in order to avoid the nasty habit of imposing our current temporal bearings on understanding that past. As the argument goes, this harnessing act enables us fully to contextualize the past, to get into the hearts and minds of our predecessors in ways that allow authentic empathic regard, to reconstruct historical agents' intentions and subsequent acts, and to develop a full understanding of the historical milieu in which these agents operated. However, as David Lowenthal pointed out, the past is a foreign country.[15] I take him to mean, at least in part, that the act of bracketing out positionality and limiting the way it is imposed, such that we can fully comprehend the foreign-ness of the past, largely is unavailable to us. I take him to say that our sociocultural bearings are all we have. Without them, no interpretation, no meaning-making process, and no understanding, historical or otherwise, is possible. We have no place to stand outside our present bearings from which we could make sense of the past. I read Carl Becker, in *Everyman His Own Historian*, to be have said virtually the same thing.[16]

Empathy as Necromancy

In Shemilt's lengthy attempt to delineate the notion of historical empathy, he begins with Collingwood's assertion that all history is the history of what our predecessors thought.[17] The historian's task necessitates that she inquire into the past for the purpose of "re-enacting experience by rethinking ideas. . . ."[18] Quoting liberally from Collingwood, Shemilt seeks to link the "rethinking of ideas" to the process of empathy. To get there, he employs Collingwood's definition of historical knowledge and the role of the historian in producing it. Collingwood defined historical knowledge as "an activity of thought, which can be known only in so far as the knowing mind re-enacts it and knows itself to be doing so. To the historian, the activities whose history he [sic] is studying are not spectacles to be watched, but experiences to be lived through his own mind. . . ."[19] However, Shemilt notes that this description of historical knowledge and the role the empathic historian plays in producing it have been the subject of considerable debate among historians. As a result, Shemilt traces out three "competing portraits of Collingwood's empathizing historian."[20]

The first portrait "sees the historian as a 'psyche-snatcher,' a 'stealer of souls' who *literally relives the thoughts and feelings* of his [sic] subjects."[21] The psyche snatcher is obligated to align the literal re-enactment of the thoughts and feelings of those studied with the actual known facts. However, if the historian can improve upon the factual record, then she has license to "exercise [her] prerogative as Caesar [crossing the Rubicon] . . . and tell us what the great man would have thought had he had the occasion to formally rehearse his thoughts or to explain himself after the event."[22] Shemilt criticizes this portrait on the grounds that it probably is impossible for any of us to relive the moments in question in any literal way. Re-enactments or empathic reconstructions of "things as they really were" are simply out of reach for very common-sensical reasons, leaving us to observe cynically with Voltaire that such historical efforts amount to little more than a joke the living play upon the dead.

The second possible portrait of Collingwood's empathizing historian demonstrates greater promise by Shemilt's lights. He refers to it as "the time-traveller." The time-traveller projects his own psyche into past events, "mentally reliving events from the situation, though not necessarily from the standpoint, of the other."[23] This empathizing historian must have detailed knowledge of the events in question, but is not required to literally correspond with other minds. Nonetheless, this historian eschews speculative autobiography, because she is committed to a valid and reliable treatment of the available evidence. That someone did thus and so because they were thinking this or something else may follow from an evidence trail examined in great depth by the historian. Empathic regard is a consequence of the time-traveller's careful study and diligence. Claims to deep empathy and their appearance in historical scholarship are therefore warranted.

Shemilt recognizes problems with this portrait as well. For example, he notes that this view presupposes some transhistorical science of human nature.[24] In other words, Caesar's thoughts and feelings can be understood by twentieth-century historians because human nature has not changed much over time. The same scientific rules of human action apply as well today as they did, say, in the Roman Empire. This position, however, is a questionable assumption at best.

The third portrait is that of the empathizing historian as "necromancer." This historian is a sorcerer who conjures "apparitions of, but not from, the past to appear and address the present in language of the present."

> As the 'necromancer' conceit suggests, the historian hides his epistemological machinery behind a persuasive illusion. Yet no charlatanism is involved for the pleasingness and persuasiveness of the illusion is the measure of the machinery. [T]he 'necromancer' conjures a vision of past action that a contemporary audience will find recognizable, intelligible and plausible.[25]

Shemilt claims that the necromancer *adduces* intentions and motives from the known facts. Unlike the time-traveller, no logical *deductive process* is at work here, no deduction that occurs from the deep historical knowledge and understanding of human nature the time-traveller builds up. As a result, the necromancer can make no ontological claims about that which she reconstructs. The resultant is more construction than reconstruction.

Shemilt finds the portrait of the empathizing historian as necromancer "exceedingly dubious" with respect to what Collingwood had in mind. Because it is construction rather than reconstruction, the necromancer can offer little that is more epistemologically convincing than what we find in our everyday experience. All the necromancer can do, according to Shemilt, is to place a sentinel at the door of presentism. The skill of the sentinel, however, turns out to be as dubious as the portrait itself. Of the three portraits, Shemilt favors the "time-traveller." The weight of his critiques of both the "psyche-snatcher" and the "necromancer" indicate the degree to which he finds Collingwood's empathizing historian neither literal idealist soul-stealer nor crafty magician, but a careful, deductive inquirer, taking justifiable license with the evidence at her disposal.

At first glance, most would want to agree with both Collingwood's and Shemilt's empathizing historian as time-traveller. We want the appearance of the stronger ontological and epistemological claims the time-traveller appears to offer. We reject the psyche-snatcher and the necromancer as common-sensically silly and as master of seduction respectively. The time-traveller appears to be the historical scholar who can provide a window onto a world that may well seem impenetrable to us. In the view of Ashby and Lee, the time-traveller takes us where so few go, to the world of contextualized historical empathy (level 5). Both the psyche-snatcher and the necromancer seem only to get us to everyday (level 3) or restricted historical empathy (level 4) because their claims to empathic regard are ontologically and epistemologically insufficient. In short, what they offer is not to be trusted.

However, my analysis of Lynn's reading of Zinn and of Zinn's text itself indicate that neither is a time-traveller. Zinn does not appear to write as a fully-empathizing historian (unless we concede that he might be a time-traveller with regard to his characterizations of the southeast Native American tribes and their plight). Rather, he appears to be much more the necromancer, the magician who disguises his epistemological machinery under cloak of rhetorical illusion. The measure of his success can be gauged by the emotional, empathic reactions elicited in a reader such as Lynn—angst-ridden, guilt-laden responses by design. Zinn sponsors empathic construction, not reconstruction. He seeks to conjure up a vision that connects with readers' contemporary understandings of the world.

For the enchantment to work, his tale, in part at least, must be intelligible, recognizable, and plausible by the present-day standards of his readers. Unlike the consensus accounts of the 1950s that celebrate Jackson, describe him in terms of his "nation-expanding" historical context, and appear to justify (or ignore) his treatment of the Cherokee (in itself its own version of empathy by necromancy), Zinn cannot take his late-1990s readers to a single meaning. Many readers whose historical positionalities were shaped in the roiling forge of the 1960s and 1970s and their aftermath likely would find such a univocal celebratory account at least implausible, if not unrecognizable. The success of Zinn's sorcery is measured in Lynn's connection to his account: her expression of resentment about her European ancestry, her feeling of guilt for the actions of someone she has never met and does not fully understand, and the manifestation of genuine empathic regard for the plight of those who were victimized by the resented.

For Lynn's part, her limited prior knowledge of the period permits little more than the degree of empathy that she expresses. Although a reasonably skilled reader, Lynn appears to lack the type of specialized strategic, historical critical reading capacities that might incline her to interrogate Zinn's scorcery, questioning the way he contextualizes events, the point of view he adopts, and the sources upon which he relies.[26] Her late twentieth-century positionality and the way she imposes it on the text connects with Zinn's portrayal in a way that we can conjecture Zinn most likely hoped it would. However, she does not achieve time travel here. Hers is empathic response via necromancy. Given this text and this reader, a different result seems difficult to imagine.

Possibly the example I have offered, Lynn's reading of Zinn, simply is a poor one, that the choice of Zinn's text and Lynn's response to it reflects a uniquely egregious case of empathy by way of necromancy. However, on closer examination, we find that no matter how carefully Collingwood's empathizing historian adheres to the evidence, she cannot separate herself from her positionality in a way that permits the sort of time travel Shemilt has in mind in his second portrait. What interpretive edge or angle would Zinn's account convey if he observed all the evidence and told the tale from within the context and from the perspective of both Jackson and the Southeast Native Americans, simply chronicling events as Hayden White's "chronicler" might?[27] White observes that even chroniclers imposed their positionalities on events by making choices about what to include and disregard in their accounting practices. And even if it were possible to assume this quintessentially neutral stance, the twentieth-century historian writing about Caesar or Andrew Jackson must still cast her account in way that makes it "recognizable, intelligible and plausible" by the lights of twentieth-century readers.[28] Otherwise little connection to Caesar or Jackson would be possible because the past of each would be seen as an inaccessible foreign country.

Hayden White also has observed that historians' texts simply are littered with their use of tropes.[29] Even their historical emplotments involve heavy reliance on tropics of discourse. In these respects, I take him to be describing moves that historians must make to render our ancestors intelligible to themselves and us. These discursive practices necessitate empathy by necromancy, by sorcery, and the machinery of illusion. In this way, White, along with Becker and more recently Lowenthal, represent a line of thinkers who challenge us to accept not only empathy as necromancy, but much of historical thought as a practice in creative construction rather than reconstruction.[30] Under these circumstances, Shemilt's notion of time travel seems extraordinarily difficult if not impossible. No matter how much we attempt contextualization (as authors and readers), we can only approach the past from the standpoint and deportment of where we are now, from the inescapably historicized positions we presently hold.

From Empathy to Historical Contextualization

Where does this discussion leave us with respect to the question of the relationship of empathy and im/positionality to historical understanding? What after all should those of us interested in history education teach about empathic regard?

I believe that the emphasis on historical empathy is misplaced in several respects. Working from the foregoing analyses, historical empathy cannot be achieved in any fully direct, unmediated way. In this sense it is a relative achievement, not possible in any complete sense, and hardly predictable. If it surfaces at all, it arises from a transaction between the inquirer and the historical artifact (e.g., secondary source, primary document, archeological find). The transaction is tempered continually by the inquirer's positionality (which turns on a set of tacit assumptions) as it intersects with that of the producer of the artifact. We can get to no outside location—one shorn of our historical positionalities—to determine the degree to which empathy we, or others, express is either fully contextualized or some extension of everyday regard. All we can point to is the extent to which we rely on the available evidence, the traces and residue from the past. Even those shards, however, require interpretation, and that interpretive act is couched within a historicized, present-day context, and surrounded by implicitly-held temporal bearings that *prescribe and direct the interpretive process*. Perhaps this difficulty is why Ashby and Lee refer to the achievement of historical empathy as a mysterious accomplishment.

To the extent that we can talk about empathy at all, what remains for discourse on historical empathy is a discussion of the degree to which an inquirer's cognitive processes reflect more or less historically contextualized thought and understanding. What this discussion would focus on are not levels or stages of empathy, or empathy at all, but the *mental acts of historical contextualization* and the pedagogical processes by which these acts can be sharpened. If empathy happens to follow from engaging the mind in contextualizing the past, then all the better. However, attempt to account for and to explain empathic regard, push, stratify, and level seems counterproductive. What we might talk about and stress instead are questions such as:

- How does the evidence permit this or that judgment of a historical agent's actions?
- What other ways can these actions be understood given the evidence available?
- How can the evidence be assembled in different configurations to help me maximize the sense I can make of the larger context of the period in question?
- What might be the various attributes of that historical context given the evidence at hand?
- What types of thinking must I do in order to build an understanding of this context?
- How aware am I and must I be of the assumptions that I am making?
- How do my assumptions influence the way I interpret the evidence and attempt to contextualize events and actions?
- What would it take to see things from (a) different angle(s)?

In other words, the question is not of empathy *per se*, but, rather, it is one of the thought processes required to construct a sense of historical context.

As with empathy, though, the process of learning to contextualize the past requires traversing some difficult cognitive terrain. However, whereas empathy appears to be a mysterious accomplishment, contextualization turns on more readily definable cognitive performances. For example, it involves deliberate acts that entail several tightly interwoven elements:

(1) exposure to a wide array of rich historical materials (e.g., a variety of narratives, primary sources, film, newspaper accounts, photographs) on a particular topic investigated in depth;

(2) the relentless examination of one's positionality modeled by all within a community of inquirers (e.g., Why do I interpret—that is, impose my present temporal bearings on—this account this way? What assumptions do I make about the world and historical knowledge that dispose me to understand the past the way I do?); and

(3) an equally relentless pursuit of opportunities within this community of learners and inquirers to discuss the positionalities of producers of historical artifacts and how they represent the historical context of the period in question.

What distinguishes more from less contextualized historical thought is a matter of strategic competence in dealing with and adjudicating among historical artifacts and the positionalities that frame them, the capacity to develop and then draw on prior knowledge of events and agents in question, and a recurring self-examination of one's own positionality.

From Contextualization to Self-Understanding

How do we know for sure that our thought is more, rather than less, historically contextualized? As with the concern about levels of empathy and their expression, we simply cannot tell.[31] Sorcery no doubt will play its role as we impose our current temporal bearings, our positionalities, on that which we inquire about. However, this issue is not primary. The concern here is with the thinking process itself, with obtaining specialized strategic competence, and the role it plays in teaching and learning the capacity to reflect on the assumptions we make about the past and about ourselves. In Collingwood's description of the way in which historical knowledge is produced, he touches on what appears to me to be the key to the direction I am suggesting. Collingwood argues that,

Historical knowledge is knowledge of what mind has done in the past, and at the same time it is the re-doing of this, the perpetuation of past acts in the present.

[I]t is an activity of thought, which can be known only in so far as the knowing mind re-enacts it and knows itself to be doing do.[32]

Collingwood senses the role our own awareness of "an activity of thought" must play in the process of constructing historical understandings.

In many ways, however, historical thought can result only principally in self-understanding. To stress again, making sense of those who have come before us through such things as empathic regard comes about by way of the machinery of illusion, or necromancy. And once more, we have not found a method for getting outside our own historicized positionalities in a way that precludes the sorcery in which we must engage to go back in time and make some sense of our predecessors. We need not lament this situation; nothing is necessarily nefarious about such a necromantic undertaking. To the contrary, if the thought processes involved in contextualizing—that is, "re-enacting"—the past (and all this requires by way of specialized, strategic thinking about and dealing with historical evidence) can be wedded with "knowing ourselves to be doing so," then we learn much more about who we are, about our historical positionalities, and about the way we wield them. I believe that this prospect is one of the most compelling reasons for any study of history and for asking children and prospective teachers to study it. Otherwise, the pursuit smacks of mere antiquarianism.

Accepting empathic regard as an act of sorcery forces us, I think, to continually re-examine the illusions we project on our ancestors and their actions and intentions. Such re-examinations push us to look more closely at how we work with historical evidence and attempt the contextualization process. In turn, this pursuit demands that we understand ourselves more fully. I can think of few better warrants for teaching and learning history.

Notes

1. H. Zinn, *A People's History of the United States* (New York: Harper Collins, 1980), 138.

2. Zinn, *A People's History*.

3. For a more detailed account of Lynn's reading of Zinn, see B. VanSledright and P. Afflerbach, "Reconstructing Andrew Jackson: An Exploratory Study of Two Prospective Elementary Teachers' Readings of Revisionist History Texts," *Theory and Research in Social Education* (in press).

4. See D. Harlan, *The Degradation of American History* (Chicago: The University of Chicago Press, 1997), 191.

5. R. Ashby and P. Lee, "Children's Concepts of Empathy and Understanding in History," in *The History Curriculum for Teachers*, Christopher Portal, ed. (London: Falmer Press, 1987), 62-88, esp. p. 63.

6. See D. Shemilt, "Beauty and The Philosopher: Empathy in History and Classroom," in *Learning History*, A. Dickinson, P. Lee, and P. Rogers, eds. (London: Heinemann, 1984), 39-84; and D. Shemilt *History 13-16 Evaluation Study* (Edinburgh: Holmes McDougall, 1980).

7. See Ashby and Lee, "Children's Concepts" 81.

8. See Shemilt, "Beauty."

9. See Shemilt, "Beauty," 55, 64-65.

10. See Ashby and Lee, "Children's Concepts"; R.G. Collingwood, *The Idea of History* (Oxford: Oxford University Press, 1946/1994); and Shemilt, "Beauty."

11. For example, see J. Brown, A. Collins, and P. Duguid, "Situated Cognition and the Culture of Learning," *Educational Researcher* 18 (1989): 32-42; J. Lave, "Situated Learning in Communities of Practice," in *Perspectives on Socially-shared Cognition*, L. Resnick, J. Levine, & S. Teasley, eds. (Washington, DC: American Psychological Association, 1991), 63-82; and J. Lave and E. Wegner, *Situated Learning: Legitimate Peripheral Participation* (New York: Cambridge University Press, 1991).

12. For example, see K. Barton and L. Levstik, "'It Wasn't A Good Part Of History': National Identity and Students' Explanations of Historical Significance," *Teachers College Record* 99 (1998): 478-513; T. Epstein, "Deconstructing Differences in African-American and European-American Adolescents' Perspectives on U.S. History," *Curriculum Inquiry* 28 (1998): 397-423. K. O'Connor, "Narrative Form and Historical Representation: A Study of American College Students' Historical Narratives" (paper presented at the Conference for Pedagogic Text and Content Analysis, Harnosand, Sweden, 1991); P. Seixas, "Historical Understanding Among Adolescents in a Multicultural Setting," *Curriculum Inquiry* 23 (1993): 301-327.

13. B. VanSledright, "On The Importance of Historical Positionality to Thinking About and Teaching History," *International Journal of Social Education* 12 (1998): 1-18. See also B. VanSledright, "The Nature and Role of Positionality in Historical Thinking and Understanding" (paper presented at the annual meeting of the American Educational Research Association, Montreal, Canada, April 1999).

14. See P. Lee, "Historical Imagination," in *Learning History*, A. Dickinson, P. J. Lee, and P. Rogers, eds., 87-112.

15. D. Lowenthal, *The Past Is a Foreign Country* (Cambridge: Cambridge University Press, 1985).

16. C. Becker, *Everyman His Own Historian* (New York: F.S. Crofts & Co., 1935).

17. See Shemilt, "Beauty," and Collingwood, *The Idea*.

18. See Shemilt, "Beauty," 40.

19. Collingwood, *The Idea*, 218.

20. Shemilt, "Beauty," 41.

21. Shemilt, "Beauty," 41, my emphasis.

22. Shemilt, "Beauty," 41.

23. Shemilt, "Beauty," 41.

24. Shemilt, "Beauty," 42-43.

25. Shemilt, "Beauty," 43.

26. See S. Wineburg, "On The Reading of Historical Texts: Notes On The Breach Between School and Academy," *American Educational Research Journal* 28 (1991): 495-519.

27. H. White, *The Content of the Form: Narrative Discourse and Historical Representation* (Baltimore: Johns Hopkins University Press, 1987).

28. Shemilt, "Beauty," 43.

29. H. White, *Tropics of Discourse: Essays in Cultural Criticism* (Baltimore: Johns Hopkins University Press, 1978).

30. Becker, *Everyman*; Lowenthal, *The Past*; see also, F. Ankersmit and H. Kellner, eds., *A New Philosophy of History* (Chicago: University of Chicago Press, 1995).

31. For a more lengthy discussion of historical contextualization and its limits, see R. Berkhofer Jr., *Beyond the Great Story: History as Text and Discourse* (Cambridge, Mass.: Belknap Press, 1995), especially chapter 2.

32. Collingwood, 218; my emphasis.

Chapter 5

Crossing the Empty Spaces: Perspective Taking in New Zealand Adolescents' Understanding of National History

Linda S. Levstik

> Learn your own history, because that is the basis on which your identity is built, and it is that which will allow you to get on living with one another, Maori, Pakeha, and Pacific Islanders . . . . Then you wouldn't be worried whether or not we were bullying you because we are big and you are small.
> —Former U.S. Ambassador to New Zealand, Josiah Beeman[1]

Ambassador Beeman's admonition to learn history provides an interesting point of departure for a discussion of historical thinking and perspective taking in an international context. To begin with, it is rich in irony. There are the oddities of that last sentence—are New Zealanders supposed to realize that they aren't being bullied, that size isn't the cause of the bullying, or that U.S. bullying isn't worth worrying over? Then there is the amazing claim that learning "your own history will allow you to get on living with one another." A brief review of his own country's troubled history in this regard might have given the Ambassador pause. Attention to the debate over the history curriculum in New Zealand should have brought him to a full stop. But the Ambassador is much like many others who assume that there is a universal history "out there" just waiting to be learned. He appears confident that such a framework will reconcile disparate groups and allow them to move on to more important things—"living with one another" rather than worrying about U.S. bullying, for instance. In practice, of course, history is a much messier enterprise than Ambassador Beeman seems to think.

There is no single way of making sense of the past, especially in multicultural, post-colonial nations where groups and individuals call on different historical narratives to either reinforce or overturn the status quo. As a growing number of studies show, ethnoracial, gender, family, and class affiliations influence historical understanding.[2] And, despite Ambassador Beeman's claims to the contrary, a nation's geoposition influences historical thinking. As I will suggest throughout this chapter, where a people perceive themselves to be situated globally—their relations with other nations and how distant from centers of power they feel themselves to be—shapes how history is perceived, taught, and learned.[3] Studying global as well as more local influences suggests alternatives to current conceptions of what it means to make sense of the past, and underscores the importance of cross-national comparisons of historical thinking, especially in regard to perspective taking.

A Sociocultural Perspective on Historical Thinking

Cognitive theorists and researchers in other disciplines have argued for some time that cognitive development takes place within a sociocultural context that establishes the parameters of expert practice.[4] As learners move from novice to more expert practice they learn to use an array of cultural tools. In the act that we conceive of as historical thinking learners or agents exercise their agency through the use of the cultural tools available in social settings for particular purposes at a particular historical moment.[5] Of course cultural tools represent *potential* rather than *actual* activity. It is only through use that some portion of their potential is realized. In this sense, learning is a form of mediated action where the available cultural tools both facilitate and constrain practice. The term *history* applies to an array of such tools—asking historical questions, evaluating evidence, organizing events chronologically, building interpretations, creating historical narratives, and more. Each of these tools developed over time to meet particular social and cultural purposes related to making sense of the past. As a result, historical thinking is not so much an individual as a social act framed and constrained by elements which are themselves sociocultural constructs. Historical thinking develops in the interactions and tensions between and among thinkers, settings, means (tools), and purposes.

Historians may privilege one set of cultural tools over another, or one purpose or stance toward history over another, but they are not the only members of society who need or want to make sense of the past. Various groups engender a sense of pride in community by recalling a past that not only explains communal roles and rules, but sustains and empowers groups and individuals in contemporary struggles.[6] Through ceremonies and celebrations, arts, architecture, and artifacts, monuments and memorials, media and family practices, different groups send powerful and often contradictory messages about the meaning of the past.[7]

Individuals, too, make personal use of the past. Some people derive pleasure from surrounding themselves with artifacts of the past, taking on the role of someone from the past, or simply knowing a great deal about a specific historical event or individual. Still others seek insight into human experience, or hope understanding the past will enable them to act more intelligently and humanely in the world.[8] Some simply want to understand how things came to be the way they are. Most people probably incorporate more than one of these stances in their understanding of history, appropriating some of the cultural tools sanctioned by historians while ignoring—or never being exposed to—others. Consider, for instance, the kind of historical thinking suggested by the information exhibition stance common in many schools. History is not employed as a system of analysis, as a means of connecting to a larger community, or as an approach to understanding the human condition. Instead, it functions as an opportunity to display data, either for personal gratification or to avoid failure and its accompanying humiliations. In classrooms where this is the primary approach to history, students are unlikely either to be introduced to or to employ concepts such as evidence, significance, interpretation, empathy, or perspective taking, even though these cultural tools are fundamental to other stances towards history. Of course different learners act within and against the possibilities and constraints of different contexts. One student may acquiesce to the expectation that history is little more than an accumulation of information; another may rebel, seeking other ways of understanding the past. In the case of the latter, other settings, other purposes, access to other cultural tools, or the character of the individual student may supercede the classroom context.

National Narratives in Multicultural Societies

I find one of these cultural tools—national historical narratives—especially interesting. Narratives of national history serve a wide array of purposes, challenging our understanding of what it means to "think historically." This is particularly the case in multicultural nations where competing narratives not only make it difficult to agree on what constitutes national history, but challenge students' willingness to develop empathy for or take the perspective of those perceived as "other." In a multicultural society, *when*, *how*, and *if* groups and individuals are included in the nation's historical narrative is fraught with controversy. Because national history is often understood to explain how groups and individuals connect with the larger society, it takes on uniquely personal significance. Indeed, perceiving oneself or one's group as connected to the past may provide a sense of personal as well as collective worth.[9] In contrast, individuals and groups left out of historical narratives may perceive themselves and be perceived by others as second-class citizens, cut off from the rights and privileges enjoyed by more favored citizens.[10] In New Zealand, for instance,

Alton-Lee, Nuthall, and Patrick documented some of the ways in which racial hierarchies were introduced and reinforced in the social studies classroom through a systematic elevation of European experience over that of native peoples.[11] Seixas too, noted that the tradition of Western history prevalent in Canadian schools could force a "minority" student either to "[build] a significant past around his or her own particularistic concerns or [adopt] the authoritative grand narrative while relegating self and family to the margin outside of 'really' significant history."[12] Studies in the United States suggest, too, that students there often struggle to reconcile a national narrative of American exceptionalism, freedom, and progress over time with the persistence of problems related to race, gender, class, and ethnicity. These students evoke the official narrative, shaping it to address their concerns with equity and "fairness."[13] Unfortunately, as Wertsch argues,[14] their lack of in-depth knowledge about the narrative to which they have access constrains their ability to frame alternative narratives or effectively critique the ones with which they disagree. Schools in Northern Ireland, on the other hand, face a different challenge. In this country a narrative of nation-building, national progress and national identity would be extremely difficult to sustain. As Barton notes, "stories of the origin and development of contemporary political and social relations [in Northern Ireland] are too controversial to present in primary schools and most other public institutions."[15] Schools direct attention away from personal and national connections to the past, focusing instead on how different people lived in the past. Not surprisingly, students in Northern Ireland tend to conclude that the purpose of studying history is to learn about other people and how they live.

National Narratives and Perspective Taking

As these studies demonstrate, national narratives can have a powerful influence on students' historical thinking. While this finding has a number of implications for the development of historical thinking, I wish to focus on the impact of national narratives on *perspective taking*. By this I mean the ability to recognize some of the sociocultural and political forces that shape human behavior, now and in the past.[16] In focusing on perspective taking, I am arguing that understanding *why* people acted the way they did in the past, not just *how* they acted, is an important aspect of historical thinking. *Why* people acted as they did is, of course, an elusive question. It requires an imaginative leap across the space between self and "other." This is not to suggest that imagination is all that is necessary. Perspective taking requires combining imagination with the other tools of history described earlier. And even when we combine these tools we only approach, but never fully understand, the attitudes, beliefs, values, and "givens" of another time and/or place. [17]

While it may seem reasonable, to the extent possible, to try to understand the past in its own terms, perspective taking is an extremely divisive issue, especially in multicultural, post-colonial nations. Debates surrounding the U.S. history standards and Smithsonian exhibits stand as examples of the depth of hostility even modest attempts to present different perspectives on national history curricula can generate.[18] Similar arguments swirl around alterations in the history curriculum in New Zealand. Middleton and May describe the situation in New Zealand as one in which "'conservatives' primary objective is to preserve religious or other traditional values; 'liberal-left' arguments . . . conceptualize education mainly as a means of achieving democracy and equality; and the . . . 'libertarian-right'. . . emphasises—to varying degrees—individualism, competition, privatisation and diversity in a free-market setting."[19] Add to this "Maori political movements, minority ethnic/cultural interests, various feminisms and other movements for sexual equality, and advocates for particular educational or religious philosophies" and it is clear that the history curriculum is not neutral territory. As in the United States, the social studies curriculum in New Zealand (of which history is a part) became a forum for the expression of many of these competing interests. The 1997 Ministry of Education curriculum document acknowledges these perspectives, but in the end takes the stand that the purpose of social studies is to "enable students to participate in a changing society as informed, confident, and responsible citizens."[20] In order to accomplish this task, the Ministry suggests organizing social studies into strands (social organization, culture and heritage, place and environment, time, continuity and change, resources and economics) and processes (inquiry, values, social decision-making) aimed at providing students with, among other things, "essential learning about New Zealand society."[21] This represents a departure from the traditional emphasis, prior to secondary school, on culture study rather than national history. The move to solidify national history in the schools also presents educators with the task of deciding what of New Zealand's past constitutes a history appropriate for use in schools.

While other countries with racially and ethnically diverse populations adopted the rhetoric if not the reality of multiculturalism, New Zealand is officially bicultural (Maori and Pakeha).[22] In a bicultural formation, "a kind of parity between indigenous and white settler cultures becomes crucial."[23] This policy is challenged daily by the multicultural reality of life in New Zealand. Indeed, in the revised social studies curriculum, the New Zealand Ministry of Education calls for attention to bicultural *and* multicultural aspects of New Zealand history. In accord with the bicultural aspect of this mandate, the Ministry charges educators not only with recognizing and valuing the "unique position of Maori in New Zealand society," but with examining issues of racism, promoting non-racist attitudes in the school and wider community, studying the effects of colonization on Maori and Pakeha, and tracing the influence of Maori culture on New

Zealand's social, cultural, political, and religious beliefs and systems.[24] After acknowledging "the importance to all New Zealanders of both Maori and Pakeha traditions, histories and values" the Ministry also charges schools with recognizing the multicultural nature of past and present New Zealand.[25] Finally, schools are reminded that students may need to meet more than one set of cultural expectations. Arguing for the importance of perspective taking, the Ministry urges that students "consider how past experiences and actions are perceived, interpreted, and revised and how these perceptions and interpretations may influence people's views and actions in the future."[26]

As is generally the case in curriculum development, this is not the disinterested, distanced, "reasoned objectivity" advocated by some as the aim of history education.[27] Rather, the specifics of the situation in New Zealand yield a national history curriculum that is complex, multivocal, contested, and in flux. Recognizing the potential disparity among versions of history encountered in different cultural settings—families, neighborhoods, racial and ethnic communities, for instance—educational policy makers recommend a pluralist curriculum for specific sociopolitical purposes. On the one hand, students are encouraged to acquire the cultural tools that will enable them to develop and express sub-national (i.e., Maori) group identities. On the other hand, they are expected to take on a national identity that is assumed to prepare them for active participation in debate about the character and direction of the nation.[28] To order to direct attention to the different systems of ethnoracial classification used in New Zealand, including consideration of the various constituencies empowered or disempowered by these classifications, educators are expected to introduce three cultural tools: "inquiry," "values exploration," and "social decision-making."[29] Students are then expected to use these tools to study social justice and welfare issues, cultural diversity, and respect for the environment in historical context. Next, they are to use what they have learned to suggest possible strategies for dealing with these issues in the present and future. In sum, history and social studies are expected to involve identification, imagination, and perspective taking, employ analytical skills common to the discipline of history, and encourage students to be socially active citizens. Earlier drafts of this document evoked a firestorm of criticism. Some critics argued that it focused too much attention on national history—the current social studies curriculum emphasizes world cultures prior to secondary schools—while others claimed that it represented a form of political indoctrination rather than the rigorous, reasoned study they associated with history.[30]

This, then, was the backdrop against which I investigated adolescent New Zealanders' perspective taking in the context of national history. When I began my work the new curriculum was not fully in place. The Ministry of Education had distributed guidelines and recommendations, and the public dispute over the history curriculum had at least temporarily dropped out of the headlines. I interviewed students who were familiar with the old social studies curriculum—

largely the study of world cultures rather than the study of national history. I was interested in what ideas and understandings these students brought to national history, what influence their study of world cultures had on their conceptions of a national past, and what, if any, national narrative they employed in assigning historical significance to people, ideas, and events connected to New Zealand's past. I wondered, too, about their willingness to take on perspectives other than their own.

Setting and Procedures

The study was conducted in four schools in New Zealand. Three of the schools were within a large urban area and the fourth was located in a small community within the commuter shed for the same urban area. The socio-economic status of schools in New Zealand is described in *deciles* from one (lowest) to ten (highest). The schools in the study included one each of decile one, eight, nine, and ten. Students were identified by school personnel to represent a range of achievement levels and an equal number of boys and girls. In addition, I specifically requested access to Maori, Pacific Islander, and European/Pakeha populations. Because each school drew on the surrounding neighborhood for its students, and neighborhoods tended to be predominantly one group or the other, interview groups were also predominantly one group or the other. Maori and Pacific Islander children were concentrated in the "decile one" school. A second school (decile ten), largely European in ethnicity, had a number of Asian students, relatively recent immigrants to the neighborhood, and two Asian children (one each from China and Hong Kong) were included in the interview pool there. One child in the commuter shed school (decile nine) identified as part Maori, none as Pacific Islander or Asian; at least four children in the fourth school (decile eight) self-identified as having some Maori heritage. Two children self-identified as North American, one Canadian, and one United States American (although he was born in New Zealand, he considered himself American because his parents were born in the U.S.).

I developed a semi-structured interview similar to one used in a previous study with American adolescents.[31] This included a task requiring students to choose from among a set of twenty-three captioned historical pictures, as well as a set of broader questions designed to explore their understanding of historical significance. These were derived from a variety of sources in the U.S. and New Zealand.[32] In order to make comparisons between the American study and this one, I attempted to select pictures in categories similar to those used in the U.S. study—political/military, social (including attention to race, class, ethnicity and gender), technological, and economic history. I then met with a public historian in New Zealand whose work involves introducing school-age children to national history in museums and (previously) living history contexts. I also visited historic sites, museums, and a living history park, read curriculum guidelines, reviewed children's literature on New Zealand, met with colleagues with expertise in New Zealand's children's literature, sat in on portions of a teacher training program, attended an educational conference, and interviewed teacher educators as well as teachers in training to broaden my understanding of the larger context for history teaching and learning. After considering this background information, I narrowed my original set of pictures down to twenty-three and tested them with a class of teachers in training.[33] As a result of this feedback, I eliminated a picture that failed to elicit much interest or provoke conversation. The final set of pictures, captions, and interview protocol are described in Appendices A and B.

I audiotaped interviews with 49 students between the ages of eleven and thirteen, and conducted all interviews with single-sex groups of either three or four students.[34] In addition to asking questions from my formal protocol, I frequently probed students' responses in order to explore more fully the reasoning behind their answers. Following the interviews I transcribed the tapes, tabulated students' choices, analyzed interview transcripts and drew conclusions from them through a process of analytic induction. After identifying thematic strands in students' responses, I subjected the transcripts to a systematic content analysis in which I categorized responses according to coding categories based on those strands, and to categories developed in the U.S. study. I then analyzed the coded data using cross-case analysis and constant comparison. During the process of coding and analysis, I explicitly searched for differences in girls' and boys' explanations, and for differences between age groups.[35] The resultant set of descriptive generalizations form the basis for my discussion of children's perspective taking in the context of a loosely constituted and fluid "master narrative" of national history. [36]

Coming to Terms with the Master Narrative

As I began my interviews in New Zealand I recalled the national image typical of the American adolescents I had studied previously. Not unlike their adult counterparts, these U.S. students perceived their nation to be exceptional— possessing a unique set of freedoms and opportunities guaranteed by the Bill of Rights and supported by a beneficent technology. Not only did they expect their nation to expand these freedoms and opportunities to previously disenfranchised groups and individuals, they also expected the United States to set a moral standard by "stand[ing] up for people," and "help[ing] other countries."[37] Curious about New Zealanders' national self-perception, I began by asking a New Zealand public historian what he considered to be the prevailing national self-image. He described a pride in national difference, a pioneering spirit, sense of initiative, and willingness to experiment. A Kiwi, he suggested, was thrifty, practical, and handy, able to "fix anything with a bit of #8 wire." Referring to the experience of WWII, he called up an image of Kiwis fixing up and using what their more wasteful American counterparts threw away. This image largely matched what other sources said of late nineteenth- and twentieth-century New Zealanders.[38] To some extent, these same sorts of things are said of any pioneering people. If pioneers maintain their hold on the "frontier," their descendants generally perceive them as resilient, industrious, and the like. What makes New Zealand's pioneer myth especially interesting is that it exists alongside an even larger sense of living on the edge, not just of a frontier, but of the world. As one prominent New Zealand author suggests, "our strength is in our independence, our boldness, and in being sufficiently on the edge of things to be able to assess what is happening elsewhere. . . . We are the well at the bottom of the world."[39] The "archetypal" New Zealanders sprung from this well—"good keen men" and "independent women"—have a "healthy disrespect for authority and [rely] more on their own sense of what's right and what isn't."[40] This image of an inventive, clear-eyed margin that speaks truth to power is part of the national narrative reflected in students' responses during the interviews.

Living on the Clear-Eyed Margins

Perhaps the image of marginality strikes an American so clearly because it is such a contrast to (U.S.) American students' assumption of the centrality of their nation not just to their own lives but to the world. In contrast, New Zealanders described their country as distant from centers of influence and somehow "behind" the rest of the world. All students, for instance, expressed surprise that New Zealand created the world's first old age pension and only one knew that New Zealand had been among the first to give women full suffrage.[41] A common response to events from New Zealand history was to assume that New Zealand was "last." As one girl picked up the picture of women voting, for instance, she said, "Let me guess, we were probably last with that" and her peers laughingly agreed. In all but two groups students asked me if they were "as smart as other kids in the world." They commented, too, on how little the rest of the world—particularly Americans—knew of New Zealand. "You probably know all about America," Linlee commented. "And we know about America, too. But they [Americans] don't know much about here." A boy in another group made a similar point, explaining that "you have American history in your schools, and we don't have anything like that."

Part of this response may be explained by the overwhelming influence of American and British media, to say nothing of American commercial hegemony. Because of the high production costs of television in a country with a relatively small market for advertisers, New Zealand commercial television is dominated by cheap American and British imports. The film market is also dominated by imports, most often from the United States. But this is only a modern sign of a colonial past that focused New Zealanders' attention on Britain and the West, rather than on themselves, the Pacific, and Asia. Not only did New Zealanders fight for the British Empire and adopt many cultural and social patterns from Britain, but Britain was their major trading partner. In addition, while colonialism did not have the benefits Maori had hoped would come from the Treaty of Waitangi,[42] there is a sense among some Maori that British imperialism was preferable to the depredations of war and settlement that preceded it.[43] Finally, because New Zealanders' independence from Britain came peacefully, they did not need to establish a clear and separate national identity in quite the way rebelling colonies such as the United States, Kenya, or India did. As a result, New Zealand's national narrative remained reasonably fluid, with a curriculum that more often focused outward toward other places than inward on national history.[44]

Given the centrality of their colonial experience, the continued friendly relations with Britain, and the current political, social, and economic influence of the United States, it is hardly surprising that students express interest in Britain and the United States. It is also understandable that they sometimes described a David-and-Goliath–like relationship with both. This was particularly apparent as students discussed banning nuclear ships from New Zealand's waters as well as New Zealand's protests against French nuclear tests in the Pacific. While only two groups selected each event as a final choice for the timeline, one or the other often stayed in the pool of pictures until the very end of the selection process. More importantly, both pictures invariably generated a good deal of conversation among the students. In considering the significance of these pictures, for instance, students generally began by discussing their aversion to nuclear "stuff," conflating nuclear power with nuclear bombs and the testing of those bombs in the South Pacific. In a statement typical of this sort of response, Rene argued that antinuclear protests "stopped nuclear bombs." Similarly, a group of boys explained that "it's so dangerous—nuclear power isn't so bad, but nuclear bombs and stuff [are]." They commented that "if we had nuclear stuff we'd have to spend a lot more money on stuff we don't need."

Once students established that nuclear weaponry and testing were problems, they moved on to discuss American intervention in New Zealand's affairs. Knowing that the United States tried to force New Zealand to allow nuclear-powered vessels into New Zealand's waters, the students described the United States as "stubborn" and an international "bully." "The United States threatens New Zealand's defense," Kyle argued. When Ellen suggested that the United States "wouldn't like it if we tested in *their* waters" Sally added that "what you do to them [the United States], they'll do it back." "Yes," Ellen said, reflecting a common concern across groups, "they could bomb you." In another group, Joseph explained that "if they [New Zealanders] didn't protest, we could have been blown away." Ellen could not understand why the United States failed to realize that the ban on nuclear power and nuclear testing was good because the oceans "wouldn't get bombed anymore. You can't drink water that is contaminated." With the ban in place, Alexi said, "everybody might survive." Ultimately, though, the students thought that the United States should not intervene in New Zealand's business, regardless of whether New Zealand's policies were good. As Jason argued, "we can do whatever we want in our backyard." And, echoing Ihimaera, Alexi suggested that New Zealand "just might have something to teach the rest of the world" about this issue.[45]

The Moral Weight of the Past

These early adolescents wielded their national narrative in interesting ways. Although they were unclear about some (or even most) of the details of some events, they retained a sense of the moral weight of the past. New Zealanders stood up for what was right, even when they "could have been blown away" by a behemoth such as the United States. Because they perceived that their nation could not easily intervene in the affairs of other nations, they recognized the importance of paying attention to other parts of the world. This allowed them to imagine learning from as well as teaching other people valuable lessons learned from history. They regularly ascribed significance to events that, in their minds, did just that. "Just to say that Kiwis did actually go over [to fight in World War II] and help out, you know what I mean? That is important," Kiri explained. Karen argued for the inclusion of World War II on the basis that it "put New Zealand in touch with other people," and Kiwis learned from these encounters, too. As Stefan explained, "sometimes, especially like the Jews in WWII, they thought, 'Oh, if we just go along with it, it's not going to get too bad' but it just kept getting worse, and worse, and worse." New Zealanders "learned that you just don't tolerate any type of racism or anything."

Teaching the world was, from the students' perspectives, a challenging proposition. While they saw themselves as paying attention to the rest of the world, they did not think the world returned that attention. As a result, events that centered world attention on New Zealand were deemed significant. When students selected Captain Cook's explorations for the timeline, for instance, one criterion was that Cook's reports back to England "told the world about [New Zealand]." Acknowledging that Cook and the Endeavour weren't the first Europeans to mention the islands, students nonetheless marked Cook's trip out because, as Chris explained, "he wasn't the first, Abel Tasman was the first, but [Cook] told the world about it." Tom added, "he told *Europeans*." All but three groups (all three at the predominantly Maori/Pacific Islander school) also added Edmund Hillary[46] to the timeline because his explorations of Everest and Antarctica attracted international attention and "people learned from them." Other pictures such as women's suffrage and the pension were identified as significant because they were "firsts." As Reed explained, women's suffrage was significant because New Zealand was "first to give females the chance." "That will always be in the history books," Arden said. Reed added that this was like "Jenny Shipley. She'll always be in the history books, too, so like the first female Prime Minister." By providing a moral lesson to the rest of the world, too, students thought both women's suffrage and the old-age pension enhanced New Zealand's international status. Stefan was most articulate about this argument:

> Because New Zealand was the first country to give women the vote, and that's important because all people should be treated equally, and New Zealand's the first country to kind of figure that out. They kind of break away from the tradition that women were weaker and shouldn't be allowed to do stuff like that and should just stay at home, and they broke that tradition. Yeah, and it worked, and Kate Sheppard[47] helped and stuff and that just led to stuff all over the world, or the "first world" anyway, and women were allowed to work and vote.

Overall, this national narrative encouraged students to see their country as a participant in a reciprocal relationship with Western nations. New Zealand learned from the West, usually about how other people met and solved or failed to solve problems. In return New Zealand offered the world a different perspective—the water from the well at the bottom of the world, if you will. New Zealand emerged as a strong ally of the West, but with a willingness to resist pressure from Western powers and an insistence on what students perceive to be moral, just, and *fair* treatment of people.

Fairness was an important criterion for determining historical significance among these students. Two of their top choices for the timeline, women's suffrage and the Treaty of Waitangi, along with education and the pension were, from the students' perspective, ultimately about fairness. In sharp contrast to their American and Irish contemporaries, *every group* identified women's suffrage as one of their choices for the timeline. The Treaty of Waitangi was selected by all but two groups, making it the third most often selected picture (Captain Cook's explorations tied with women's suffrage), education was chosen by seven groups, and the pension by five. Students explained that all four pictures were significant, at least in part because they demonstrated the move toward "equal opportunity" and "fairness" for all New Zealanders.

In considering the significance of women's participation in New Zealand history, for instance, each group declared that equal participation in public life was "only fair." Even in the one group of boys where there was a brief suggestion that women's suffrage had nothing to do with them, they ultimately included it on the grounds that women "helped run the country" and therefore the right to vote was "quite important."[48] A few students also suggested that males and females might think differently about the significance of women's suffrage, but even this was a distinctly minority viewpoint. As one group of boys pointed out, with more women in the population than men it was only fair that both groups vote. Boys also argued that women were "just as important" as men, could do the same kind of work, and possessed skills that were necessary to the country.[49] In discussing women's contributions to New Zealand history, they noted that educating women as well as men for jobs was important because women who have skills can "go on and teach other people how to do it." Girls said similar things, adding that, because men always had power and there was "discrimination against woman-kind," it was especially important that women have the vote. "Men would roll over us more" without the vote, one girl explained. "It's only fair that women have an equal say." Jason pointed out that the country needed the labor of both men and women, especially during the wartime and Depression, and that it made no sense to discriminate. Moana declared that if "men have everything . . . it isn't fair."

Among the predominantly Maori and Pacific Islander groups, there was additional discussion regarding the length of time it took for women to get the vote. In one group, Kiri lifted up the picture of women voting, read the caption, and asked, "1893, eh? And why not before that?" Her classmate, Tiana, nodded, equally unimpressed. "When did *men* first get to vote?" she asked. In a group of boys, Tama asked what there had been to vote *for*, suggesting "votes for women are important, unless men couldn't vote either." When Peter explained that "before only men voted," Tama declared "then women getting to vote, that's only fair!"

Interestingly, after declaring that it was only fair that women and men share equally in public life, students in each group also acknowledged gender inequities in private life, especially in families. Women worked more at home, they agreed. Shawn explained that "less men take care of the house" and that would need to change "to make it more even." Several noted that seeing women in public positions—Prime Minister Jenny Shipley for instance[50]—provided important "role models for other women." These public figures, they argued, were evidence that women "can do the job same as a man." "Yes," Ames said, "They can do exactly the same jobs [as men], and then other women learn that they can do that, too." Several of the boys cautioned that despite the prominence of some women, inequities remained. Hamilton explained that women did not have equal numbers in Parliament, nor did they run as many businesses as men. Tama and Meara mentioned that women did more work at home "because they have the babies," a point made by at least one student in each of the girls' groups.

Seven groups also selected state support for education as an instance of fairness "because it gave everyone, rich or poor . . . the right to read, and to an education, so when they grow up to get jobs, they would know how to read and write." Before that, Reed said, "just the people who could afford it could go to school, then, like everyone could." As did most of the students who commented on the significance of education, Ames thought that public schooling made it possible for "everyone to get an equal education. Most schools in New Zealand now are pretty much equal." They agreed, too, that an equal education meant an equal chance at employment. In fact, every group mentioned this as an argument for the importance of education, whether they eventually put it on the timeline or not. As Kiri noted, "a lot of people, especially in this area [around the decile one school] wouldn't be able to go to school, and there's a lot of people, if it was for money, they wouldn't be able to go to school. It's like we're the next generation, and we need to be able to work so we make money and so we can bring up our families." "You can't do much without an education," agreed Tiana.

Although all groups indicated that giving retired people a pension was "only fair," only five selected the pension as among the eight choices for the timeline. Nonetheless, their conversations as they considered the pension illustrates the function of "fairness" as an organizing principle in their historical thinking. This was particularly vivid, too, because the Shipley administration had just cut cost-of-living increases for pensions and at least one student in each group was able to explain something about the controversy this caused. Students in two of the schools (decile one and decile eight) were clear about the inability of adults to put aside enough money for their old age. When asked why that was so, Riwia responded by explaining that raising a family absorbed most people's income and left them little to save. "They've worked all that time, and taken care of all of us," she said. "It's only fair that we take care of them when they get old." Students in the wealthier schools were less specific, expressing concern, as Judith did, that "without [the pension] some old people just wouldn't survive," or suggesting that the pension was not historically significant because "it would have happened eventually anyway."

In assigning significance to events representing "learning from others," "teaching the world," and "fairness," these students crafted a historical narrative with distinctive moral underpinnings. They imagined that their national history could provide them with a glimpse of "what should be and what is not yet."[51] They identified pieces of evidence that, strung together, provided them with some assurance of a particular kind of progress over time, some notion that good would ultimately triumph. A fundamental part of this progress was the extension of "fairness." To some extent, their belief in the significance of the extension of fair treatment to all people allowed them to recognize that there were different perspectives on events. This was particularly so when they knew the people or were associated with them in some way. At the same time, their lack of historical background left them with little understanding of what might constitute those perspectives. They could imagine *themselves* in a particular historical situation, and they recognized the importance of different perspectives in relation to their studies of distant countries, but they lacked the historical depth to understand alternative realities *in their own country*. Particularly in regard to race and ethnicity, they struggled to imagine other perspectives.[52]

Imagining Other Perspectives: Race and Ethnicity

Just as the persistence of racial and ethnic tensions challenged U.S. children's national narrative of American exceptionality and progress, so too did they generate confusion and controversy among the New Zealand students. It was one thing for them to represent issues that took place far from home as examples of fairness, or as moral lessons for other nations. They could apply their "Quest for Fairness" narrative to the holocaust, for instance, but struggled with how to explain where "fairness" lay in disputes over land or fishing rights at home. Was the Treaty of Waitangi, for instance, an example of fairness? All of the students agreed that it was, yet failed to agree about what kind of fairness was at issue. From the perspective of most of the Pakeha students, the Treaty resulted in sharing land, and they perceived sharing as fair. That "Maori and Pakeha could both settle in New Zealand and not fight over the land" was reiterated in all but one of the predominantly European New Zealander groups. Yet individuals in each group acknowledged that the Treaty had not worked out fairly. Stefan tried to explain what happened: "[The Treaty] is where the Maori decided to get along with the Whites, supposedly, and Whites were actually coming to New Zealand." In this instance, Stefan presented the story as most European New Zealand students told it—an agreement whereby Maori and Pakeha decided to get along. But Stefan adds a "supposedly," indicating that this commonly told narrative may not be true. In fact, he does not believe it, and suggests an alternative story: "The Treaty was sort of a passport for Whites to come to New Zealand but it didn't work out quite the way the Maori had thought it would. They got ripped off, some of the land, you know. The Whites bought it for three purple beads and a musket *'cause the Maori didn't know the value of property* (emphasis mine)." In this version of events, "sharing" is not an issue. The Maori lose their land out of a combination of Pakeha greed and Maori ignorance. While Stefan understands that the Maori lost their land, he does not have a framework that might explain that event from a Maori perspective. The only story to which he has access is one that explains the loss of land as a scam that might have been prevented had the Maori understood the Western notion of "the value of property." As a result, as Alexi explained, "we've got Maori claiming land now." Her classmate Ellen agreed, "The Maori want land the Pakehas have."

Not all of the students saw the loss of Maori land as either unfair or relevant to present disputes. Sally explained that the Treaty was "important for Maori because they got to *keep* land, and forests, and fisheries. It was between the Maori and the English. Pakehas." Alan made a similar point, explaining that

Maori used the Treaty "whenever there's something wrong. They always go back to the Treaty and find something that helps." Dougal agreed, explaining that "they say they didn't get enough land." When asked if this was an accurate assessment of the Maori's situation, Dougal responded by saying "It's hard to tell what Maoris should have had, because there's lots of different tribes and things. . . . There must have been something wrong with the Treaty because there's still trouble over it." After listening to her peers explain that people were still fighting over the fairness of the Treaty and its aftermath, Rachel shrugged her shoulders, dismissing the entire dispute, and said, "well, *Maori* do." In her opinion the fight was one-sided and more of a concern to Maori than to any other New Zealanders.

As had their Pakeha peers, Maori and Pacific Islander students agreed that the Treaty of Waitangi was significant because it was about fairness—"how Maori would be treated"—but understood the issue rather differently than did most of the European New Zealand students. Ripeka explained that the Treaty was "how the Maori and the Pakehas came together to make a compromise about land, that's what I think, and just to think that the Pakehas tricked . . . they signed this bit of paper that said, well, we'll have this kind of land and that sort of land." Her classmate, Irihapeti interrupted, saying "Well, what I'm going to say is, the Treaty of Waitangi, its about fighting over your land, and if the teachers were to go over *that* . . . there would be a *lot* more to tell than just a few little battles they had." Ripeka agreed, adding, "it would be, because like Pakehas don't actually rely on the land that much, do you know what I mean? The Maori used the land as much as they could, and I think we could learn from that, from the things they've left behind." In another group, Kiri explained that she thought the Treaty was important to her as a Maori, "because I want to be part of that past, and what happened with Maoris."

When asked what might have happened without the Treaty, issues of cultural power and racism became more specific and further complicated students' notions of fairness. Without the Treaty, there would have been no queen, most agreed, though Hamilton was sure that someone else would have colonized New Zealand. "The French, probably," he said. Reed and Paul, however, thought that the country would have stayed Maori and "White people would have to live like Maori, rather than the other way round." Paul added, "The Maori people could live where they wanted." When I asked if Maori had been able to live where they wanted under British rule, the four boys in this group said that had not always been the case. "Maori are protesting this now," Paul said. "Before they owned it, but . . ." his voice trailed off. Frederick explained that "some people don't like the White people," and was cut off immediately by Reed, who said "and some Whites don't like Maori." "Without the Treaty," Paul said, "then the Maoris and the Whites would be fighting." In another group, Hamilton suggested that it "would be fair to give [the land] back" but it would be very complicated. "I reckon everyone should have the same like, should all be equal. You shouldn't get anything just because you're Maori, or you shouldn't get anything just because you're Pakeha." Reed had a different idea about what was fair. "The Maori," he said, "when their ancestors signed the treaty, they said they could have that land. . . . They could have said we don't want you on our land, it's ours, but they let us come here." "Yes," Robert said, "and then we took all their land." Frustrated, Robert said, "I think we should all just live peacefully." When asked how that might be accomplished, Reed precipitated this lively exchange:

Reed:	Send them all to Auckland!
Robert:	NO!
Frederick:	Give them back what's rightfully theirs!
Researcher:	And that would be?
Reed:	It was all theirs before Cook came.
Robert:	So they should have?
Reed:	All of it? Maybe not all of it, but quite a bit of it?
Robert:	More than 50%.
Frederick:	No.
Reed:	No, they didn't have to let us take it.
Frederick:	Now they want it back.
Reed:	Now that we've taken over.

None of the Maori or Pacific Islander students engaged in this sort of exchange. While they thought the Treaty was important, and that it represented an occasion when Maori were dealt with unfairly, they did not mention returning land to Maori people. They suggested instead that the Treaty represented an opportunity for coexistence lost to greed—the Pakeha could have learned to use the land more wisely if they had worked with rather than against the Maori. In fact, coexistence appeared in every group as a corollary of students' fairness principle of historical significance. Just as they had argued that certain events were significant because they represented matters of fairness, students also argued for the significance of events that brought diverse people to New Zealand. As Kiri explained in regard to the Treaty of Waitangi, "that's how the Maori and the Pakeha came together." Similarly, Captain Cook's explorations were significant because they precipitated European immigration to the islands. "He told all the Europeans about us," Hamilton said, "and they came here."

When students selected the first Polynesian settlement in New Zealand for the timeline, they explained their choice by saying, "They were the first people to come in contact with, eventually." Immigration, too, represented one way in which New Zealand became more diverse. "[Immigration] is a good thing," Reed explained. "If they hadn't have come way back then there wouldn't be as many cultures in New Zealand." When asked why that was a good thing, Reed explained that "people can learn off of each other, like different languages and things like that. I think that's pretty important, because like lots of people that come from other countries can learn from our culture and we can learn off them and what's different between their home country and ours." After listening to Reed, Robert suggested that this gathering of people learning from each other had a larger significance, too. "Like our governments and theirs would be like closer because you see on like the news that different countries are fighting and all, and if they [the immigrants] come to our country they will think that this is not a bad place." Reed interrupted, "and not fight with them?" "Yeah," Robert said. Among this group of four boys, three had relatives who were first generation immigrants. "My dad was born in Zimbabwe," Reed said. "My Auntie was born in England," added Arthur. Paul's aunt was born in Scotland. Only Robert claimed to be a "full-on Kiwi." Asked if that meant none of his ancestors had been immigrants, Robert said they were "Kiwis all the way back."

Unlike the "Quest for Fairness" narrative that was positively perceived across all groups, some students had reservations about coexistence and about immigration. As I noted earlier, some of the Pakeha students expressed discomfort with what they understood of Maori complaints about loss of land and culture. In this instance, however, students from Maori and Pacific Islanders as well as Pakeha backgrounds expressed discomfort with aspects of immigration. In one group of Maori and Pacific Island boys, for example, an argument erupted over the inclusion of immigration on the timeline. When Witi suggested putting it on the timeline, Peter adamantly refused. "I don't like it! It's not important!" he declared. Witi objected, saying, "That's no kind of reason." Peter continued to object, exclaiming that there were already enough immigrants in the country. "That's sad," Witi said. "If we didn't let immigrants in, than she [the researcher] wouldn't be here." When I explained that I was a temporary visitor rather than an immigrant the conversation moved on to who immigrants were. "Are they just poor people, or can anybody be an immigrant," Tama asked. "Some of us wouldn't be here," Witi explained, "if it weren't for immigrants." Peter, however was adamant. "Jenny Shipley's giving all the Chinese people everything." Tama agreed. "They're the ones who've got more than most people." "And," said Peter, "it should be for the ones who are born here." These comments were, at least in part, a reflection of the recent influx of Asian immigrants, some in the wake of the return of Hong Kong to the People's Republic of China. In at least two groups, too, immigration was associated with the presence in the community of refugees from the former Yugoslavia. In the end, only five groups included immigration on their timeline. This marks an interesting contrast with their peers in the United States who tended to view the U.S. as a nation of immigrants and understood themselves as the direct descendants of immigrants.[53] In contrast, the New Zealand students recognized immigration as part of their history, but tended to perceive themselves either as "full-on Kiwi," Maori, or Pacific Islander. As I asked each group about their own immigrant history, one boy described ancestors emigrating from Ireland in the face of the potato famine, four students mentioned emigration from China and Hong Kong, and at least one person in each of the twelve groups identified British ancestry. Maori and Pacific Islander students provided the most richly elaborated discussion of their immigration and ancestry. When asked what would happen if children didn't learn about this aspect of the past, Kiri said "I think you would feel empty. . . . It's just like people who are fostered, and they don't have any parents, and they ask, 'how did I get here,' that sort of thing."

A Preference for Perspective Taking at a Distance

Overall, students reported that they were less interested in studying New Zealand history than in learning about other parts of the world. As one girl, Heather, explained in response to a question about her historical interests, "being in New Zealand, you're expected to say New Zealand, but I know the general outline, you know, but that wouldn't be like my favorite subject. I'd like somewhere different, like India, or Egypt, with the mummies." All twelve interview groups expressed interest in learning about the United States, eight groups preferred Britain, and three wanted to study India. Students in four groups mentioned that they either already had or intended someday to live in the United States and "needed to know about your history." "I lived in America," Hamilton explained, "and I reckon they've got a more interesting history because before with the slaves and stuff, that's probably more interesting than any of our history. I'd pick to study about the slaves and stuff." Other students who had lived or traveled in Canada, Australia, and Japan thought these countries more interesting than New Zealand. In each group students expressed interest in studying "really different kinds of places" or people and events in the news, "for instance this new guy in Serbia and stuff." When asked why they felt this way, students explained that these places, people, or events were more interesting and that it was "important to know what people were doing before your time." As one boy, Tainui, noted, "I think it's just like soap operas and that sort of thing . . . a show like Shortland Street" [a popular television soap opera]. Tainui also suggested that teachers might consider the soap opera aspects of history as they planned instruction. "Maybe if they were making it like that, but we didn't know we were learning," he mused. "If they were going to teach us something?" Other students suggested that learning the history of distant peoples made them "think differently about stuff," and "understand a different point of view." No doubt some of this can be explained by a curricular focus on world cultures. Students had more background knowledge of India or Egypt, for instance, than of New Zealand's history. In addition, as Tainui suggests, learning about people in other parts of the world is a bit like watching a soap opera, or, perhaps, reading a novel. In the context of a distant place and past, students contemplate other perspectives with relative safety. Investigating the perspectives of people in Ancient Egypt or India, for instance, does not necessarily challenge students to reconsider the perspectives of their own local communities of identification.

Conclusion

Student responses indicate that they were better prepared to "think differently" and "understand a different point of view" in regard to distant rather than local "others." One feature of their willingness to consider alternative perspectives in international contexts was their belief that it was important to do so. Students in the U.S. might also be better prepared to engage in perspective taking outside of national history, but they expressed little need to learn about other countries. Unlike their New Zealand counterparts who *preferred* to study about other parts of the world, the American students tended to think it was more important to study their own national history. Perceiving themselves as the teachers of the world, they were not inclined to think they had much to learn from the world. New Zealanders, on the other hand, have access to a national narrative that inclines them to pay attention to the world beyond their shores. The fluidity of this narrative, with relatively few fixed points of reference or reverence, leaves students open to the possibility of learning from as well as teaching other people.[54] The students I interviewed were willing—even anxious—to engage in dialogue with other parts of the world. As I mentioned earlier, part of this has to do with geoposition and the distribution of global power, as well as the specifics of the colonial past, and perhaps to the fact that they were being interviewed by someone from another country. It should not be surprising, however, that a small island nation distant from the Western centers of power with which it is culturally and politically allied should focus outward, nor that its children should reflect this orientation. Such an orientation may not focus a great deal of attention on national history, but it does incline students to recognize that alternative perspectives prevail in the world, and that it is important to understand these perspectives.

New Zealand students' willingness to recognize different perspectives in distant places stands in marked contrast to their discomfort with perspective taking in more local settings. Membership in local communities of identification makes it difficult for these students to take the perspective of local "others." Thus Stefan, operating within a global setting, claims that New Zealanders learned from the distant Nazi Holocaust that racism is always wrong, while Reed, operating within a local setting suggests that all Maori move to Auckland. It is not that Reed does not know that an alternative perspective is possible. Indeed, some of his peers vigorously protest against his views. Rather, taking on a different perspective on this issue would require a degree of separation from Reed's own community of identification and involve a level of discomfort for which he is unprepared. Because Reed identifies with European New Zealanders he does not want to understand a Maori perspective. He has a personal stake in believing that the Maori somehow gave the land away—they could have said no, he declares—and shouldn't complain now about their choices in the past. Reed cannot distance himself enough from a European perspective to consider any other. In addition, the national narrative available to him provides little help. Reed and his peers have not studied national history. What they have available to them is a history cobbled together from bits and pieces—holiday celebrations, media presentations, family, literature, and the like. Some have a richer array of information from which to choose. Stefan, for instance, is an enthusiastic participant in workshops held at the local history museum where he has worked with artifacts and primary sources. In his comments, too, he references discussions with his family about issues of race, gender, and ethnicity. Some of the Maori and Pacific Islander students also have access to historical narratives rooted in their own communities of identification. They recall exposure to the Whakapapa, stories told on the *marae*, visits to former homesites and the like as sources of their historical information. Most, however, have very little historical information at their disposal. As a result, they do not have particularly *historical* schema to apply to these oddments about the past. Instead, they apply social relations schema—fairness, morality, getting along together—and link them in a familiar narrative arc—characters in the past experience some crisis, they rise to the occasion, meet and overcome the challenge, learn from the experience, and share what they've learned with others. This narrative allows students to retain their sense of identification with the past and to see their nation or community of identification and, by extension, themselves, as moral. It does not, however, provide them with the tools necessary to make sense out of the continuation of inequity, injustice, or immorality in the nation or local community.

Despite students' difficulties with perspective taking in a national context, New Zealand's new curriculum challenges schools to focus more on perspective taking in national history at a much earlier age. If the Ministry's recommendations are followed, instruction would engage children from primary school onwards in in-depth inquiry into issues of social justice from past to present. The curriculum designers express the hope that historical study of this kind will provide students with some of the tools necessary for effective citizenship. The responses of the students in this study and the experience of other nations suggest caution in assuming that this will be the case. First of all, national history is invariably contested. As a result, groups and individuals attach enormous importance to the form history takes in school. Given the politically charged consequences of curricular choices, it will be a challenge for teachers to approach national history from the perspective suggested in the curriculum documents. This is not to suggest that national history be ignored; rather, that perspective taking presents a different set of challenges in national history than it does in more distant, less personal and less highly charged settings. Second, neither students' willingness to look beyond their own position, nor their curiosity about the lives of other people in other places and times necessarily prepares them to deal with perspective taking in their own nation. We know very little about making that imaginative leap, especially in relation to historically rooted and persistent social problems. These youngsters appear to have an advantage in their outward orientation and their willingness to cross the spaces between themselves and distant others. Perhaps the combination of careful attention to developing the tools of inquiry and the content of history suggested in the new curriculum standards will help students apply perspective taking to their own history. North American examples are not promising in this regard. These New Zealand adolescents, however, tend to combine an emphasis on connecting to a personal past—as do American students—with an expectation that history teaches about how other people lived—as do Northern Irish students. It is the latter understanding, if nurtured, that may help them to understand national history in ways more likely to meet the goals of the proposed curriculum. It will be interesting to see what impact an earlier introduction of national history will have on this process, and whether the suggested emphasis on inquiry, perspective taking, and social justice survives in the classroom.

Appendix A
Materials Used in Interview Task:
Captions and Picture Descriptions

Materials consisted of twenty-three laminated photocopies and accompanying captions (captions are written using New Zealand standard spellings), as described below:

First Polynesians. The first Polynesians came to New Zealand beginning in about 950 B.C.E. According to tradition, a voyager named Kupe named the country Aotearoa. In the 1300s a wave of immigrants arrived, possibly from Hawaiiki, in outrigger canoes. They brought taro, yam, kumara, the rat, and the dog. They settled on the islands, and lived there for over three hundred years before Abel Tasman named the country Nieuw Zeeland.

Captain Cook. Captain Cook and the *Endeavour* arrive in New Zealand in 1769. Cook soon learned that Maori inhabitants of the islands were powerful, aggressive, and brave. Cook sailed all around New Zealand, producing an accurate map of the country that was used for the next 150 years. This voyage put New Zealand on the European map of the world.

Treaty of Waitangi. In 1840, after years of warfare, some 50 Maori chiefs signed the Treaty of Waitangi, ceding sovereignty to the Queen of England. In return, the Queen guaranteed the Maori possession of the lands, forests, fisheries, and other property. The treaty was never ratified, and within ten years was held by the Pakeha courts to be invalid. Despite this, the date of the signing is generally held to be the "founding day" of New Zealand as a British colony. The treaty remains a source of disagreement and civil dissent.

Gold Rush. When gold was discovered on the South Island the gold rush brought thousands of miners to New Zealand, increasing the population of the South Island, and changing New Zealand's economy. Gold became New Zealand's largest export.

Land Wars. In 1860 Wiremu Kingi's claim to the Waitara started the Maori Land Wars; vast tracts of land were confiscated from rebel groups.

Immigration. Immigration is an important way in which the population of New Zealand changes over time. From the first Polynesians who came to Aotearoa to people from Asia and Eastern Europe who enter now, immigration has been a part of New Zealand. In the 1870s the government helped European immigrants and their families to settle in New Zealand. Today, people of Maori, Pacific Islander, European, and Asian ancestry form the population of New Zealand.

Education. When the central government took over the responsibility for primary education in 1877, school committees could compel (force) all children between 7 and 13 to attend school. This was an important addition to the responsibilities of central government and a move that made it possible for all children, rich or poor, to at least learn to read and write.

Railroads. With the coming of the railroads huge new tracts of land opened up for settlement. As new settlers moved away from towns, conflicts over land ownership often arose.

Dunedin. In 1882 the first refrigerated cargo ship left New Zealand for England. Once cargo could be kept cold, New Zealand could export meat as well as wool. Sheep became a very important part of the New Zealand economy.

Women's Suffrage. New Zealand was one of the first countries in the world to grant women the right to vote. While some states in the United States allowed women to vote in some elections before 1893, they couldn't vote in national elections until more than twenty-five years after women got the vote in New Zealand. Despite the vote, women could not serve in Parliament or be Cabinet Ministers. They were active, however, "behind the scenes" and in reform activities.

Pension. A typical scene at the post office when old age pensions were paid out (1898). The pension was considered a citizen's right, earned by years of paying taxes. At first, this money was given only to men who were very poor and had "good morals." Later it was extended to all those who contributed to the pension system. This was the first old age pension in the world.

John Seddon. Richard John Seddon began a new, democratic style of politics in New Zealand. Under his administration, a number of reforms occurred that appeared to give "ordinary" people more power. Seddon sought all the publicity he could get, such as this picture from a construction project, to advertise the public works and railway construction projects begun during his administration.

Cook Islands. In 1901, New Zealand annexed the Cook Islands. Cook Islanders now make up about one-fifth of New Zealand's population.

Cars. The development of the car gave people freedom of movement, which led to rapid changes in New Zealand society. Automotive import and the classroom.

Notes

1. C. Brett, "The Beastly Beatitudes of Josiah Beeman," *The Press*, 30 April 1999, 5.

2. B. A. VanSledright, "And Santayana Lives On: Students' Views on the Purposes for Studying American History," *Journal of Curriculum Studies* 29 (1997): 529-557.

3. K. C. Barton, "'You'd Be Wanting to Know About the Past': Social Contexts of Children's Historical Understanding in Northern Ireland and the United States" (paper presented at the annual meeting of the American Educational Research Association, San Diego, California, 1998); K. C. Barton and L. S. Levstik, "'It Wasn't a Good Part of History': National Identity and Students' Explanations of Historical Significance," *Teachers College Record* 99 (1998): 478-513; Linda S. Levstik, "European, Pacific Islander, and Maori Students' Understanding of Historical Significance" (April 1999); Y. Su, "Changing Minds: How Elementary Social Studies Textbooks Both Reflect and Change Society," *International Journal of Social Education* 12 (1999): 76-104; J. V. Wertsch, *Mind as Action* (New York: Oxford University Press, 1998).

4. B. Rogoff, *Apprenticeship in Thinking: Cognitive Development in Social Context* (New York: Oxford University Press, 1990).

5. Wertsch, *Mind as Action*; J. V. Wertsch, P. Del Rio, and A. Alvarez, eds., *Sociocultural Studies of Mind* (Cambridge: Cambridge University Press, 1995).

6. K.C. Barton and L.S. Levstik, *National Identity*; Linda S. Levstik, "The Relationship Between Historical Response and Narrative in a Sixth-Grade Classroom," *Theory and Research in Social Education* 28 (1986): 114-119; L. S. Levstik and K. C. Barton, "'They Still Use Some of Their Past': Historical Salience in Elementary Children's Chronological Thinking," *Journal of Curriculum Studies* 28 (1996): 531-576.

7. A. K. Appiah & A. Gutmann, *Color Conscious: The Political Morality of Race* (Princeton: Princeton University Press, 1996); B. Barber, *Jihad vs. McWorld* (New York: Ballentine Books, 1996); J. Bodnar, *Remaking America: Public Memory, Commemoration, and Patriotism in the Twentieth Century* (Princeton: Princeton University Press, 1992); T. J. Friedman, *The Lexus and the Olive Tree* (New York: Farrar, Straus & Giroux, 1999); D. W. Cohen, *The Combing of History* (Chicago: Chicago University Press, 1994); M. Kammen, *Mystic Chords of Memory: The Transformation of Tradition in American Culture* (New York: Vintage, 1991).

8. M. Greene, *Releasing the Imagination: Essays on Education the Arts and Social Change* (New York: Teachers College Press, 1995).

9. Greene, *Releasing the Imagination*.

10. K.C. Barton and L.S. Levstik, *National Identity*; Bodnar, *Remaking America*; T. Epstein, "Makes No Difference if You're Black or White? African American and European American Adolescents' Perspectives on Historical Significance and Historical Sources" (paper presented at the annual meeting of American Educational Research Association, New Orleans, 1994); P. Seixas, "Historical Understanding Among Adolescents in a Multicultural Setting," *Curriculum Inquiry* 23 (1993): 301-327.

11. A. Alton-Lee, G. Nuthall, and J. Patrick, "Reframing Classroom Research: A Lesson from the Private World of Children," *Harvard Educational Review* 63 (1993): 54-84.

12. P. Seixas, "Mapping the Terrain of Historical Significance," *Social Education* 61 (1997): 27.

13. K. C. Barton, "'You'd Be Wanting to Know About the Past': Social Contexts of Children's Historical Understanding in Northern Ireland and the United States"; Barton and Levstik, "National Identity"; Epstein, "Makes No Difference"; Levstik & Barton, "Historical Salience"; VanSledright, "Santayana Lives."

14. Wertsch, et al., *Sociocultural Studies*.

15. Barton, "Social Contexts," 49.

16. S. Foster, "Using Historical Empathy to Excite Students About the Study of History: Can You Empathize with Neville Chamberlain?" *The Social Studies* 90, (1999).

17. Foster, "Historical Empathy"; Greene, *Imagination*; Tom Holt, *Thinking Historically: Narrative, Imagination, and Understanding*, in D. P. Wolf, ed., *The Thinking Series* (New York: College Entrance Examination Board, 1990).

18. C. Hartman, "McConnell Decries Exhibits' 'Political Correctness,'" *Lexington Herald Leader*, Thursday, July 29, 1999, A8; G. Nash, C. Crabtree, and R. Dunn, *History on Trial: Culture Wars and the Teaching of the Past* (New York: Knopf, 1997).

19. S. Middleton and H. May, *Teachers Talk Teaching, 1915-1995: Early Childhood Schools and Teachers Colleges* (Palmerston North, New Zealand: Dunmore Press, 1997), 9.

20. Ministry of Education, *Social Studies in the New Zealand Curriculum: Getting Started* (Wellington, New Zealand: Ministry of Education, 1998), 8.

21. Ministry, *Getting Started*, 10-11.

22. The term *Pakeha,* or foreigner, refers to non-Maori. While it can be a pejorative, it remains in use in public documents and was used by the students and teachers alike to describe themselves and others. It is also used throughout the Ministry of Education documents to refer to non-Maori.

23. N. Thomas, "Kiss the Baby Goodbye: Kowhaiwhai and Aesthetics in Aotearoa New Zealand," *Critical Inquiry* 22 (1995), 116.

24. Ministry of Education, *Social Studies in the New Zealand Curriculum* (Wellington, New Zealand: Ministry of Education, [Te Tahuhu o te Matauranga], 1997), 21.

25. Ministry, *Social Studies*, 8.

26. Ministry, *Social Studies*.

27. Foster, "Historical Empathy."

28. D. A. Hollinger, "National Solidarity at the End of the Twentieth Century: Reflections on the United States and Liberal Nationalism," *Journal of American History* 84 (1997).

29. Ministry, *Social Studies*.

30. R. Openshaw, "Citizen Who? The Debate Over Economic and Political Correctness in the Social Studies Curriculum," P. Benson and R. Openshaw, eds., *New Horizons for New Zealand Social Studies* (Palmerston North, New Zealand: Educational Research and Development Press, 1998), 19-42.

31. Barton and Levstik, "*National Identity.*"

32. See, for example, S. Coney, *Standing in the Sunshine: A History of New Zealand Women Since they Won the Vote* (Auckland: Viking/Penguin Books, 1993); P. Crawford, *Nomads of the Wind: A Natural History of Polynesia* (London: BBC Books, 1993); A. Salmond, *Two Worlds—First Meetings between Maori and Europeans* (Viking, 1991); K. Sinclair, *The Oxford Illustrated History of New Zealand* (Oxford, Great Britain: Oxford University Press, 1989).

33. The teachers in training had undergraduate degrees in a variety of fields and were working towards initial certification.

34. In one group only two boys participated. All other groups had three or four.

35. Because differences by gender or age were rare I have chosen to provide examples of responses that represent both sexes and a range of grade levels throughout this paper.

36. I use the term "master" to imply that colonial histories tend to be the history of the colonists/masters rather than of the colonized/mastered. A "master" narrative tends also to become the official narrative sanctioned in the curriculum, and the one for which students are accountable on tests of academic achievement.

37. Barton and Levstik, "National Identity," 490.

38. Coney, *Standing in the Sunshine*; W. Ihimaera, *The Legendary Land: Auckland* (Auckland: Reed Publishing, 1994); Sinclair, *History*.

39. Ihimaera, *Legendary Land*, 32.

40. Ihimaera, *Legendary Land*, 151.

41. While women in some other places (i.e., Wyoming, Utah, Pitcairn Island, and the Isle of Man) could vote before women in New Zealand, New Zealand was the first country in the world where a campaign for women's suffrage was victorious (see Coney, *Standing*).

42. The Treaty of Waitangi is generally considered the beginning of British colonial rule in New Zealand. Although never ratified, Maori and Pakeha agreed to submit themselves to British sovereignty in exchange for the cessation of warfare, not just between Maori and Pakeha, but among Maori as well. Land settlements made as part of the Treaty are still disputed and were not upheld in practice.

43. D. Cohen, "New Zealand no longer tries to be 'more English than England,'" *The Christian Science Monitor,* 1998.

44. Openshaw, "Citizen Who?"

45. Ihimaera, *Legendary Land*.

46. Hillary was not one of the set of pictures presented to students. Instead, he was spontaneously suggested by students in response to being asked if I had left anything significant out of the pictures that they were using.

47. K. Sheppard (1847-1934) was a key figure in the women's movement in New Zealand. She had strong views on electoral reform, prison reform, international peace and arbitration, vegetarianism and health, as well as women's rights. She kept in contact with her American and British women's rights colleagues and her success was noted by them in their work (see Coney, *Standing*).

48. At the time of this study Jenny Shipley was Prime Minister of New Zealand and several women had just been elected to mayoral seats.

49. One group of boys suggested that women were "probably more important" than men because "they look after the homes and all, most of the time, and they have the babies." A New Zealand colleague suggested that this response might have been reflective of a recent unit of study that included attention to puberty, reproduction, and the like.

50. This claim was made despite the students' almost universal dislike for Mrs. Shipley. Their disapproval was never attributed to Mrs. Shipley's gender and, when asked, they almost always pointed out that there were a number of women in public life—Helen Clark, for instance—whom they supported.

51. Greene, *Imagination*, 3.

52. Greene, *Imagination*, 3.
53. Barton and Levstik, "National Identity."
54. While individual students had some background information on people and event pictures on the timeline task, only Cook, the Treaty of Waitangi, and Prime Minister Jenny Shipley were universally familiar. Edmund Hillary appeared to be the other national figure with whom most students were familiar, and was the most frequently suggested addition to the timeline.

Chapter 6

Teaching and Learning Multiple Perspectives on the Use of the Atomic Bomb: Historical Empathy in the Secondary Classroom

Elizabeth Anne Yeager and Frans H. Doppen

In an earlier chapter of this book, "The Role of Empathy in the Development of Historical Understanding," Yeager and Foster suggest that the central question of historical empathy exercises is: Why did an individual or group of people, given a certain set of circumstances, act in a certain way? Historians must bring this question to their inquiry in order to understand the events, actions, and words of key figures in the historical record. This chapter addresses the idea of historical empathy by arguing that the development of historical empathy in students is a considered and active process, embedded in the historical method, that involves four interrelated phases: the introduction of an historical event necessitating the analysis of human action, the understanding of historical context and chronology, the analysis of a variety of historical evidence and interpretations, and the construction of a narrative framework through which reasonable historical conclusions are reached. In this chapter, we discuss two exercises in historical empathy with high school students, focusing on the subject matter of World War II because of its centrality to the high school history curriculum and because of its breadth of moral and political dilemmas. In addition, the topic of World War II has generated ample primary and secondary source material that is relatively easy for teachers and students to use in the classroom.

Portal's[1] research informed our efforts to design questions for studying aspects of the development of students' historical empathy. The questions were based on his suggestions and written so that students would be able to project their own ideas and feelings into an historical situation, to encounter the "element of paradox" so that they could distinguish the period they were studying from their own, to employ a collection of reference materials and contemporary sources appropriate to the topic at hand, to encounter "a particular person or situation in terms that extend beyond the merely typical to encompass the unique circumstances of the case," and to use a two-sided narrative "where the inadequately empathic relationship between the historical participants leads to misunderstanding, conflict, (or) tragedy."[2]

Truman's Decision to Use Atomic Weapons: A Preliminary Study and Writing Exercise

In this exercise, eight high school juniors (two African American females, two African American males, two white males, one white female, and one Asian-American female), studying United States history at the time of this exercise and divided into two groups of four, read accounts related to Truman's decision to use atomic weapons in Japan. One group read an account from a standard high school history textbook. The other group read a variety of excerpts from sources including Richard Haynes' *The Awesome Power*, John Hersey's *Hiroshima*, Michihiko Hachiya's *Hiroshima Diary: Journal of a Japanese Physician*, Yoichi Fukushima's *Children of Hiroshima*, Rachelle Linner's *City of Silence*, Peter Wyden's *Day One*, Japanese army manuals, Kelly and Whittock's *The Era of the Second World War*, articles from *Foreign Affairs*, Harry S Truman's memoirs, and other recollections from prisoners of war, Manhattan Project scientists, Winston Churchill, and Paul Tibbets (see appendix A for a complete listing). After their reading, the students wrote responses to this question:

> Based on the evidence you have at hand, construct a reasonable explanation of why you think Truman ordered the bombing of Hiroshima and Nagasaki. What factors affected his decision? What were his options? What were the short- and long-term effects of his decision?

The students completed their task in the school library during regular school hours. They were given no model or specific guidelines for completing the writing assignment, and they took as much time as they needed to finish their work. None of the participants appeared to struggle with the task; all of them produced coherent, well-rounded responses to each question (approximately two to four pages per question for each participant).

We examined the students' work, wrote notes and research memoranda of our initial reactions to the data, then shared these notes with each other. Through ongoing discussion, we developed characterizations and conclusions about the data, and we holistically analyzed each written response for patterns and trends, thus creating a well-rounded portrayal of the students' thinking.

We present two main findings from this exercise. First, we offer insights into students' understandings of historical empathy with specific illustrations from their responses to the questions. More importantly, we demonstrate the difference that the available evidence and contextual/chronological information made in the two groups' understandings and empathic responses.

This task was highly preliminary in nature; its emphasis was solely on the participants' engagement with the sources and questions that were developed for this exercise. Portal and others cited in the introduction to this study have argued that students' exposure to particular historical sources and to appropriate "empathic questions" are important starting points in their inquiry; thus, we wanted to study specifically how exposure to these sources and questions might stimulate empathic responses among the students in this study. Later in this chapter, we describe a more in-depth, teacher-directed classroom empathy exercise.

Discussion of Historical Empathy Writing Exercise

Because many history teachers tend to use a single "standard" textbook in their classrooms, we wanted to find out whether the students who used only a single school history textbook in this empathy exercise yielded substantially different empathic responses from the students who read from the large array of primary and secondary sources that were assembled in order to provide multiple perspectives and insights on the decision to bomb Hiroshima and Nagasaki.

The textbook devoted two chapters to the prelude, actual events, and aftermath of World War Two, evenly covering the home front and the European, North African, and Pacific theaters of the war. About a page and half were devoted to the atomic bombing of the two Japanese cities (this was a considerable amount compared to other texts that were considered, one of which dealt with the bombing in a few sentences). The textbook account that was used opened with the stated point of view that an all-out invasion of the Japanese islands would have been devastating for both sides in the conflict, commented on the intransigence of Japanese leaders and the resistance of the Japanese people, described Truman's newness as president at the Potsdam Conference, and implied that he went along with Stalin and Churchill. The textbook also described the strength of American industrial power and scientific knowledge, but also the American fear of German scientific progress and competition. The bomb was described as both a remarkable and devastating weapon; casualty counts were provided with no description of the nature and consequences of an atomic bombing. The conditions of Japan's surrender and the resultant peace treaty were briefly described. No reference was made to Japanese perspectives, the role of the Soviet Union, or any opposing viewpoints or alternatives to the bombing decision.

The students in the textbook group had very limited historical material and information with which to employ aspects of empathic thinking described earlier. Hence, their capacity to draw upon a rich variety of evidence in order to analyze context, use hindsight to explore the complex circumstances and consequences of Truman's decision, and explore the beliefs, values, and feelings of the participants was restricted.

Not surprisingly, the students in the textbook group generally responded to the designated question by reciting the facts presented in the textbook. In response to this question, regarding Truman's decision to drop the bomb, all agreed that the bombing was an either/or proposition, a simplified choice between American and Japanese lives. Truman had only two options: invade Japan or use atomic weapons to end the war. None of the students in this group had enough information to consider Truman's other possible options (for example, the implications of Truman's option to drop the bomb in a sparsely-populated area simply to demonstrate the power of this new weapon). Secondly, the only short-term effect of the bombing that the students in this group mentioned was their agreement that Truman bombed Japanese cities in order to save even more lives, especially American ones, and that he probably did save many lives by doing so and ending the war quickly. A representative comment made by one student, June, was as follows:

> I believe Truman ordered (the bombing) because Japan was not willing to surrender unconditionally, even though they had been given an ultimatum. Truman had two choices: he could have invaded Japan, which in turn would have resulted in hundreds of thousands of American casualties, or he could . . . order the bombing. He intelligently chose the atomic bomb.

The other students in the group gave similar responses, and all scattered verbatim passages from the textbook account throughout their arguments.

A few picked up on the textbook's description of Truman as "new to the job," asserting that Truman acted partly because he *was* new and therefore unsure how to act. Another student, Latanya, followed the text's implication that Truman bowed to pressure from Stalin and Churchill at Potsdam, arguing that the latter two leaders were the "forces" compelling Truman to act because he "didn't know what to do . . . he was still young in the way the President is supposed to conduct his duties." A third student, Deion, explained that "the forces that affected (Truman's) decision weren't really forces, they were individuals . . . Churchill and Stalin."

Finally, the only other short- or long-term effect of the bombing that these students mentioned was their general agreement that the bombing of the two Japanese cities was tragic and devastating. Deion ventured that the United States could never again be "at peace" with Hiroshima and Nagasaki because of the bombing. However, all concurred that the bomb "got things over with quickly," which, in the long run, was the point of Truman's decision.

The other group in this study used a wide range of sources representing a variety of perspectives on Truman's decision, its implications for the end of World War Two and for foreign policy in the postwar era, and its effects on Japan. Cooper and Downey, in previous studies of children's historical understanding,[3] concluded that students with access to a wide variety of good historical sources were able to construct valid explanations and suppositions about sources in order to try to understand how people in the past may have felt and thought and to begin to explain attitudes and values different from their own. The students in the second group of this study exhibited the same characteristics.

Generally, the students in the second group appeared to have read the material carefully and incorporated information into their written responses without simply copying phrases and passages from the material as if they were on a search for correct answers. Rather, they tended to shift among perspectives in the sources and to synthesize information into their own coherent explanations and conclusions. When appropriate, they quoted historical actors cited in the sources in order to support their views.

First, these students offered multiple, interconnected reasons for Truman's decision. All mentioned the argument that he was concerned with saving American lives; however, this factor did not figure as prominently into their explanations as it did with the textbook group. Each student in the second group developed his or her own "angle" on the bombing, featuring one or more other factors that made this a complex decision for Truman. Like the students in Dickinson and Lee's study of historical empathy, who attempted to explain why the emperor Claudius decided to invade Britain, the participants in the second group of this study showed some understanding of the fact that people in the past saw things differently from those in the present, according to the specific situations in which historical actors found themselves.[4]

In this study, two students, Tameka and Rasheed, gave explanations of why Truman decided to use the atomic bomb, based on some combination of the following factors: 1) to fulfill an obligation initiated by President Roosevelt; 2) to demonstrate American power to the world, especially to the Soviet Union, at a time when U.S.-Soviet tension was fermenting; 3) to justify the time, effort, and cost that had gone into the Manhattan Project; 4) to exact revenge for Pearl Harbor; 5) to satisfy Truman's personal pride and need to demonstrate presidential leadership. Another student, Michael, based his argument mainly on the "demonstration of power" perspective:

> I think that (Truman) wanted to show the world that the U.S. was the number one country. He could have ordered the bombings to show that nobody should mess with the U.S., since now they have such a great weapon. The reasoning

officially was that he wanted to save human lives in the long run, get Japan to surrender, and avoid a land attack. All of these reasons I don't believe too much. Truman had many other options that he could have taken but didn't.

While the students in the first group had no information on other options available to Truman, the students in the second group did. In fact, all of them listed some of the other avenues he could have taken to end the war in a less cataclysmic way: test the bomb on "some remote island to show Japan how powerful the bomb really was," "destroy an uninhabited area of Japan," wait for "conventional methods to work because Japan was getting ready to surrender anyway," or "prewarn Japan about the bomb or show their top leaders a testing." However, they concluded, to use the words of another student, Karen, that "these options were thought not to be very convincing, a waste of time, and a waste of fissionable material."

Interestingly, Karen offered yet another perspective on why Truman acted as he did: the fact that Truman himself had limited information on what his options were. As she explained:

> Truman ordered the bombings because he was not well-informed and was only hearing the side that wanted the bomb. . . .The forces that affected his decision were. . . .his military advisers and the information they were giving him. . . .Truman's advisers told him the bomb should be used as a terror weapon, to produce 'the greatest psychological effect against Japan' and to make others aware of the new power that America had. The objections that were made about the bomb were not made known to the President, or only a few were.

Most agreed that the pro-bombing perspective predominated among Truman's military advisers, who exerted considerable influence and were the primary force behind his decision. However, Karen was the only one who specifically mentioned *Truman's* limited viewpoint because of his lack of access to multiple perspectives on the situation.

With regard to the short- and long-term effects of Truman's decision, the students in the second group generally agreed on the following: the Japanese surrendered quickly, many "innocent" lives were lost, widespread "suffering" and "destruction" ensued, "overall shock" spread throughout the world, and the United States established its global power. Michael argued that the "long-term effects were greater" because "with Truman's order the world had seen the first true mass destruction weapon, and this showed that the U. S. owned the most powerful weapon on the planet." Karen agreed that the strategic implications were vast, adding that, with the use of the bomb, "Soviet participation in the war would no longer be as essential . . . and this would ultimately strengthen Truman's position." Michael also introduced another perspective that would have a long-term impact: the United States "now had to deal with the problem of being looked at as a murderer." He said, "Everyone knew that Japan was getting ready to surrender, and that they were looking for peace before the first A-bomb was ever dropped. So the U.S. had to deal with the question of "why?"

Truman's Decision to Use Atomic Weapons: A Teacher-Directed Classroom Exercise

The same historical event was the focus of an extension to the previous study, this time with a group of 88 sophomore students in four separate sections of world history at the same school. The participants included 49 male and 39 female students who were 15 or 16 years old. Of the students, 53 were white, 27 African American, and 8 Hispanic.

To ascertain the students' preexisting knowledge about Truman's decision to use the atomic bomb, the world history teacher gave a pretest to all the students in which they answered the following four questions:

1. In what year did the United States drop the first atomic bomb?
2. Which are the only two cities on which an atomic bomb has ever been dropped?
3. Why did the United States decide to drop the atomic bomb? List as many reasons as you can think of.
4. Did the United States do the right thing when it decided to drop the atomic bomb? Explain your opinion as fully as possible.

The teacher designed a classroom exercise that focused on developing the students' historical empathy through an analysis of eighteen documents on President Truman's decision to use the atomic bomb against Japan (see appendix B). Documents 1-3 were excerpts from three World History textbooks commonly found in American high schools, while documents 4-7 were excerpts from three films that each present a different perspective. Documents 8-18 presented several other perspectives including those of historians, political leaders, and victims of the bombing. The teacher gave some direct instruction about the historical events surrounding the development and use of the atomic bomb, but kept direct instruction to a minimum in order to encourage the students to do their own historical thinking, as in Bohan and Davis's study on historical thinking.[5] The teacher's introductory lessons provided a time line of significant events and a presentation on the nature of historical empathy.

Next, the students were divided into heterogeneous groups of four. Each student received a copy of the eighteen documents and an investigation sheet with questions intended to guide the group's "think aloud" sessions. The investigation sheet was based on Foster's suggestions:[6]

1. Who is the author, and when and where was the source published?
2. Is this a primary or secondary source? How reliable does it seem?
3. How does this source support or reject Truman's decision to use the bomb?
4. How does this source support or contradict other sources?
5. What does the author's perspective tell you about his or her possible intentions?
6. Why did Truman decide that using the atomic bomb against Japan was necessary?
7. Why did Japan not surrender after the United States dropped an atomic bomb on Hiroshima?
8. Why did the United States drop a second atomic bomb on Nagasaki three days after it bombed Hiroshima?
9. What role did the Soviet Union play in the decision to use the atomic bomb against Japan?
10. What role did Great Britain play in the decision to use the atomic bomb against Japan?
11. What justification can be given for the use of a weapon as destructive as the atomic bomb?

After completing their "think aloud" sessions, each group wrote a report on its findings, which one member had to present to the class. For the report, each group followed a format in which the members listed arguments and cited documents in favor of and against Truman's decision, followed by questions for further group inquiry.

As a follow-up activity, students prepared a museum display on this historical event and presented it to the rest of the class. To give them further insight into the controversial nature of such a display, the students read a letter to the Smithsonian from 52 prominent historians. Dated July 31, 1995, the letter raised numerous objections to the Smithsonian's scheduled Enola Gay exhibit. In their displays, the students were encouraged to present multiple perspectives on the use of the bomb to avoid the kind of criticism that had been raised against the Smithsonian exhibit. The teacher offered suggestions on what to include in the display, such as maps, timelines, and other pertinent illustrations. The students then independently conducted research in the library and on the Internet to gather information to include in their displays.

As a concluding assignment, all students wrote a personal, reflective essay in which they presented their individual, personal perspectives on the use of the bomb. Also, one week after the completion of the unit, the students completed an unannounced posttest identical to the pretest. Three weeks later, they were given a final opportunity to provide qualitative feedback through an anonymous questionnaire with the following questions:

1. Did you like the unit on the decision to use the atomic bomb? Why or why not?

2. How was this social studies unit different from others you have studied?
3. Did you like learning about the decision to use the atomic bomb from multiple perspectives? Why or why not?
4. What are some things you learned from this unit?
5. Was studying the decision to drop the atomic bomb useful or meaningful to you? Why or why not?
6. Is it possible to know "the truth" about the decision to use the atomic bomb or any other historical event? Why or why not?

Discussion of Historical Empathy Classroom Exercise

The pretest revealed that one fourth of the 88 students did not know what year the United States dropped the first atomic bomb. While more than one third of the students knew that the atomic bomb was first used during the 1940s, only nine students specifically knew that 1945 was the correct answer. Eleven students believed that the atomic bomb had first been used during the early 1960s, perhaps during the Cuban missile crisis. Eleven students knew that an atomic bomb had been dropped on both Hiroshima and Nagasaki. More than half of all students were able to list Hiroshima as the site of an atomic bomb explosion.

When asked to list as many reasons as possible why the United States decided to drop the atomic bomb, one fourth of the students could not list a single reason. The majority, however, were able to list one or two reasons. "To show American strength" and "to end the war" were each listed 20 times, "to seek revenge for Pearl Harbor" was listed 15 times, whereas "to conduct a scientific experiment" was listed 12 times. The desire "to kill Japanese nationals" was listed six times, whereas "to save lives" and "Japan's refusal to surrender" were each mentioned only twice.

Finally, the students clearly were divided about the morality of the decision to use the atomic bomb. Twenty-five students strongly believed that it was right, while 35 students strongly believed it was wrong. The rest of the students either wrote that they did not know or were not sure, or simply left the space blank. The main reasons students gave to argue that the bombing was the right decision dealt with the saving of lives and money, ending the war and showing America's power to the world. Arguments to the contrary focused mainly on the belief that it is wrong to kill innocent people. A few students also referred to nuclear fallout and the destructive effect of the atomic bomb on the environment.

Nearly all students worked diligently throughout the "think aloud" sessions. They were often involved in serious discussions about the evidence a particular document provided. All groups completed the sessions in two or three regular 50-minute class periods, and most decided to use the strategy of systematically answering each question for each document and determining whether it supported or rejected Truman's decision. While some groups were more meticulous in citing sources than others, their reports were reflective of the in-depth discussions that occurred throughout the "think aloud" sessions.

The group discussions yielded interesting insights. One group wrote that it acquired

> . . . a sense of many points of view of both primary and secondary sources which help us get a better idea of what it was really like. Truman's decision was probably the most difficult decision he had to make in his presidency and maybe in his life time. He had the power of this incredible bomb and the well being of his country, but also the guilt of the people this bomb could and did indeed destroy.

Another group wrote:

> Our group is undecided as to whether Truman was right or wrong. We feel that there are many facts that are not presented correctly or are controversial. . . Questions that we feel have not been answered are the amount of American and Japanese casualties, whether Japan was ready to surrender, and why Japan and the United States were at war in the first place. Once these questions are answered we may be able to form a conclusion.

Some groups were unable to reach a consensus, and thus one reported:

> Our considerations are split. Two of the members believe that it was good to drop the bomb the first time but not the second. Without the bomb, warfare would have cost more lives on both sides. The United States along with other nations would have been forced to invade and many would have died in combat. The two other members believe it wasn't good to drop the bomb at all. The bomb was a very destructive device and shouldn't have been used at all. In the Trinity test they saw the impact of the bomb as it completely demolished the tower from which it had been dropped.

Yet another group argued:

> Some of the things that we were unclear about were whether or not Japan knew about America's decision to drop the bomb and the power and destruction that the atomic bomb would leave behind. Another thing was how close Japan was to surrendering before the bomb was dropped. It was basically Japan against the world and maybe a simple threat to use the atomic bomb would have scared them into surrendering.

Although they raised these concerns, the group nonetheless decided that the "dropping of the atomic bomb was the right decision at the time." Addressing some of the same concerns about Japan's knowledge of the bomb, another group suggested that "if we wanted to destroy the morale of the Japanese, why didn't we just drop the bomb on the imperial palace?"

Throughout the museum display project, the students showed enthusiasm about the opportunity to exhibit what they had learned. They were often involved in vehement discussions about the layout as well as content of their poster board display. In nearly all groups, each student was actively involved in the effort to create a quality display, and many students came in after class hours to complete the assignment.

The museum displays revealed that the students paid a great deal of attention to the layout. Most displays had a somber black and white color scheme, while the illustrations included professional looking borders. Nearly all groups chose to include maps of Hiroshima and Nagasaki, as well as brief timelines with significant dates and events. For their illustrations, students chose such images as Little Boy and Fat Man, Paul Tibbets, the atomic mushroom cloud, the damage caused by the atomic bomb, victims of the atomic bomb, and President Truman.

Most groups, however, struggled with the content part of their display. It was difficult for them to write their own text for their displays. Almost all groups also found it difficult to create a display that presented multiple perspectives, including non-American ones, on the use of the bomb. Only a few of the displays included materials related to domestic disagreements over the use of the bomb. Most displays focused largely on the actual bombings of Hiroshima and Nagasaki and their aftermath.

In the final reflective essay, the students revealed their personal perspectives. For example, in defense of Truman's decision, a student wrote that "the pros outweigh the cons. . . .Japan should have surrendered at least after the first bomb." Another argued that the bomb "cut losses to a minimum and drew the war to an end quickly"; still another stated that "the Japanese were trying to kill us and if they had the atomic bomb, they would have used it" and that the bomb "put fear into the minds of other countries."

Some students questioned the president's decision, arguing that the use of the bomb was unnecessary because Japan was ready to surrender as long as they could keep their emperor. As one student stated, "We could have demonstrated to the world the power that the U.S.A. had with the atomic bomb," perhaps "on some deserted island," and that the "scientists at Los Alamos [had] encouraged" Truman actually to do so.

Many students were able to make clear references to multiple perspectives in their individual essays. One student wrote:

The pros and cons balance each other out pretty well. . . .From the American side it was the right thing to do because it won the war for them, they didn't care about the Japanese when they were at war with them. From the Japanese side it was the wrong thing to do because they were ready to surrender, just not unconditionally which would make them lose their emperor.

Another student wrote that surrender would have come sooner if America had withdrawn its demand that the Japanese give up "their emperor system. . . .The United States should have also given some time after the first bombing for talks of surrender to take place instead of dropping a second bomb." In addition, this student wrote:

> The Soviet Union had promised to enter the war in early August, which would have likely forced Japan to surrender. Japan knew . . . that it could not take on a fight against the United States, Britain and Russia. The United States also dropped the bomb for reasons that should never have played a role in the decision. The U.S. wanted revenge against the Japanese for bombing Pearl Harbor and to prove their superiority to the Soviet Union who became a chief rival in the postwar.

Looking into the future, others wrote that "the bomb was a good thing because now all the world knows how much desolation and destruction" it causes and that "hopefully we will have enough sense not to drop it ever again." Also, referring to the U.S. role as international arbitrator in today's world, another wrote that if the United States had become "involved sooner, there would have been another resolution" and that using "its power in places like Kosovo can help prevent violent bloody wars, like World War II, from happening again in our future."

The posttest revealed that nearly all students were able to identify that the bomb was used during the 1940s. Eighty-two of the 88 students were able to identify 1945 as the correct year. Similarly, all students were able to identify Hiroshima, whereas 84 were able to identify both Hiroshima and Nagasaki as the bombing targets.

More importantly, perhaps, more students were able to list multiple reasons for the use of the atomic bomb. Nearly three out of five students listed two or three reasons; dropping the atomic bomb to end the war quickly remained the most often listed reason (58 times). Other reasons listed included showing American strength to the Soviets and the rest of the world, justifying the scientific research and expense of the Manhattan Project, attempting to prevent further loss of American lives, and Japan's refusal to surrender unconditionally. Revenge for Pearl Harbor was listed by a few students as well.

Finally, while the number of students who decided that the use of the bomb was the wrong decision remained basically unchanged, those who supported the decision increased by about ten percent to more than one out of three. The number of students who listed a mixed "yes and no" response nearly doubled to about one out of seven. In addition, while approximately ten students wrote a somewhat unclear response, no students wrote "I don't know" or left an answer blank.

In terms of the questionnaire results, students overwhelmingly responded that they liked the unit and found it interesting. They believed that the unit gave them a chance to "learn about the pros and cons" of President Truman's decision; they liked focusing on "one aspect of the war" in such depth. Furthermore, they learned to "understand the reasons why the atomic bomb was used," and they "got to voice [their] opinions about what [their] great-grandparents did." The small handful of students who indicated that they did not like the unit did so because they either did not like studying the horror of war or did not like group work.

Many found the unit "different" than what they were accustomed to doing in social studies class because they had never been able to decide for themselves about particular historical events, and the project gave them "the chance to see a different side of the world and what we think about the United States." One student wrote that he learned not "just the textbook side" but got to "use other sources and realize others' views." Others responded, that it was "most interesting because of the depth," that they had to do "most of the work [themselves]," and that it helped them to "learn quicker and develop communication skills." This unit "makes you search for the important information yourself," wrote yet another.

Students indicated that they liked learning about history from different perspectives. While some felt that the unit "changed our minds and that we now feel completely different" about this historical event, others wrote that although it "opened [their] eyes," it did not change their opinions. Echoing the research of Bohan and Davis,[7] some students wrote that "if you take a little bit from both you can kinda figure out your own perspective" and "learn how [the use of the bomb] both hurt and helped." They also expressed a few problematic notions. For example, some stated that they enjoyed learning that "there are two sides to every situation"; most students continued to interpret the use of the bomb as an issue that affected the United States and Japan only.

Discussing what they had personally learned from the unit, most students responded by listing facts. However, when asked whether the project was useful or meaningful to them, many made either explicit or implicit references to having learned how to empathize. Many felt they had learned how Truman made his decision to use the bomb, given the circumstances he was in, and how decisions "can [affect] the whole world." While a small group of students did not find the unit useful because "it wasn't going to help [them] get through life," most found it meaningful because it made them "appreciate life more," or because they were able to "be a judge on a piece of history" and that it helped them to "understand the legacy [they] were receiving." One student wrote that her view "has changed from completely disliking the decision to disliking but understanding it."

Finally, while a few students believed that "the truth" can be known, mostly by finding more information, nearly all students maintained that this is not possible. These students said, for example, that "people rarely ever say what they are truly thinking," and that everybody "sees the world differently, especially history." Some even alleged that "governments [seek] to hide [the truth]." Many students believed that unless one actually had been present in a particular historical event or circumstance, the complete truth could not be known. Others, however, wrote that it is "human nature to interpret things the way we see or feel about them" and that " 'the truth' is what people allow themselves to see and believe." One student simply wrote, "It's all a matter of perspective."

Conclusions About the Two Studies

The results of the two studies reveal several interesting findings that relate to the teaching and learning of historical understanding in general and to the development of historical empathy in particular.

1. The students in both studies who had access to a wide variety of sources and perspectives, for the most part, viewed Truman's decision to use the bomb in relatively complex terms. Most were able to identify multiple perspectives, possibilities, and lessons to be learned from the decision. They also infused their own perspectives on Truman's decision into the empathy exercises in reasonable and appropriate ways. Most of the students exhibited characteristics of rational "hindsight" in their responses to the questions as they explored multiple perspectives and explanations for the decision. Clearly, the rich array of contextual information available to the students was key to their ability successfully to engage in the historical empathy exercises.

2. The investigation questions that the teacher provided in the classroom exercise effectively assisted students in analyzing the meaning and value of the historical sources they used. In fact, the questions helped the students to stay focused on the information and perspectives that could be mined from their sources—rather than drawing solely on their own emotions or opinions—in order to develop reasoned conclusions and explanations.

3. Even though the exercises broadened the students' understandings of why and how Truman made his decision and what the ramifications were, many of the students still expressed the view that there are essentially two sides to this issue. Not surprisingly, an American perspective on the bomb figured prominently in their viewpoints, although most were able also to demonstrate some understanding of a Japanese perspective. However, they were unable to see beyond the two countries that appeared to be most directly affected by the use of the bomb. Thus, despite inclusion of British and Russian perspectives in the documents and specific questions on the investigation sheet, almost no student was able to incorporate either of these perspectives into their explanations. One possibility to help students avoid a "them and us" perspective might be to design an empathy exercise with historical events that do not involve the United States. At any rate, this narrow focus on two sides to an historical event is an issue that perhaps future research and teachers will need to address.

4. While most groups were able to write a narrative in which they cited multiple sources and presented multiple perspectives, they were unable to do so in their museum displays. As the producers of the Smithsonian exhibit

surely discovered, it is difficult to develop and present a consensus on such a controversial issue as the use of the atomic bomb. Likewise, the students found it difficult to decide how to transfer the multiple perspectives they had learned about to a museum display. Most groups were simply unable to develop a group process to accomplish that goal. We believe that the museum display activity is worth trying because it has the potential to engage students in dialogue, debate, and consensus building. However, we realize that the possibility also exists that students will fail to reach consensus or will have difficulty conceptualizing their displays. Either way, we believe that teachers should closely monitor this activity, help students to facilitate their group discussions and processes, and be prepared to lead a constructive discussion analyzing the success, failure, and/or results of the museum activity.

Conclusions

As these two studies show, the teaching of historical empathy is a challenging experience that has the potential to engage students in worthwhile historical thinking, judgment, and explanation. It also clearly is a time consuming activity to focus on one single event for so long. We found that the teacher's preparation of such a unit involves many hours in the selection of materials and the development of learning activities. In addition, the teaching of the unit takes a long time. Teachers who wish to do historical empathy exercises necessarily will be faced with decisions about depth versus coverage, and from a practical standpoint, will probably have to decide on a few historical topics that they want to focus on for historical empathy exercises.

Most of the students discussed in this chapter responded enthusiastically and intelligently to the empathy tasks they were given, and many indicated that history seemed more meaningful and significant to them when they studied it this way. Teachers can help students to reflect on history, to see that history offers understanding, and to broaden their notions of what is historically significant.[8] VanSledright argues that as students genuinely try to learn in more depth about what happened in history, to make sense out of what happened, and to understand why people did what they did, they are also able to do their own perspective taking and decide what an event in the past means to them as young people living in today's world.[9]

The results of these two studies also show that students learn history better and in greater depth when the teacher acts as a facilitator and they have to "do history" themselves. Therefore the traditional role of the teacher as the deliverer of knowledge must be reexamined and transformed into one in which he or she guides the students towards the construction of personal, yet reasoned, perspectives and explanations. As students try to make more sense out of the past by "doing history" themselves, they may be able to develop a deeper understanding of decisions made by previous generations. Thus they may come to realize that history always involves an interpretation of the past from multiple perspectives with implications not only for the present but also for the future.

Appendix A
Sources Used in Historical Empathy Writing Exercise

1. From *The Awesome Power: Harry S. Truman as Commander in Chief*, by Richard F. Haynes (Baton Rouge: Louisiana State, 1973).
2. From *Hiroshima* (1946), by Jon Hersey.
3. From *Hiroshima Diary: The Journal of a Japanese Physician August 6–September 30, 1945*, by Michihiko Hachiya, translated and edited by Warner Wells (Chapel Hill: University of North Carolina, 1955).
4. From *Children of Hiroshima*, edited by Yoichi Fukushima (Tokyo, Publishing Committee for "Children of Hiroshima," 1980).
5. From *City of Silence: Listening to Hiroshima*, by Rachelle Linner (Maryknoll, N. Y.: Orbis Book, 1995).
6. Poem by Toge Sankichi from *Hiroshima: Three Witnesses*, edited and translated by Richard H. Minear (Princeton, N. J.: Princeton University, 1990).
7. From *Day One: Before Hiroshima and After*, by Peter Wyden (New York: Simon and Schuster, 1984).
8. From *Widows of Hiroshima: The Life Stories of 19 Peasant Wives*, edited by Mikion Kanda, translated by Taeko Midorikawa (New York: St. Martin's, 1989).
9. Photograph of Hiroshima after the bombing (1945).
10. Excerpts from Japanese army manual issued during World War II.
11. From *The Era of the Second World War* (1993), edited by Nigel Kelly and Martyn Whittock.
12. From *No High Ground*, by Fletcher Knebel and Charles W. Bailey (New York: Harper and Row, 1960).
13. From "The Atomic Bombing Reconsidered," in January/February 1995 issue of *Foreign Affairs*, by Barton J. Bernstein.
14. From *The Memoirs of Harry S. Truman*, by Harry S. Truman (New York: Da Caper, 1955).
15. British newspaper cartoon published in 1945 after bombing.

Notes

1. C. Portal, "Empathy as an Objective for History Teaching," in C. Portal, ed., *The History Curriculum for Teachers* (London: Falmer Press, 1987): 89-99.

2. C. Portal, "Empathy," p. 97.

3. H. Cooper, "Children's Learning, Key Stage 2: Recent Findings," in M. Booth, H. Moniot, and K. Pellens, eds., *Communications of the International Society for History Didactics* 16 (1995): 55; M. T. Downey, "Perspective Taking and Historical Thinking: Doing History in a Fifth-Grade Classroom" (paper presented at the annual meeting of the American Educational Research Association, San Francisco, California, 1995).

4. A. Dickinson and P. Lee, "Investigating Progression in Children's Ideas about History," in M. Booth, H. Moniot, and K. Pellens, eds., *Communications*: 37-47.

5. C. H. Bohan and O. L. Davis Jr., "Historical Constructions: How Social Studies Student Teachers' Historical Thinking is Reflected in their Writing of History," *Theory and Research in Social Education* 21 (1998): 173-197.

6. S. J. Foster, "Using Historical Empathy to Excite Students about the Study of History: Can you Empathize with Neville Chamberlain?," *The Social Studies* 90 (1999): 18-24.

7. C. H. Bohan and O. L. Davis Jr., "Historical Constructions: How Social Studies Student Teachers' Historical Thinking is Reflected in their Writing of History," *Theory and Research in Social Education* 21 (1998): 173-197.

8. P. Seixas, "Students' Understanding of Historical Significance," *Theory and Research in Social Education* 22 (1994): 281-304.

9. B. A. VanSledright, "'I don't remember — the ideas are all jumbled in my head': 8th graders' reconstructions of colonial American history," *Journal of Curriculum and Supervision* 10 (1995): 317-345.

Chapter 7

Perspectives and Elementary Social Studies: Practice and Promise

Sherry L. Field

Research on empathy and the historical thinking and understanding of children has emerged in the last two decades as an important area of inquiry. The work of a growing cadre of researchers has enhanced our understanding of the ways in which students learn history and think historically.[1] A key component of historical thinking and understanding is empathy. Ashby and Lee suggest that its meaning is "difficult to pin down."[2] Empathy is generally defined in broad terms, as reflected by the meaning advanced in *The American Heritage Dictionary*, Second College Edition:

> Empathy—n. the identification and understanding of another's situation, feelings, and motives

To teachers of young children, teaching for empathy typically is understood as helping children to gain historical perspective and to understand others. Noddings acknowledges that, although children may not fully comprehend the reality of another person or group of people, that they can build toward such an understanding. She notes that caring transcends intellectual understanding and moves toward "feeling with" others.[3] Ashby and Lee add another layer of meaning to the notion of historical perspective; they support the importance of helping children "acquire a disposition to empathize, and to develop strategies for its successful achievement." They indicate that looking "from someone else's point of view" is critical to the achievement of empathy.[4]

Consideration of acts of gaining perspective in American elementary schools is at the heart of this inquiry. *Perspective* derives from the Latin, *perspicere*, to inspect: *per* (intensive) + *specere*, to look. Carr wrote about the idea of perspective in this way: "It does not follow that, because a mountain appears to take on different shapes from different angles of vision, it has objectively either no shape at all or an infinity of shapes."[5] Implied in Carr's imagery is the notion that "what matters are the angles of vision. Essential questions are about traveling all the way around the mountain, seeing the whole picture, gathering all the necessary information, and becoming aware of the wide range of different perspectives."[6] Likewise, important questions about perspective should be asked in elementary school classrooms every day by teachers who are helping their students make sense of the world around them and acquire necessary social studies knowledge, skills, and attitudes. In order to better understand the sense that students are making of social studies and their notions of multiple and single perspectives, it is important to discern how they have learned about social studies. Equally important is knowledge about how their teachers have learned to teach about social studies, how they learn and have learned about social studies themselves, how they teach about social studies to children, how they consider and write about their practice, and how their practice has been reported in educational writing for teachers. Much of the research about children's historical thinking has been conducted with children at the fifth grade level (ages) and above. It is essential, therefore, to gain a sense of how these children may have learned and had prior experiences with history and how their concepts (and distorted ideas) may have developed. Investigating the rhetoric of practice of a popular social studies journal for elementary school educators enables us to examine one of many possible sources of information.

This study offers a glimpse into the status of teaching and learning about perspective as indicated by articles published in the twelve volumes of *Social Studies & the Young Learner* from September/October 1988 (Volume I) to March/April 2000 (Volume XII). *Social Studies & the Young Learner*, published quarterly for elementary school teachers, by the National Council for the Social Studies for elementary social studies teachers, is the only journal in the United States that focuses specifically on elementary social studies. Articles found in *Social Studies & the Young Learner* include those written by an array of social studies educators: social studies methods professors, elementary school teachers, graduate students, school district curriculum directors, school administrators, museum curators, and project coordinators. The content of articles typically found in the journal ranges from statements of advocacy to curriculum ideas to reports of practice.

Data for this study were collected in the following ways: First, copies of all issues of *Social Studies & the Young Learner* were collected for study. Next, each issue was carefully read to identify articles whose purpose included a focus on the broad concepts of perspective, perspective taking, recognizing perspective, and understanding multiple perspectives. The focus on perspective varied considerably from one topic or article to another. Some articles did not have an identifiable perspective focus, whereas others contained one or more instances of focus on perspective. Some of the articles identified for analysis included more than one of the identified categories of perspective. After articles were identified, I analyzed each and coded instances of perspective. Five major categories of perspective emerged from the data. These included: 1) personal perspective, 2) cultural perspective, 3) civic-community perspective, 4) chronological perspective, and 5) histori-biographical perspective.

Personal Perspective

Sixteen articles in *Social Studies & the Young Learner* contained a recognizable focus on personal perspective. They contained content themes of self, sense of identity, human motives, major life events, sense of place, and commonalities and differences among people. One overarching theme seemed to connect the notion of learning about personal perspective described in these articles. That is, children should learn a great deal about themselves and their surroundings in order to utilize this knowledge to understand what they learn about others. Children should be taught that they have a perspective, that their perspective is important, and that their perspective may differ from those of other people. Early learning about the self serves as a foundation for learning about the larger world.

Banks advocated recognition that the "cultural, ethnic, religious, and national boundaries that divide, often sharply, the world's peoples into groups" in order to cooperate and solve global problems, and that people can do so "only when they function in equal-status situations and when they perceive their fates as shared."[7] Ladson-Billings endorsed a pedagogy intended to "empower[s] students, through the use of their home and community cultures, to make connections. . . ."[8] Turkovich and Mueller posited that "we each belong to a myriad of cultures and multicultural education is simply learning about all aspects of ourselves" while supporting teachers to include information about issues such as gender, age, religion, and sexual identity in the curriculum for young learners.[9]

Several authors also noted the importance of self-discovery and self-identity as a topic in the elementary social studies curriculum. McKinney and Fry reported their experiences and follow-up with twenty teachers who engaged in a summer graduate course about the creation and use of life stories with children. After completing the course, twelve of the twenty teachers affirmed the value of using personal life stories with their own students. They also noted that mutual respect increased between teachers and students, the self-esteem of students increased, and sensitivity and understanding among students increased.[10] Chicola and English described the utility of children learning about themselves spatially by participating in various activities at home and with their parents. Foremost among these activities was the construction of a "Me" Map following an outline of the child's form.[11] Barclay, Benelli, and Wolf structured a personal change unit of instruction around literature about birthdays and personal events in the life of a child.[12] Czartoski and Hickey's Personal Heritage Project occurred in an upper-elementary classroom with students serving as personal researchers.[13] Schwartz revealed the benefits gained by her kindergarten students during their parent-assisted personal history studies. She "wanted [her] students to be able to share who they were and who their families were" to expand their ideas and concepts about family and to develop their literacy skills. During the year-long study, her students had opportunities to expand their school learning into their homes as their parents assisted them with research and composition of their personal stories.[14] Porter promoted the role of the student as historian in various ways among which was the incorporation into the elementary social studies curriculum of a family study to include literature and personal research.[15] Miller advocated the benefits of having students engage in the work of biographers by pairing younger and older children. Together, the children interviewed and wrote stories about the lives of their partners. By performing roles of biographer and interviewee, students gained firsthand knowledge of historical perspectives and life experiences.[16]

Native Spanish-speaking first grade children explored the meaning of family in Dallas, Texas, and Antigua, Guatemala, in a bicultural exploration developed by Main, Wilhelm, and Cox. According to the authors, "this unit of social study... emphasized cultural and family awareness and pride. . . . By enlisting their parents in their research about their immediate family and community, the pupils gained knowledge and self-esteem. One girl in Main's class glowed with pride as she explained to her peers that her mother made valves for artificial hearts."[17] Students in Athens, Georgia, and Hualien City, Taiwan, similarly explored their personal perspectives as they made decisions about what should be included in a video and e-mail exchange intended to provide information about the lives of third grade children in each location. Their unit of study helped to alleviate commonly held misconceptions about Taiwan and the United States. Importantly, students reflected about how they wanted to represent themselves and their perspectives about their lives to distant children by way of the video tape they produced and the multimedia projects they created.[18] During their units of instruction on food, clothing, and shelter, first and second grade students in Michigan developed a sense of self-efficacy and examined their personal perspectives. As the authors explained, patterns of growth in students' sense of self-efficacy were evident during their study of cultural universals because "they provide[d] natural opportunities for students to contribute ideas, examine choices and tradeoffs, and influence and regulate their social experiences and decisions."[19]

Two scholars described the personal perspective that children should accomplish in economic terms. According to Passe, young children gain perspective by performing chores, earning money, shopping at local stores, and venturing outside the confines of home.[20] Personal perspective may be realized, alternatively, when children realize that they are responsible for their own actions, that they have the power to make choices, and that ethics are at play when children make choices.[21]

Children need to learn to take perspectives about themselves and their surroundings. They are not islands. Rather, they have relationships and their abilities to "see" themselves in different settings should enable them better to understand what they learn about other people in sharply different cultural settings.

Cultural Perspective

In tandem with concepts of personal perspective, pedagogy that emphasized cultural perspectives was reported by many authors in *Social Studies & the Young Learner*. Indeed, forty-two articles manifest this concern. Broad concepts about culture advanced in these articles included understanding the nature and facets of culture, identifying and challenging prejudice and stereotyping, recognizing that everyone has a culture, learning about people of various cultures in the United States, and learning about the cultures of people all over the world. Frameworks for considering culture, advocacy for reducing prejudice and stereotypes, suggestions for literature and for unit and lesson plans, information about Asian and Middle Eastern cultures, information and suggestions for teaching about Native Americans, and reports of classroom practice were themes that necessitated cultural perspective taking on the part of young learners and their teachers.

Frameworks or guidelines for teaching about cultural issues were presented in various ways. Banks posited a hierarchy for multicultural curriculum development and teaching comprising four components—contributions, additive, transformation, and social action[22] and presented research findings to support multicultural education in schools. He suggested six strategies to reduce prejudice in students. They included integrating positive ethnic and racial groups in teaching, helping students to differentiate the faces of outside racial and ethnic groups, and involving children in vicarious experiences with racial and ethnic groups.[23] Ladson-Billings offered additional strategies to combat prejudice and stereotyping that included attending to curriculum materials for negative and erroneous information, infusing the curriculum with multicultural content, and embracing culturally relevant pedagogy.[24]

Developing a sense of wonder about the world, of encouraging positive attitudes toward learning about a country, and of building learning skills that connect with future learning were learning goals mentioned by Hoge and Allen.[25] They outlined key features of universals of culture about which children need to gain perspective and compare with their personal perspectives. Passe spoke of the "need to provide perspective" as one of the challenges for elementary social studies teachers, in addition to the need to: 1) move away from "expanding environment" curriculum, 2) focus on important issues, 3) portray leaders in balanced ways, and 4) portray society realistically.[26] Finding ways to sensitively portray the Holocaust story for children was a topic explored by Totten. He specified activities to reduce prejudice and initiate perspective taking about the subject.[27] Pang and Evans provided helpful guidelines for teachers to nurture Asian Pacific students in their classrooms and to dispel stereotypes about them.[28]

In addition to the general guidelines for teachers mentioned above, authors directed teachers to reduce prejudice and stereotypical beliefs or perspectives in specific ways. Wade stressed the importance of exploring prejudice and stereotyping with white children,[29] and the critical nature of introducing and speaking openly about religion and sexual orientation in social studies classes.[30] Byrnes addressed teaching about religion to young children.[31] Schram wrote about how he resolved issues of children's preconceived stereotypical ideas about international guests in the classroom,[32] and Wingfield and Karaman suggested ways to dispel stereotypes about Arabs.[33]

Using literature to teach children about others, although not a new strategy for teaching cultural perspective, was addressed specifically six times in *Social Studies & the Young Learner*. For example, Banks provided examples of books that lent themselves to discussions about stereotypes and reducing prejudice.[34] Other recommended children's literature addressed learning about culture through its folk tales and stories[35] and considering human rights across cultures.[36] DeCoker and Ballou compared the treatment of Japan in two children's nonfiction books,[37] whereas Bernson directed teachers to utilize fiction free of stereotypes to teach about Japan.[38] Cordier and Perez-Stable reviewed numerous titles that offered accurate information about Latinos.[39] Their article was one of only two that specifically addressed Latino culture to be found in the twelve volumes of the journal.[40]

Three articles specified constructive content knowledge intended to inform teachers about life in Japan and Germany. Eisenstadt proposed appropriate cultural universals for teaching about Japan,[41] and Field and Labbo concentrated on one aspect of Japanese culture, schooling. They drew upon children's natural interest in learning about daily lives of children in other parts of the world and children's personal perspectives of their own daily lives.[42] Shortly after the unification of Germany, Blankenship provided up-to-date information on the daily lives of contemporary German children.[43]

In addition to gaining cultural perspective by studying children around the world, children's preferred method to gain cultural perspective is studying cultural and ethnic groups at home. Both Harvey and Geoghegan offered consistently thorough information to help educators teach non-stereotypical lessons about Native Americans.[44] Franklin, Roach, and Snyder suggested bias-free literature selections to complement a study of Native Americans.[45] In an article about teaching concepts, Parker provided examples for teaching about North American Indians. He urged teachers to "study several examples, not just one . . ." to avoid superficial concept development.[46]

Three articles appearing in a specially-themed issue titled "Rethinking the Holidays" urged teachers to focus attention on and be sensitive to the ways in which they presented the concept of holidays to children. Recognizing that "celebrations of holidays in a culturally diverse society can be problematic," and that "Christian holidays often receive more recognition than the holidays of other religions," Naylor and Smith offered implications for policy decisions within schools. They observed that "children can study the social functions of holidays— legitimacy, preservation, and cohesion and how holidays help us acquire a common identity."[47] Suggestions for viable activities for children included their consideration of the religious and secular nature of holidays and exploration of the symbolic images that represent them.[48] Lockledge, Hanson, and Corbin identified the celebratory aspect of various holidays and offered lesson ideas for teachers.[49]

Five articles featured lesson or unit plan suggestions for teachers based on cultural topics. Turkovich and Mueller illustrated their plan to study color in a multicultural context.[50] Laney and Moseley showed how children could conduct critical investigations about people by playing the role of archaeologist or anthropologist and solving a cultural mystery.[51] Also advocating the presence of archaeology in elementary school classrooms, Black suggested several activities related to the cultural significance of corn in the Americas and of taking perspective by simulating archaeological findings.[52] The use of culture kits, or collections of artifacts to represent a culture or country also was promoted.[53] Finally, Wasta and Scott provided a unit plan designed to highlight the culture of China.[54]

Seven reports of classroom practice dealt with cultural issues. These included the use of literature and response activities, bicultural explorations enhanced by use of the Internet, service learning based on the Rainforest, local community history, and global education.[55]

Cultural perspectives acknowledge both differences and similarities as a function of children studying other people's lives and ways and patterns. In school social studies, pupils do not seek cultural universals in simplisms, but they note details and recognize nuances within complexities. Such perspective taking offers children freshened views of peoples throughout the world.

Chronological Perspective

A number of articles about the acquisition of chronological perspective appeared periodically in issues of *Social Studies and the Young Learner*. They included efforts to help children realize the nature of time, the passage of time, sequencing of events, and historical time periods. Four categories were determined for this theme, including frameworks or guidelines, lesson or unit ideas, use of literature, and reports of classroom practice.

Researchers found that "certain time concepts are accessible to children as young as six," that children in the elementary grades could address broad time categories with relative success, and that "children's use of time terms and their apparent understanding of time concepts are related not just to age but to instruction."[56] Complementing the research findings of Levstik, Parker noted a general sequence for learning a concept. He then illustrated this sequence with an example from a classroom study of North American Indians. A key component of the study included having student groups research and answer questions, during which they were to illustrate with a timeline the period in which a North American Indian group flourished.[57]

Examples of a few other lessons and units that focused on chronology also appeared in the journal. For example, six key historical themes were introduced by Reed. They were accompanied by suggested learning activities to enhance each theme. Three themes included the following attention to chronology-related learning objectives: to describe how things happen and change, to understand how things happen and change, to discover what life was like long ago, and to recognize that some things change and some things stay the same.[58] Laney and Moseley planned for children to "become detectives, using clues to interpret within their personal frames of reference," as professional social scientists do, when challenged with the task of discovering "who packed a suitcase."[59] Moulton and Tevis promoted the use of photographs and the inquiry process by asking children to survey various historical photographs from their community and "decide which photograph is older."[60] Project GREEN (Global Rivers Environmental Education Network) was explained in *Social Studies & the Young Learner*. In her recommended unit of study based upon the project, Simmons invited children to interview community members about a nearby river or stream. All of the questions were chronological in nature: How long have you lived in the area? What was the river like when you were my age? Did you use the river in different ways than we use it now? What are your hopes for the river in the next century?[61] The final unit idea was based upon children's use of the inquiry skills needed by archaeologists to learn about key historical eras in the Americas.[62]

Three articles promoted the use of literature to teach children how to think about and interpret the passage of time. Porter endorsed several books for teachers that highlighted historical inquiry, use of artifacts, and personal and family history research.[63] The children's literature advocated by Field, Labbo, and Brook was categorized to help children reflect about micro-, meso-, and macro-time periods. For young children, considering micro time—encompassing months, days, hours, minutes, and seconds—and meso time—encompassing millions of years, millennia, centuries, and years—was considered to be most helpful.[64] The cross-curricular activities and literature addressed by Aronson, Galbo, Schulz, and Shawkey were "designed to help students in grades 3-6 broaden their understanding of time and of the 'neighbors' who live in their own or other time zones."[65]

The work done by Andel with her fourth grade students modeled active learning about time. As they were engaged in a sustained archaeological dig of several century-old homes in their community, students dug, discovered, washed, recorded, classified, and placed various artifacts on a timeline.[66] Another related project involved younger students working with their teachers to research and create personal timelines. These timelines included annotated drawings to depict major life events and build concepts related to personal time and change.[67] Finally, a "Youngster, Oldster" unit of study was conducted by a group of first grade students. Concepts addressed included those of aging and life passages, with the theme, "aging is an opportunity for continuous growth and development." Students considered the time-related questions: How old is old? What is the process of aging? They participated in intergenerational activities to develop essential knowledge and skills and adopt helpful attitudes. Their activities included interviewing familiar and non-familiar older adults, creating pictorial genograms, conducting surveys, and visiting nearby retirement centers.[68]

Civic/Community Perspective

Enrichment of childrens' civic and community perspective was addressed many times in *Social Studies & the Young Learner*. These efforts included an understanding of the need to develop in children a perspective about their community and others, to help them learn to become civic participants, to help them recognize and participate in work for the common good, and to model the concept of caring.

The lead article in the inaugural issue of *Social Studies & the Young Learner* examined the ethics of citizenship education, based upon the Socratic notion of knowing and of acting for the common good. It provided a framework for teaching the concept of civic/community perspective and considered how to impart the value of virtue and the action of caring to young children.[69] Classroom lessons "support[ed] the development of care: for ourselves, our neighbors, and the larger world around us."[70] Three goals later were posited for civic/community perspective: conceptual, process, and affective.[71] Wade conceptualized a key social studies goal of promoting active citizenship through "practical, hands-on experiences in which students identify community needs, develop action plans, and put their ideas into practice."[72] Alter developed a framework for the inclusion of concepts of care and empathy in her alternative model to traditional elementary social studies curriculum.[73] Her framework included the following empathetic concepts: K-1, "human diversity"; 2: "belonging"; 3: "human needs in the community"; 4: "diversity in the nation"; 5: "the struggle for democracy"; and 6:

"image and reality." The overarching question of including values in the social studies curriculum was addressed by Larkins, who suggested various integration techniques.[74] Addressing a similar concern, Wade provided strategies to assist teachers in expanding students' views of heroes and heroines beyond that of "superhuman gods" to include women, children, and people of color.[75] Others stressed the need to teach economic concepts in concert with community studies in order that students develop a schema for the concept of community.[76] The concept of first understanding the classroom as a socio-political community and then using problem solving to overlay the importance of rights, responsibility, and interaction was supported in another article.[77] Perhaps Wade's comments best summarized the nature of teaching for civic/community perspective: "Citizenship can only be learned meaningfully within the context of community, and the school is the sole institution available to all children to learn about the roles, rights, and responsibilities of being a community member."[78]

In the past decade, educators developed unique unit and lesson plans with civic-community perspective themes for inclusion in the journal. One unit of study encouraged a writing process called "We-Search" to promote civic competence.[79] Two sources highlighted the use of historical photographs and postcards to gain historical perspective about the community.[80] Patton planned a unit in which children studied the topic of homelessness from the perspective of their own community, read literature on the topic, heard from guest speakers, and participated in field trips.[81]Another unit focused on community studies with an emphasis on the concept of caring and culminated in a group community project.[82] A unit on citizenship education stressed that "participation . . .[is] an approach to help . . .form realistic perceptions of leadership . . .and to practice citizenship behavior."[83] A recommended study of sports heroes was viewed as an opportunity to involve children in a meaningful, ethics-based series of lessons.[84] Perspective taking was clearly at the heart of Anderson's suggestions for teaching freedom of speech to elementary students. She noted, "While it is essential that children become conscious of perspective . . .perspective consciousness is very difficult to achieve and must be distinguished from opinion which 'is the surface layer, the conscious outcropping of perspective.'"[85] Similarly, engaging children in discussion groups during which they could reflect on one of five teacher-assigned situations was suggested as another strategy to help students gain a sense of perspective.[86] Finally, one article discussed the use of the Internet to enhance service learning projects. In order to engage their students in "reflective deliberation," teachers were advised to pose the following questions to elicit a sense of perspective: "What are environmental issues and why are they important? Who is interested in environmental issues? What government regulations and policies about the environment exist?" and to guide their students to appropriate Internet sites for answers.[87] Alhough diverse in content, each unit of study or series of lessons presented the concepts of perspective taking and civic-community awareness.

Children's literature was recommended for development of community perspective in four articles. Cordier and Perez-Stable cited several books meant to evoke a sense of understanding about Latino communities.[88] Sandmann and Ahern wrote two articles for upper grade students that highlighted books that would "extend students' learning beyond the text . . .and provide valuable . . .perspectives."[89] Moore related how she planned to introduce a citizenship unit of study to her fifth grade students by sharing quality children's literature about homelessness and the elderly. She wanted to set a goal of working for the "common good" of community members and to culminate her lessons with a service project.[90]

Stories of elementary school children learning about their communities by active and challenging means were reported by many authors in *Social Studies and the Young Learner*. The work of teachers from Tess Corners Elementary School in Wisconsin allowed K-5 students to explore their community through their Museum-in-Progress program. Photographing the community in order to study its architectural details was one memorable activity.[91] Several articles dealt with young children's first experiences exploring their communities and gaining civic-social knowledge and skills. Children in grades 1-3 in Red Bridge School in Kansas City participated in Walk Around the Block, a comprehensive community study that includes advocacy, caring, and understanding. Students learned about their city by publishing a student newspaper, creating art to represent their advocacy, participating in restoration projects including that of the local train station, and "adopting" Kansas City buildings and the people who work in them, thereby getting to know them on multiple visits.[92] Second grade students at Mary McLeod Bethune School in Central Harlem learned about their community and the people for whom streets in their neighborhood were named. When they discovered that all those people were men, they began the successful political process to have 134th Street, on which their school was located, renamed after educator Bethune.[93] First grade students in Denton, Texas, learned about the perspectives of older people in their community during their "Youngster, Oldster" unit of study.[94] Third grade students in Washington used a process called Storypath to explore their community.[95] Third and fifth grade students in Pennsylvania critically examined issues of concern in their respective communities, that included land development and open space, playgrounds, the use of abandoned housing, and youth curfews. In many instances, their efforts led to city council hearings and positive action.[96] Sixth grade students in Washington State studied public policy issues through structured classroom discussion and gained multiple perspectives about the desire of the Makah tribe of Neah Bay to participate in legal whale hunts for food and ceremonial purposes.[97] The activities of fifth grade children engaged in a microsociety, during which they participated in the creation of a working community in their school to include a marketplace, bank, judicial system, advertising, employment commission, and newspaper were reported.[98] Learning about the economy of Long Island prompted a fifth grade class to consider deeply multiple perspectives related to the concept of "progress."[99]

Various projects enabled children to encounter multiple perspectives from people in their own community, and in the larger world community. These efforts included social action projects in Texas, Chicago, and Washington, D.C.; an Internet project between students in Nebraska and Bosnia; an Iowa project to develop understanding and advocacy for children in the Rainforest; and a tea ceremony project initiated by special education students at the Museum School in Yonkers (PS 25), and joined by children from the Japanese School of New Jersey.[100]

Histori-Biographical Perspective

The final theme advanced by this study is that of histori-biographical perspective. It may be developed as teachers work with their students toward reasoning, thinking about causality and effect, acquiring contextual knowledge, considering evidence, discriminating, and gaining a biographical point of view. An analysis of articles with historical perspective taking as a topic merited the following categories: advancement of pedagogy, lesson and unit strategies, literature as a springboard for historical thinking, and classroom practice.

A few articles advocated practical pedagogy to help children realize historical perspective. In the first of two themed issues on elementary school history published in *Social Studies & the Young Learner* in the past twelve years, Levstik reported four constructs from a review of the research literature on children's historical thinking and learning: 1) the importance of context, 2) the connection between history and narrative, 3) the importance of connecting with the present, and 4) the importance of experience in dealing with time and history. She elaborated that "evidence in history is particularistic, and interpretation is dependent on the historian's perspective."[101] Six goals and themes of history were reported by Reed: 1) civilization, cultural diffusion, and innovation; 2) human interaction with the environment; 3) values, beliefs, political ideas, and institutions; 4) conflict and cooperation; 5) comparative history of major developments; and 6) patterns of social and political interaction. Two learning objectives were included for each. For themes one and six, "to develop historical empathy" was a clearly stated objective.[102] Using quality resources to plan for classroom episodes "to recreate historical moments, events, and circumstances in role-play or simulation environment" was recommended in one article.[103] Key strategies for promoting children's perspective taking and writing, including simulated newspaper reports, advice columns, editorials, memoirs, obituaries, protest letters, and slogans, were supported in the journal.[104]

Although only four articles dealt generally with the topic of history to advance pedagogy, eighteen articles shared history-based lessons and unit plans with some focus on historical perspective. A themed issue on Columbus's Quincentennial contained several particularly helpful in the provision of providing teachers with accurate and relevant information from multiple perspectives.[105] Harvey wrote lessons that provided insights into Native American perspectives, including biographical readings about contemporary Native Americans.[106] Field and Labbo advocated critical reading of biographies and perspective-taking activities intended to promote an insider's perspective.[107] A "gender rights" simulation was offered in an article about women and empowerment. In it, children were to experience gender discrimination incrementally as a springboard for research and study during Women's History Month.[108]

The topic of war provided rich content for several unit and lesson publications. One activity suggested learning about World War II by having students interview grandparents, other relatives, and neighbors. Children's questions were intended to elicit responses from their interviewees that would illuminate for them a perspective about the home front as well as the battle front.[109] Suggestions were given to help students understand the Holocaust by humanizing the story and using first-person accounts.[110] Perspectives on Hiroshima from World War II to contemporary times were provided in a third article about World War II.[111]

Specific processes to explore history were advocated by others in the journal. For example, thematic teaching at Ramirez Elementary School in Lubbock, Texas, "helped children make connections across subject areas and [provided] them with rich literacy situations." Children were especially drawn to biographies during interdisciplinary units.[112] Engaging pupils in artifact inquiry was considered a valuable process toward thinking about and interpreting a time period.[113] Likewise, investigating primary sources, in this case, letters from William Barrett Travis at the Alamo, was the subject of a creative unit of study which required students to interpret his point of view.[114] A teacher in Cleveland, Ohio, shared her succes with teaching the process of historical method to her students, and helping them to "have an historian's eye, to use the historian's tools, and to enjoy the historian's passion."[115]

The final group of lesson and unit articles highlighted diverse subjects. Helping children to understand an array of holiday celebrations around the world, including their history, was one focus.[116] Investigating a geographical region around St. Louis from the perspective of a Cahokia trading empire existent in 1000 A.D. was another.[117] Igniting children's historical imaginations was the topic of an article based upon a visit to a reconstructed historical site in Barkersville, British Columbia.[118] Exploring the history and significance of rice to the country of Japan and its people was also featured.[119] Finally, researching the lives of a Civil-War-era family via the Internet was offered as a unit replete with meaningful research into primary source documents.[120]

The efficacy of literature as a teaching tool in elementary social studies classes was highlighted in several journal articles. Children's literature was offered as an important resource in articles about teaching elementary history.

Seen as a helpful tool in helping students gain historical perspective, literature was promoted as an inspiration for student's writing and analysis of a historical period. For example, strategies to supplement the social studies content with literature included debating issues brought out in novels, making diary entries and double-entry journaling, writing newspaper accounts of historical events,[121] and assembling character charts, a method by which children illustrate and explain motivations and personalities of their selected characters.[122] In addition to writing about them, some features encouraged teachers to have students role-play historical figures from other continents.[123] In-depth study of related pieces of literature was recommended as another effective method to gain historical perspective.[124] Studying history with the help of children's trade books to elicit a sense of time was also stressed.[125]

Many classroom settings were the subject of articles about histori-biographical perspective and elementary social studies. Learning about the American Revolution, community history, and life in pioneer times were popular topics. One class of third and fourth grade students from Illinois, for example, utilized children's literature, in the form of biographies and historical fiction, during an American Revolution study. It should be noted that "children's views were colored by the author's interpretation of events and characters. The teacher . . .has a great deal of influence relative to the perspective children will have."[126] In Yukon, Oklahoma, fifth grade students participated in a Revolutionary War unit of study that included writing letters to understand others' points of view.[127] Children attending Pepperell Intermediate School in Opelika, Alabama, learned about the Colonial Period, the American Revolution, and events leading up to the Civil War during four-week units culminating in Community Heritage Week, "a five-day extravaganza of interrelated activities around the three themes being studied." They dressed in costume, learned songs typical to the eras, danced, and role-played.[128] Second grade students made personal connections to the events about pioneer life on the prairie portrayed in the trade books they shared in their literature discussion groups.[129] Exhibiting thematic planning and teaching, two teachers in Florida reported their state history study with an emphasis on African American history which featured four types of questions for historic understanding: informational, empathetic, methodological, and analytic/evaluative.[130]

Zarnowski reported her work with a sixth grade classroom teacher and her students in New York. Over a period of several years, she used literature as a springboard for reflective study about various topics. They ranged by subject from comparing past and modern plagues to reading and writing about people to asking critical questions to elicit thoughtful responses to studying and developing empathy for the children of the Great Depression.[131] Fifth grade students in New York made empathetic connections to people in their local and larger world community as they investigated the question, "Has progress been made in our community?"[132]

The last category of articles reporting classroom practice focused on the use of a particular methodology to enhance perspective taking. Teachers in Bellevue, Washington, and El Campo, Texas, shared their units of study which encompassed locating and analyzing historical photographs, writing creative stories about the photographs, and role playing the action depicted in illustrative scenes.[133] Chilcoat used the basic elements of street theater to develop units and teach about slavery and the desegregation of Central High School in Little Rock, Arkansas. Students researched the topics, wrote scripts, made puppets or illustrations, and acted out the historical stories.[134] Teachers from Tess Corners Elementary School in Muskego, Wisconsin, helped their students "transform the school into a rainforest" by following techniques formulated by Museum-in-Progress, such as investigating artifacts, designing and planning the exhibit, and documenting knowledge.[135] In addition to dramatizing historical events and making exhibits to represent them, students in Missouri participated in another type of historical inquiry during an authentic archaeological dig. Prior to the dig, they formulated questions that helped them make inferences from the perspective of the family whose artifacts the students discovered.[136]

Concluding Thoughts about Teaching Perspective Taking to Children

This descriptive analysis of articles in *Social Studies & The Young Learner* clearly does not provide a fulsome picture of the reality of elementary school teaching and learning about perspective taking. On the other hand, it portrays how dimensions of this idea have surfaced in this journal over the past dozen years. This review offers a sense of the nature of teacher practice, both reported and suggested, that seeks improvement in elementary social study.

Especially important is that American elementary social studies teachers appear increasingly aware of the needs and opportunities to help young children gain different perspectives on their world. They and their pupils certainly are not prisoners of a curriculum that walls off attention to cultures and eras according to a sometimes outdated scope and sequence. Consequently, each year, many pupils increasingly study such that they better understand themselves and their relationships to others in different places. Pupils continue to seek verified information and ways of knowing. They also encounter both the desirability and necessity of differing perspectives on the social studies of significance to them.

This perspective taking is plural. Other contributions in this book properly focus on historical perspective taking. Teachers of young children, however, seem intuitively to understand that these pupils need much experience in perspective taking of all varieties. Thus, they emphasize perspectives that are personal, cultural, chronological, civic/community, and historical. Likely, as they recognize the validity of claims and opportunities for historical perspective taking, elementary school teachers will shift some of their emphases to this form from other categories. That prospect, however, is an agenda item of the future and surely will build on teachers' contemporary practices of perspective taking.

Importantly, elementary social studies teachers understand that children can and do learn to take perspectives at a young age. Evidence from this review also substantiates another understanding: children need to return often, certainly at different grade levels, to tasks of perspective building; such construction is not a once and forever matter. Also, children need informed adult assistance; perspective taking ordinarily does not just "happen."

Additionally, this review calls attention to several matters of significance to increased and robust teaching about perspective taking to children. Surely, the initial preparation and continuing education of elementary school teachers must include increased attention to legitimate historical sources and procedures that include empathizing/perspective taking. Also, teachers will find use for literature, artifacts, and thematic studies in their promotion of perspective taking. Teachers simply must have enriched substantive background such that they can do in fact what they want to do: to teach more sensitively. Curriculum materials available to teachers and pupils also must promote perspective taking. Research on historical perspective taking, commonly focused on children's thinking in the middle grades, should be expanded to include children's thought at lower academic levels. Along with other valued emphases, perspective taking and discourse about it seem essential to the development of children's social responsibility.[137] As Charlotte Crabtree noted, the power inherent in social studies and history learning serves to "expand children's ability to see the world through others' eyes, enlarges their vision of lives well lived, and of their own human potential."[138]

Notes

1. See, for example, S. J. Foster and E. A. Yeager, "'You've Got to Put Together the Pieces': English 12-Year Olds Encounter and Learn from Historical Evidence," *Journal of Curriculum and Supervision* 14 (1999): 286-317; K. C. Barton, "'I Just Kinda Know': Elementary Pupils' Ideas About Historical Evidence," *Theory and Research in Social Education* 25 (1997): 407-430; K. C. Barton and L. S. Levstik, "'Back When God Was Around and Everything': Elementary Children's Understanding of Historical Time," *American Educational Research Journal* 33 (1996): 419-454; P. Seixas, "Pupils' Understanding of Historical Significance," *Theory and Research in Social Education* 22 (1994): 105-127; B. VanSledright and J. Brophy, "Storytelling, Imagination, and Fanciful Elaboration in Children's Historical Reconstructions," *American Educational Research Journal* 29 (1992): 837-859; M. T. Downey and L. S. Levstik, "Teaching and Learning

History," in J. P. Shaver, ed., *Handbook of Research on Social Studies Teaching and Learning* (New York: Macmillan, 1991), 400-410.

2. R. Ashby and P. Lee, "Children's Concepts of Empathy and Understanding in History," in C. Portal, ed., *The History Curriculum for Teachers* (London: The Falmer Press, 1987), 62-88.

3. N. Noddings, *Caring: A Feminine Approach to Ethics and Moral Education* (Berkeley: University of California Press, 1984).

4. Ashby and Lee, 1987, p. 64.

5. E. H. Carr, *What Is History?* (New York: Alfred A. Knopf, 1964).

6. C. Gavin, A. Libresco, and P. Marron, "Essential Questions for Elementary Social Studies: Curriculum Reform for Social Action," *Social Studies & The Young Learner* 11 (Jan/Feb1999): 12-15.

7. J. A. Banks, "Education for Survival in a Multicultural World," *Social Studies & The Young Learner* 1 (Mar/Apr 1989): 3-5.

8. G. Ladson-Billings, "I Don't See Color, I Just See Children: Dealing with Stereotyping and Prejudice in Young Children," *Social Studies & The Young Learner* 5 (Nov/Dec 1992): 9-12.

9. M. Turkovich and P. Mueller, "The Multicultural Factor: A Curriculum Multiplier," *Social Studies & the Young Learner* 1 (Mar/Apr 1989): 9-12.

10. L. McKinney and P. G. Fry, "Personal Life Stories: A Strategy for Empowerment," *Social Studies & The Young Learner* 7 (Sep/Oct 1994): 7-9.

11. N. A. Chicola and E. B. English, "The Child's World: Geography Around the Home," *Social Studies & The Young Learner* 9 (Sep/Oct 1996): P5-P8.

12. K. Barclay, C. Benelli, and J. Maakstad Wolf, "Me, Me, Wonderful Me!: Acquiring Concepts of Time and Change," *Social Studies & The Young Learner* 9 (Sep/Oct 1996): 15-16, 26.

13. S. Czartoski and G. Hickey, "All About Me: A Personal Heritage Project," *Social Studies & The Young Learner* 11 (Mar/Apr 1999): 11-14.

14. S. Schwartz, "My Family's Story: Discovering History at Home," *Social Studies & The Young Learner* 12 (Jan/Feb 2000): 6-9.

15. P. H. Porter, "The Student as Historian," *Social Studies & The Young Learner* 7 (Nov/Dec 1994): 23-26.

16. F. Miller, "Biography Buddy: Interviewing Each Other," *Social Studies & The Young Learner* 12 (Jan/Feb 2000): 13-14.

17. M. Main, R. W. Wilhelm, and A. R. Cox, "Mi Comunidad: Young Children's Bicultural Explorations of the Meaning of Family," *Social Studies & The Young Learner* 9 (Sep/Oct 1996): 7-9, 14.

18. S. L. Field, L. D. Labbo, and C. Lu, "Real People, Real Places: A Powerful Social Studies Exchange Through Technology," *Social Studies & The Young Learner* 9 (Nov/Dec 1996): 16-18, 23.

19. J. Alleman and J. Brophy, "On the Menu: The Growth of Self-Efficacy," *Social Studies & The Young Learner* 12 (Jan/Feb 2000): 15-19.

20. J. Passe, "Citizenship Knowledge in Young Learners," *Social Studies & The Young Learner* 3 (Mar/Apr 1991): 15-17.

21. M. C. Schug, "Economic Reasoning and Values Education," *Social Studies & The Young Learner* 1 (Sep/Oct 1988): 6-9.

22. J. A. Banks, "Education for Survival in a Multicultural World," *Social Studies & The Young Learner*, 1 (Mar/Apr 1989): 3-5.

23. J. A. Banks, "Reducing Prejudice in Children: Guidelines from Research," *Social Studies & The Young Learner* 5 (Nov/Dec 1992): 3-5.

24. G. Ladson-Billings, "I Don't See Color, I Just See Children: Dealing with Stereotyping and Prejudice in Young Children," *Social Studies & The Young Learner* 5 (Nov/Dec 1992): 9-12.

25. J. D. Hoge and R. F. Allen, "Teaching about Our World Community: Guidelines and Resources," *Social Studies & The Young Learner* 3 (Mar/Apr 1991): 19, 28-32.

26. J. Passe, "Media Literacy in a Global Age," *Social Studies & The Young Learner* 6 (Mar/Apr 1994): 7-9.

27. S. Totten, "Telling the Holocaust Story to Children," *Social Studies & The Young Learner* 7 (Nov/Dec 1994): P5-P8.

28. V. O. Pang and R. W. Evans, "Caring for Asian Pacific American Students in the Social Studies Classroom," *Social Studies & The Young Learner* 7 (Mar/Apr 1995): 11-14.

29. R. Wade, "'Whites Are Us': Exploring Prejudice and Stereotyping with White Children," *Social Studies & The Young Learner* 5 (Nov/Dec 1992): 16-18.

30. R. Wade, "Diversity Taboos: Religion and Sexual Orientation in the Social Studies Classroom," *Social Studies & The Young Learner* 7 (Mar/Apr 1995): 19-22.

31. D. A. Byrnes, "Teaching Children Religious Tolerance," *Social Studies & The Young Learner* 5 (Nov/Dec 1992): 13-15.

32. T. Schram, "Face to Face: Stereotypes and the International Classroom Visitor," *Social Studies & The Young Learner* 5 (Nov/Dec 1992): 19-20, 28.

33. M. Wingfield and B. Karaman, "Arab Stereotypes and American Educators," *Social Studies & The Young Learner* 7 (Mar/Apr 1995): 7-10.

34. C. A. McGee Banks, "Shattering Stereotypes and Reducing Prejudice with Multiethnic Literature," *Social Studies & The Young Learner* 5 (Nov/Dec 1992): 6-8.

35. "Folk Tales and Stories: An Elementary Student's Passport to the World," *Social Studies & The Young Learner* 4 (Sep/Oct 1991), unpaged pullout section.

36. C. J. Fuhler, P. J. Farris, and L. Hatch, "Learning about World Cultures through Folktales," *Social Studies & The Young Learner* 11 (Sep/Oct 1998): 23-25.

37. G. DeCoker and M. Ballou, "Evaluating K-3 Non-Fiction Books on Other Cultures: Analyzing Two Books about Japan," *Social Studies & The Young Learner* 2 (Jan/Feb 1990): 13-15.

38. M. H. Bernson, "Beyond Momotaro: Using Fiction about Japan in the Elementary Classroom," *Social Studies & The Young Learner* 10 (Jan/Feb 1998): 24-26.

39. M. H. Cordier and M. Perez-Stable, "Latino Connections: Family, Neighbors, and Community," *Social Studies & The Young Learner* 9 (Sep/Oct 1996): 20-22, 32.

40. See also M. Main, R. W. Wilhelm, and A. R. Cox, "Mi Comunidad: Young Children's Bicultural Explorations of the Meaning of Family," *Social Studies & The Young Learner* 9 (Sep/Oct 1996): 7-9, 14.

41. M. G. Eisenstadt, "Japan for Young Children: A Cross-Cultural Approach," *Social Studies & The Young Learner* 4 (Nov/Dec 1991): 8-9, 19, 27.

42. S. L. Field and L. D. Labbo, "Stepping into Elementary Schools in Japan," *Social Studies & The Young Learner* 10 (Jan/Feb 1998): 6-10.

43. G. Blankenship, "Germany, the Search for Unity," *Social Studies & The Young Learner* 6 (Mar/Apr 1994): P1-P4.

44. See, for example, W. Geoghegan, "The Meaning of Tribe," *Social Studies & The Young Learner* 1(Nov/Dec 1988): 8-11; K. Harvey, "Teaching about Native Americans," *Social Studies & The Young Learner* 4 (Mar/Apr 1992): 7-11, 30; K. D. Harvey, "Native Americans: The Next 500 Years," *Social Studies & The Young Learner* 5 (Jan/Feb 1993): P1-P4; and K. D. Harvey, "Teaching about Human Rights and American Indians," 8 (Mar/Apr 1996): 6-10.

45. M. R. Franklin, P. B. Roach, and J. K. Snyder, "Beyond Feathers and Tomahawks: Lessons from Literature," *Social Studies & The Young Learner* 6 (Nov/Dec 1993): 13-16.

46. W. C. Parker, "Teaching an IDEA," *Social Studies & The Young Learner* 3 (Jan/Feb 1991):11-14.

47. D. T. Naylor and B. D. Smith, "Holidays, Cultural Diversity, and the Public Culture," *Social Studies & The Young Learner* 6 (Nov/Dec 1993): 4-5, 17.

48. D. T. Naylor and B. D. Smith, "Teaching about Holidays," *Social Studies & The Young Learner* 6 (Nov/Dec 1993): P1-P4.

49. A. Lockledge, T. Hanson, and D. Corbin, "Unity and Diversity: Holiday Celebrations Around the World," *Social Studies & The Young Learner* 6 (Nov/Dec 1993): 6-8.

50. M. Turkovich and P. Mueller, "The Multicultural Factor: A Curriculum Multiplier," *Social Studies & The Young Learner* 1 (Mar/Apr 1989): 9-12.

51. J. D. Laney and P. A. Moseley, "Who Packed the Suitcase?: Playing the Role of an Archaeologist/Anthropologist," *Social Studies & The Young Learner* 2 (Jan/Feb 1990): 17-19.

52. M. S. Black, "Using Archaeology to Explore Cultures of North America through Time," *Social Studies & The Young Learner* 11 (Sep/Oct 1998): 11-16.

53. G. M. Hickey, "Culture Kits for the Elementary Classroom," *Social Studies & The Young Learner* 9 (Mar/Apr 1997): P1-P4.

54. S. Wasta and M. Scott, "Building Bridges to China," *Social Studies & The Young Learner* 11 (Sep/Oct 1998): 6-10.

55. See, for example, P. G. Fry, L. J. McKinney, and K. B. Phillips, "Expanding Multicultural Curriculum: Helping Children Discover Cultural Similarities," *Social Studies & The Young Learner* 6 (Jan/Feb 1994), 12-15; P. Magnuson, "If I Were in Charge . . .Students Debate the Ideal School at Concordia Language Villages," *Social Studies & The Young Learner* 8 (Jan/Feb 1996): P5-P8; M. Main, R. W. Wilhelm, and A. R. Cox. "Mi Comunidad: Young Children's Bicultural Explorations of the Meaning of Family," *Social Studies & The Young Learner* 9 (Sep/Oct 1996): 7-9, 14; S. L. Field, L. D. Labbo, and C. Lu, "Real People, Real Places: A Powerful Social Studies Exchange Through Technology," *Social Studies & The Young Learner* 9 (Nov/Dec 1996): 16-18, 23; G. E. Hamot and M. Johnson, "Enriching Economics Through Global Education and Service Learning: 5th Graders Rally Around the Rainforest," *Social Studies & The Young Learner* 11 (Nov/Dec 1998): 18-21; H. L. Carlson and C. Holm, "Diversity and Global Studies: Elementary Children's Investigations," *Social Studies & The Young Learner* 11 (Jan/Feb 1999): 6-10; C. Gavin, A. Libresco, and P. Marron, "Essential Questions for Elementary Social Studies: Curriculum Reform for Social Action," *Social Studies & The Young Learner* 11 (Jan/Feb1999): 12-15.

56. L. S. Levstik, "Once Upon a Time Past—History in the Elementary Classroom," *Social Studies & The Young Learner* 2 (Nov/Dec 1989): 3-5.

57. W. C. Parker, "Teaching an IDEA," *Social Studies & The Young Learner* 3 (Jan/Feb 1991):11-14.

58. E. W. Reed, "Historical Themes and Activities for Primary Grades," *Social Studies & The Young Learner* 2 (Nov/Dec 1989): 6-8.

59. J. D. Laney and P. A. Moseley, "Who Packed the Suitcase?: Playing the Role of an Archaeologist/Anthropologist," *Social Studies & The Young Learner* 2 (Jan/Feb 1990): 17-19.

60. L. Moulton and C. Tevis, "Making History Come Alive: Using Historical Photos in the Classroom," *Social Studies & The Young Learner* 3 (Mar/Apr 1991): 13-15.

61. D. Simmons, "Thinking Globally, Acting Locally: Using the Local Environment to Explore Global Issues," *Social Studies & The Young Learner* 6 (Mar/Apr 1994): 10-13.

62. M. S. Black, "Using Archaeology to Explore Cultures of North America Through Time," *Social Studies & The Young Learner* 11 (Sep/Oct 1998): 11-16.

63. P. H. Porter, "The Student as Historian," *Social Studies & The Young Learner* 7 (Nov/Dec 1994): 23-26.

64. S. L. Field, L. D. Labbo, and D. L. Brook, "Teaching and Thinking for Interpretations of the Passage of Time," *Social Studies & The Young Learner* 9 (Sep/Oct 1996): 10-14.

65. M. Aronson, K. Galbo, A. R. Schultz, and J. Shawkey, "Time Traveling with Children's Literature," *Social Studies & The Young Learner* 9 (Sep/Oct 1996): P1-P4.

66. M. A. Andel, "Digging for the Secrets of Time: Artifacts, Old Foundations, and More . . . ," *Social Studies & The Young Learner* 3 (Sep/Oct 1990): 9-11.

67. K. Barclay, C. Benelli, and J. M. Wolf, "Me, Me, Wonderful Me!: Acquiring Concepts of Time and Change," *Social Studies & The Young Learner* 9 (Sep/Oct 1996): 15-16, 26.

68. J. D. Laney, J. L. Laney, T. J. Winsatt, and P. A. Moseley, "Youngster, Oldster: Aging Education in the Primary Grades," *Social Studies & The Young Learner* 9 (Mar/Apr 1997): 4-9.

69. W. Parker, "Why Ethics in Citizenship Education?" *Social Studies & The Young Learner* 1 (Sep/Oct 1988): 3-5.

70. R. Wade, "ProSocial Studies," *Social Studies & The Young Learner* 8 (Jan/Feb 1996): 18-20.

71. J. Passe, "Citizenship Knowledge in Young Learners," *Social Studies & The Young Learner* 3 (Mar/Apr 1991): 15-17.

72. R. Wade, "Community Service-Learning: Commitment through Active Citizenship," *Social Studies & The Young Learner* 6 (Jan/Feb 1994): 1-4.

73. G. Alter, "The Emergence of a Diverse, Caring Community: Next Steps in Responsive Curriculum Design for Elementary Social Studies," *Social Studies & The Young Learner* 10 (Sep/Oct 1997): 6-9.

74. A. G. Larkins, "Should We Teach Values? Which Ones? How?" *Social Studies & The Young Learner* 10 (Sep/Oct 1997): 30-32.

75. R. Wade, "Heroes: From the Famous to the Familiar," *Social Studies & The Young Learner* 8 (Jan/Feb 1996): 15-17.

76. M. C. Schug, "Economic Reasoning and Values Education," *Social Studies & The Young Learner* 1 (Sep/Oct 1988): 6-9; J. D. Laney and M. C. Schug, "Teach Kids Economics and They Will Learn," *Social Studies & The Young Learner* 11 (Nov/Dec 1998): 13-17.

77. T. E. Jennings, S. M. Crowell, and P. F. Fernlund, "Social Justice in the Elementary Classroom," *Social Studies & The Young Learner* 7 (Sep/Oct 1994): 4-6.

78. R. Wade, "Civic Ideals into Practice: Democracy in the Elementary School," *Social Studies & The Young Learner* 8 (Sep/Oct 1995): 16-18.

79. G. A. Heacock, "The We-Search Process: Using the Whole Language Model of Writing to Learn Social Studies Content and Civic Competence," *Social Studies & The Young Learner* 2 (Jan/Feb 1990): 9-11.

80. See, for example, K. T. Bucher and M. Fravel, Jr., "Local History Comes Alive with Postcards," *Social Studies & The Young Learner* 3 (Jan/Feb 1991): 18-20; L. Moulton and C. Tevis, "Making History Come Alive: Using Historical Photos in the Classroom," *Social Studies & The Young Learner* 3 (Mar/Apr 1991): 13-15.

81. M. M. Patton, "Where Do You Live When You Don't Have a House?" *Social Studies & The Young Learner* 8 (Mar/Apr 1996): 14-16.

82. A. L. McCall, J. Higgins, and A. Karrels, "Infusing a Communities Unit with the Concept of Caring," *Social Studies & The Young Learner* 4 (Nov/Dec 1991): 13-15.

83. L. E. Nielsen and J. M. Finkelstein, "Citizenship Education: Looking at Government," *Social Studies & The Young Learner* 1 (Sep/Oct 1988): 10-13.

84. A. J. Hoffman and N. L. Hoffman, "Today's Tarnished Sports Heroes: Implications for Ethics-Based Instruction," *Social Studies & The Young Learner* 1 (Sep/Oct 1988): 14-18.

85. C. Anderson, "Teaching Freedom of Speech in the Elementary Classroom," *Social Studies & The Young Learner* 4 (Sep/Oct 1991): 3-6.

86. G. Mertz, "Strategies for Teaching About the First Amendment in 4-6," *Social Studies & The Young Learner* 4 (Sep/Oct 1991): 10-13.

87. A. M. Harwood and J. Chang, "Inquiry-Based Service-Learning and the Internet," *Social Studies & The Young Learner* 12 (Sep/Oct 1999): 15-18.

88. M. H. Cordier and M. Perez-Stable, "Latino Connections: Family, Neighbors, and Community," *Social Studies & The Young Learner* 9 (Sep/Oct 1996): 20-22, 32.

89. A. L. Sandmann and J. F. Ahern, "Promoting Citizenship in the Upper Elementary and Middle Grades," *Social Studies & The Young Learner* 10 (Sep/Oct 1997): 27-29; A. L. Sandmann and J. F. Ahern, "More Children's Literature to Promote Citizenship in the Upper and Middle Grades," *Social Studies & The Young Learner* 10 (Nov/Dec 1997): 25-28.

90. K. Moore, "Heightening Children's Social Awareness with Trade Books," *Social Studies & The Young Learner* 11 (Jan/Feb 1999): 17-19.

91. P. Koetsch, "Museum-in-Progress: Student Generated Learning Environments," *Social Studies & The Young Learner* 7 (Sep/Oct 1994): 15-18, 32.

92. D. Lerner, "Walk Around the Block: My Home, My School, My City," *Social Studies & The Young Learner* 9 (Nov/Dec 1996): 30-32.

93. S. Solovitch-Haynes, "Street-Smart Second-Graders Navigate the Political Process," *Social Studies & The Young Learner* 8 (Mar/Apr 1996): 4-5.

94. J. D. Laney, J. L. Laney, T. J. Winsatt, and P. A. Moseley, "Youngster, Oldster: Aging Education in the Primary Grades," *Social Studies & The Young Learner* 9 (Mar/Apr 1997): 4-9.

95. B. R. Fulweiler and M. E. McGuire, "Storypath: Powerful Social Studies Instruction in the Primary Grades," *Social Studies & The Young Learner* 9 (Jan/Feb 1997): 4-7.

96. A. L. Rappoport and S. B. Kletzien, "Kids Around Town: Civic Education Through Democratic Action," *Social Studies & The Young Learner* 10 (Sep/Oct 1997): 14-16.

97. B. E. Larson, "The Makah: Exploring Public Issues During a Structured Classroom Discussion," *Social Studies & The Young Learner* 10 (Sep/Oct 1997): 10-13.

98. J. Hoge, "Try Microsociety for Hands-on Citizenship," *Social Studies & The Young Learner* 10 (Sep/Oct 1997): 18-21.

99. C. Gavin, A. Libresco, and P. Marron, "Essential Questions for Elementary Social Studies: Curriculum Reform for Social Action," *Social Studies & The Young Learner* 11 (Jan/Feb1999): 12-15.

100. See, for example, E. A. Yeager and M. J. Patterson, "Teacher-Directed Social Action in a Middle School Classroom," *Social Studies & The Young Learner* 8 (Mar/Apr 1996): 29-31; K. Bishop and D. Hershberger, "Real-Life Global Citizenship Connections Through the Internet," *Social Studies & The Young Learner* 10 (Sep/Oct 1997): 25-26; L. Garrison, "A Bowl of Tea with Me: A Photo Essay," *Social Studies & The Young Learner* 10 (Jan/Feb 1998): 30-32; Hamot and Johnson, 1998; C. Pereira, J. Dolenga, C. A. Rolzinski, "Teaching Citizenship Through Community Service," *Social Studies & The Young Learner* 3 (Nov/Dec 1990): P1-P4.

101. L. S. Levstik, "Once Upon a Time Past—History in the Elementary Classroom," *Social Studies & The Young Learner* 2 (Nov/Dec 1989): 3-5.

102. E. W. Reed, "Historical Themes and Activities for Primary Grades," *Social Studies & The Young Learner* 2 (Nov/Dec 1989): 6-8.

103. P. H. Porter, "The Student as Historian," *Social Studies & The Young Learner* 7 (Nov/Dec 1994): 23-26.

104. See, for example, T. A. Young and M. F. Marek-Schroer, "Writing to Learn in Social Studies," *Social Studies & The Young Learner* 5 (Sep/Oct 1992): 14-16; S. Crenshaw, K. M. Pierce, L. Riekes, S. Slane, and F. Stopksy, "Teaching History Across the Elementary Curriculum," *Social Studies & The Young Learner* 2 (Nov/Dec 1989): P1-P4.

105. See, for example, G. B. Nash, "The Consequences of 1492: Teaching about the Columbian Voyages," *Social Studies & The Young Learner* 4 (Mar/Apr 1992): 3-5; R. Moulden, "Discovering Columbus," *Social Studies & The Young Learner* 4(Mar/Apr 1992): P1-P4; C. Gorn, "The Columbian Voyages and Primary-Grade Learners," *Social Studies & The Young Learner* 4 (Mar/Apr 1992): 17-18; G. A. Levitt, P. R. Speaker, and R. B. Speaker, "Columbus and the Exploration of the Americas: Ideas for Thematic Units in the Elementary Grades," *Social Studies & The Young Learner* 4 (Mar/Apr 1992): 19-22.

106. K. D. Harvey, "Native Americans: The Next 500 Years," *Social Studies & The Young Learner* 5 (Jan/Feb 1993): P1-P4.

107. S. L. Field and L. D. Labbo, "A Pocketful of History," *Social Studies & The Young Learner* 7 (Nov/Dec 1994): 4-7.

108. M. E. Hauser and J. C. Hauser, "Women and Empowerment: Part I," *Social Studies & The Young Learner* 7 (Sep/Oct 1994): P1-P4.

109. M. E. Haas and J. K. Tipton, "The Study of World War II," *Social Studies & The Young Learner* 7 (Nov/Dec 1994): P1-P4.

110. S. Totten, "Telling the Holocaust Story to Children," *Social Studies & The Young Learner* 7 (Nov/Dec 1994): P5-P8.

111. K. Schill, "Multiple Perspectives on Hiroshima," *Social Studies & The Young Learner* 10 (Jan/Feb 1998): P5-P8.

112. M. J. Johnson and C. Janisch. "Connecting Literacy with Social Studies Content," *Social Studies & The Young Learner* 10 (Mar/Apr 1998): 6-9.

113. See, for example, R. V. Morris, "Using Artifacts as a Springboard to Literacy," *Social Studies & The Young Learner* 10 (Mar/Apr 1998): 14-16; C. Gorn, in M. McKinney-Browning, ed., "Point/Counterpoint," *Social Studies & The Young Learner*, 2 (Nov/Dec 1989): 29-31.

114. F. Miller, "Understanding Multicultural Perspectives: A Project Approach," *Social Studies & The Young Learner* 11 (Jan/Feb 1999): 22-23.

115. H. Debelak, in M. McKinney-Browning, ed., "Point/Counterpoint," *Social Studies & The Young Learner* 2 (Nov/Dec 1989): 29-31.

116. A. Lockledge, T. Hanson, and D. Corbin, "Unity and Diversity: Holiday Celebrations Around the World," *Social Studies & The Young Learner* 6 (Nov/Dec 1993): 6-8.

117. J. S. Shively, "Inquiry into a Trading Center: The Case of the Cahokia Empire," *Social Studies & The Young Learner* 11 (Nov/Dec 1998): P3-P4.

118. V. A. Green, "Extraordinary People: Mannequins and the Historical Imagination," *Social Studies & The Young Learner* 8 (Jan/Feb 1996): 4-6.

119. L. Wojtan, "Exploring Japan through Rice," *Social Studies & The Young Learner* 10 (Jan/Feb 1998): 11-14.

120. C. L. Mason and A. Carter, "The Garbers: Using Digital History to Recreate a 19th-Century Family," *Social Studies & The Young Learner* 12 (Sep/Oct 1999): 11-14.

121. J. A. Smith and D. Dobson, "Teaching with Historical Novels: A Four-Step Approach," *Social Studies & The Young Learner* 5 (Jan/Feb 1993): 19-22.

122. T. McGowan, B. Guzzetti, and B. Kowalinski, "Using Literature Studies to Promote Elementary Social Studies Learning," *Social Studies & The Young Learner* 5 (Sep/Oct 1992): 10-13.

123. "Folk Tales and Stories: An Elementary Student's Passport to the World," 1991.

124. P. Fritzer and V. Bristor, "People and Places in the Laura Ingalls Wilder Books," *Social Studies & The Young Learner* 8 (Jan/Feb 1996): 11-14.

125. See, for example, S. L. Field, L. D. Labbo, and D. L. Brook, "Teaching and Thinking for Interpretations of the Passage of Time," *Social Studies & The Young Learner* 9 (Sep/Oct 1996): 10-14; L. B. Clegg and P. K. Ford, "Historical Fiction & Fantasy for the Young Learner," *Social Studies & The Young Learner* 9 (Nov/Dec 1996): 24-26, 29.

126. J. J. Drake and F. D. Drake, "Using Children's Literature to Teach About the American Revolution," *Social Studies & The Young Learner* 3 (Nov/Dec 1990): 6-8.

127. G. LoBaugh and G. E. Tompkins, "Walking in Their Footsteps: Writing Letters to Learn about the American Revolution," *Social Studies & The Young Learner* 2 (Nov/Dec 1989): 9-11.

128. C. D. Deaton, "History and Community Resources: Teaching Children about Our National Heritage," *Social Studies & The Young Learner* 3 (Sep/Oct 1990): 6-8, 11.

129. J. A. Smith and D. Hobbs, "Did Your Family Take Baths on the Prairie?" *Social Studies & The Young Learner* 9 (Nov/Dec 1996): 12-15.

130. E. A. Yeager, F. H. Doppen, and E. B. Otani, "State History and African American History: An Interdisciplinary Civil Rights Approach," *Social Studies & The Young Learner* 9 (Jan/Feb 1997): 14-17.

131. See, for example, M. Zarnowski, "Interpreting Critical Issues: Comparing Past and Modern Plagues," *Social Studies & The Young Learner* 10 (Nov/Dec 1997): 10-13; M. Zarnowski, "Poetry about People," *Social Studies & The Young Learner* 4 (Sep/Oct 1991): 15-17, 22; M. Zarnowski, "The Question-and-Answer Book: A Format for Young Historians," *Social Studies & The Young Learner* 4 (Nov/Dec 1991): 5-7; M. Zarnowski,

"Knowing and Caring About Children of the Depression," *Social Studies & The Young Learner* 9 (Sep/Oct 1996): 4-6.

132. C. Gavin, A. Libresco, and P. Marron, "Essential Questions for Elementary Social Studies: Curriculum Reform for Social Action," *Social Studies & The Young Learner* 11 (Jan/Feb1999): 12-15.

133. See, for example, L. Moulton and C. Tevis, "Making History Come Alive: Using Historical Photos in the Classroom," *Social Studies & The Young Learner* 3 (Mar/Apr 1991): 13-15; L. Miculka, "Photographs Slide into the Classroom," *Social Studies & The Young Learner* 9 (Jan/Feb 1997): 8-10.

134. See, for example, G. W. Chilcoat, "Puppet Theatre as Method: Teaching About Slavery in the 5th Grade," *Social Studies & The Young Learner* 4 (Nov/Dec 1991): 16-19; G. Chilcoat, "How to Use Flippy Theater in Social Studies," *Social Studies & The Young Learner* 9 (Nov/Dec 1996): P1-P4.

135. P. Koetsch, "Museum-in-Progress: Student Generated Learning Environments," *Social Studies & The Young Learner* 7 (Sep/Oct 1994): 15-18, 32.

136. M. A. Andel, "Digging for the Secrets of Time: Artifacts, Old Foundations, and More . . . ," *Social Studies & The Young Learner* 3 (Sep/Oct 1990): 9-11.

137. S. Berman, *Children's Social Consciousness and the Development of Social Responsibility* (Albany: State University of New York Press, 1997), 85.

138. C. Crabtree, "Returning History to the Elementary School," in P. Gagnon, ed., *The Future of the Past: The Plight of History in American Education* (New York: Macmillan, 1989).

Chapter 8

The Holocaust and Historical Empathy: The Politics of Understanding

Karen L. Riley

The quest to understand is the single most important endeavor and ultimate goal of a student of history. As such, the history student examines historical accounts, biographies, testimonies, in addition to reading a mountain of secondary sources and sifting through countless pages of primary evidence, all in an effort to reconstruct the past in a faithful yet original way. In the case of the Holocaust and other sweeping historical events, the task of selecting sources for analysis, a first step in historical craftsmanship, is daunting. Yet, the journey to understand neither begins with nor ends with an examination of available evidence. For one, the individual researcher-student brings to the task at hand a set of unique experiences. Each person, for example, has been shaped by both the accident of birth and his or her historic moment. Secondly, as she begins to filter available sources through her personal lens, an organizing framework becomes an indispensable tool in the process of her construction of understanding and reconstruction of past events. Therefore, the quest to understand is dependent upon both the individual nature of the researcher, and the organizing principle or framework employed in the process of assigning meaning.

Today, unlike the print-rich decades of our grandparents and great-grandparents, children and adolescents who will soon enter adulthood and public life have come to understand their own world and past worlds largely through surreal electronic platforms such as movies, television, and the Internet. This space-age generation knows what it knows through mass-media presentations and visual symbols, which often discourage sustained and thoughtful attention to the past.[1] Hence, this sound byte approach to information or evidence gathering serves as a barrier to in-depth analysis and perspective taking, both of which are required for historical understanding. According to Lerner, in *Why History Matters*, this mass-media culture, influenced by television's method of short-range interpretation, often views the world and events through *present-mindedness*, or the shallow attempt at meaning, and cultivates a certain contempt for precise meaning and critical reasoning.[2] If true, teachers from kindergarten through twelfth grade will be challenged to move their students from *factoid* accumulation to critical thinking. Nowhere will the challenge be greater than in the history classroom.

Few subject areas are more susceptible to special interest intrusion than the Social Studies, especially history. As Levstik asserts, 'history is among the most controversial subjects in the curriculum,' hence, contestation over what should be taught and how draws the attention of more than a few.[3] Not surprisingly, textbook and curriculum writers often pander to these groups whose political influence frequently drives curriculum or textbook adoption. In the case of the Holocaust as an increasing topic of study in history classrooms, its political nature presents multiple challenges beyond a noble quest to understand. One challenge for teachers is how or whether to use the plethora of curricula on the Holocaust, written from any number of philosophical perspectives and for a variety of reasons, some of which can be considered egregiously self-serving, to those whose writers consider their efforts a *public service*. What's more, the Holocaust as a topic of study, unlike *Rome of the Caesars*, gives rise to intense passions which often obscure objectivity. Hence, teachers must recognize that in order for students to understand an historical event of such magnitude, they must engage a complement of intellectual skills and dispositions in order to assign meaning to the vast quantity of primary evidence and secondary sources.[4]

However, for secondary teachers, the Holocaust as a topic of study may lead them into conflict when they attempt to balance the affective with the cognitive in terms of historical understanding or empathy. Partly, this conflict may stem from Vinson's findings that history teachers are less effective than historians in dealing with historical problems because they prefer a social criticism approach rather than a social science approach to understanding history.[5] On the one hand, teachers must help students to cope with factual truths about the Holocaust—Auschwitz was an extermination camp, while Dachau was a concentration camp—and provide opportunities for them to *discover* these truths through sustained examination of sources. On the other, the search for a measure of objective truth is often eclipsed by the affective side of learning as teachers either intentionally or unintentionally romanticize the victims, perpetrators, and rescuers—all Jews were pure, all Germans were evil, all rescuers were saintly—in the pursuit of inculcating students with such feelings as compassion and outrage.[6] The danger of course is that the historical actors of the Holocaust become something other than human, a perspective that thwarts historical understanding or empathy.

Teachers can help students to guard against historical distortion and factual inaccuracy by helping them to build a framework for understanding history through a sustained analysis of historical evidence and other tools of the discipline. Acquisition of a useable and useful framework for understanding the complexities of historical events will help teachers and students avoid a reliance on any individual text or curriculum guide as an authority. Moreover, teachers in secondary social studies classrooms should reject one-dimensional accounts of historical events in favor of student investigations which encourage and incorporate both breadth and depth. Thus, the challenge for teachers who engage their students in a study of the Holocaust enter onto a field whose parameters are guarded by ideologues and where they must diligently strive to set aside their own desires to have students feel the pain of world atrocities by studying the Holocaust, and assist them with building a framework for understanding this watershed event in human history. What follows is a three-dimensional view to *doing Holocaust history*. First, I discuss the politics of the Holocaust as a challenge and sometimes a barrier to historical understanding. Second, I offer an interpretation of historical empathy as both a methodology and methodological outcome, followed by a critique of three popular curriculum guides on the Holocaust within the framework of historical empathy.

Standing History on Its Head: Understanding the Politics of the Holocaust

The politics surrounding the Holocaust may soon stand history on its head. Today, the Holocaust is on trial, or should I say, history as craftsmanship is on trial. In Great Britain, David Irving, a well-known historian, has filed suit against Deborah Lipstadt, a professor of Religious Studies at Emory University, for libel. She claims that he is a Holocaust denier who distorts the facts; he claims that he writes "real history," and that his expertise is as an historian of National Socialism, not the Holocaust. She claims that he denies the existence of such things as gas chambers at Auschwitz, a site that has stirred the emotions and passions of both Jews and Poles who view the former extermination camp as a sacred site for their respective ethnic and cultural groups. He claims that the gas chambers at Auschwitz were erected after the war. Caught in between is the idea that when something bad happens, someone is to blame, and we want our chroniclers and sages to tell us what happened. As an event of the twentieth century, we look to the experts, the historians, to tell us what occurred. However, disagreements over interpretations which were once the mainstay of scholarly debate have now turned into an exercise in political correctness and open hostility in the case of the Holocaust. This war of words will have an impact on future historians, and students of history, no matter the outcome.[7]

What makes this case so compelling is that historical scholarship is really the defendant. The warring camps are many—from the particularists, universalists, intentionists, and functionalists[8] to those who suggest that Germans are plagued by a certain *evil gene*.[9] In fact, Goldhagen's book, *Hitler's Willing Executioners: Ordinary Germans*, treats the evil-gene-concept as historical fact, a claim that has brought down the wrath of mainstream Holocaust historians. Despite the fact that Goldhagen has been largely discredited by the community of Holocaust historians—his training was in political science methodology, not historical methodology—the public's, both German and American, appetite for the atrocities of the Holocaust sustains his popularity.[10] So great is their hunger that even when it became known that the author of *Fragments* (1995)—which won the National Jewish Book Award, beating out literary works by individuals such as Elie Wiesel and Alfred Kazin—had never been in a concentration camp, wrote his work as an autobiography/testimony. Despite any falsity of purpose or fraudulent construction on the part of the author, "his work continued to attract readers."[11]

Irving's libel suit will force British jurisprudence to decide, in effect, who is telling the historical truth about the Holocaust. This decision may alter our notion of *doing history* to *doing history legally*. Yet as Guttenplan summed it up, "Though it is impolite to mention them in public, there are still a number of 'live questions' about the Holocaust."[12] As teachers and students in history classrooms begin to seek answers to some of these "live questions," they soon encounter a number of paradoxes and ironies embedded within multiple perspectives on the topic. These elements often manifest themselves in opposing ideological positions, represented by historians, psychologists, writers, dramatists, and others, whose views are often disseminated through textbook accounts and curriculum guides. Without knowledge of the political nature of the Holocaust, textbooks and prepared curricular materials often lead teachers and students away from any real investigation and towards the writers' own forgone conclusions. In one study on historical thinking, Wineburg found that textbook accounts of an historical event employ "the notion that the way things are told are simply the way things were."[13] This is certainly true of most Holocaust curricula. Thus, teachers can help to ensure that students genuinely examine historical events by first acknowledging the political nature of the topic under study. In terms of the Holocaust, one such political issue involves the notion of historical ownership which largely centers on the philosophical perspective of the particularists' camp versus the perspective of the universalists' camp; both will challenge teachers to reflect upon their own beliefs about teaching, learning, and subject matter, as well as their own positionality regarding the Holocaust prior to engaging students in historical inquiry.

For example, the perspective of the *particularist* is that the Holocaust was a uniquely Jewish event and attempts to universalize it diminishes and distorts the importance of this event to Jewish history. The *universalist*, on the other hand, seeks to include non-Jewish historical actors so that events such as the roundup and extermination of Christian clergy, Gypsies, Poles, Quakers, and political opponents, along with the euthanasia program for the physically and mentally impaired, share in historical importance with the roundup and extermination of Jews. This paradox will confront teachers as they seek to understand their own positions regarding how to approach teaching the Holocaust. Generally, teachers in this country are motivated to teach the Holocaust out of an urgency to confront domestic issues such as stereotyping and prejudice,[14] both of which contain moral messages for American youth and which fit well within the perspective of the universalists. However, in *American Youth and the Holocaust*, the writers caution teachers that "the very urge to fight this phenomenon [stereotyping and prejudice] easily turns teaching into propaganda."[15] Moreover, they say, "it is propaganda, even if it is in [the] service of good things. This must be said as harshly as possible, because otherwise good intentions tempt educators not to face the issue."[16]

According to their position, society can be changed only when the complexity of the facts are allowed to emerge. Distortion is not needed; the event itself can *mold* the consciousness of individuals. If true, the notion of ownership then serves as an obstacle to the *molding* process. For example, the historical integrity of the Holocaust is compromised when teachers attempt to draw parallels between the persecution of European Jewry and the results of stereotyping and prejudice experienced by minorities in the United States. This universal application of the themes of the Holocaust not only compromises historical understanding, it fails to do justice to real issues faced by Blacks, Hispanics, Asians, and other minorities. When teachers simply borrow events of the Holocaust in order to give students a reason to discuss present or contemporary events which directly affect their lives, they are not engaging students in historical inquiry, but rather in history as therapy. Research over the past two decades on historical thinking in both elementary and secondary classrooms has urged us to reject these one-dimensional accounts of historical events in favor of student investigations which depend on both breadth and depth.[17]

However, the drive to universalize the Holocaust is often motivated by a desire to introduce it into the K-12 curriculum—the broader the application, the more likely the acceptance. Yet, as a result of this broad-stroke approach, secondary teachers often introduce the themes of the Holocaust as topics of study, but then charge off in the pursuit of other world atrocities such as the slaughter of Cambodians by the Khmer Rouge, or the mass destruction of innocents in Uganda. Often, teachers begin to teach the "moral lessons of the Holocaust," yet find themselves really teaching about southern slavery or Andrew Jackson's Indian relocation plan and the "Trail of Tears," all of which are misguided lessons in comparative pain and not historical inquiry. While these topics are worthy of study in their own right, "the price of such universalization is the destruction of what actually happened in the Holocaust; in that catastrophe, a particular group was singled out for total destruction."[18] This dilemma—particularists versus universalists—not only involves teachers, but the entire academic community as well. Historians more than any other group involved in Holocaust studies and research, continue to be divided into several camps, those who believe that the Holocaust was a watershed event in Jewish history and those who believe that it was a watershed event in human history.

Despite the obstacles to understanding presented by opposing philosophies and ideologies, teachers can help students to construct a framework for understanding that while abundant evidence of Jewish self-help existed in places such as Auschwitz or the Warsaw ghetto, the historical record also contains instances of Jewish cruelty toward fellow victims, such as the actions of the Jewish police in the Warsaw ghetto or Jews in Berlin who sold information to Nazi officials concerning the whereabouts of fellow Jews in hiding. Or that the record also shows the baseness of countless Polish Christians toward their Jewish countrymen, while at the same time recognizing those Poles who saved Jews despite the overwhelming odds of danger to themselves and their families.[19] One set of "facts" which emerges from inquiry into the Holocaust, however, is the recognition that European Jewry became a collective target for annihilation, and the technology of extermination involved the destruction of millions of others. In that regard, secondary teachers have the curricular obligation to help their students to explore the full range of understandings contained in the Holocaust. In doing so, teachers should naturally weave together the universal and particular aspects of the event, but in an effort to assist students in a robust interpretation of the Holocaust, and not for purposes of indoctrination, propaganda, or social therapy.

Historical Empathy as Process and Outcome

Studies conducted on historical understanding, including historical empathy, within the past decade have largely confined themselves to an historical problem faced by key individuals whose actions or intentions students analyzed and then used in the construction of an historical narrative (e.g., Yeager and others' study of empathy and Truman's decision to drop the bomb, or Foster's study of Neville Chamberlain's plan of appeasement).[20] These historical vignettes allow students to focus on the actions of one figure and examine documents that relate to his actions. Embedded in this process is the element of context. While this body of work will go a long way in reforming how history is currently taught in secondary classrooms, its efforts must be expanded. For example, the political nature of the Holocaust naturally draws students to its key figures, especially of Adolf Hitler. Yet, mainstream historians of the Holocaust point to actions or inactions of bystanders and ordinary people making them key players in the Holocaust.

Additionally, the great wartime bureaucracy of Nazi Germany is generally considered a key factor in the destruction of so many millions of innocent people. Therefore, context and the antecedents to the context play a far greater role in student understanding than the individual actions of key players, including Adolf Hitler. Stern, a presidential historian at the John F. Kennedy library, warned the writers of the National History Standards that they must avoid three temptations: presentism, telling only part of controversial stories, and underestimating students' ability to understand history's complications and ambiguities. Historical empathy then as a process and outcome offers us a framework from which we can help students to begin the arduous task of examining multiple perspectives without imposing a personal bias or prejudice as they attempt to understand and interpret the paradoxes and ambiguities of the Holocaust.[21]

Empathy as a process, whose framework incorporates four key constructs, owes much to the body of research on historical thinking. Accordingly, discussions on historical thinking and how students learn and know history usually deal with such notions as the role of memory versus facts, historical imagination, context, the nature of historical sources, detection of bias, conflicting accounts, and the ambiguous state of historical conclusions.[22] In crafting an historical account, the historian must assign weight to all of these elements and more. For students new to the historical process, historical empathy as an organizing framework, a set of dispositions critical to the historical endeavor, is invaluable. While authors such as Ashby and Lee, Portal, Rogers, and Shemilt,[23] have, over the past two decades, expanded and added depth to our understanding of what historical empathy is or is not, I find that the explanation of empathy offered by Yeager and others contains a set of well-articulated constructs that make up the core processes of historical methodology. In addition, this particular empathetical model contains an added dimension, that of outcome.[24] Therefore, we might understand empathy to be both the process of historical craftsmanship and its end result.

If empathy is to be useable as a tool with which to understand the Holocaust, we must first examine its four components or constructs included in Yeager's discussion: introduction and analysis of the event, including the perspectives of the historical actors; context and chronology; evidence, including interpretations of other historians; and construction of a narrative framework through which historical conclusions are reached.[25] The first construct deals with the introduction of an historical event that involves an analysis of human action. However, the topic of the Holocaust rests upon a wide historical stage with scores of historical actors, often categorized as perpetrators, victims, or bystanders. The problem most teachers encounter is what to teach or introduce about the Holocaust because the question most students ask is, *How could something like this happen?* The vastness conjured up by this question often leads teachers away from inquiry and drives them towards a one-dimensional account usually found in textbooks or curriculum guides. Yet, this need not be the case. By asking the question, What will I have to understand before I can approach understanding the question *How could something like this happen?* one begins the process of understanding by selecting categories for examination. While the body of literature on historical empathy generally focuses on the introduction of one event within the context of a *meta-event*—Truman's decision to drop the bomb, which is an event within the *meta-event* of World War II—the central question, *How could such a thing have happened?* leads us away from understanding one actor or event and compels us to investigate multiple actors and categories. Thus, we must expand this first construct to include sweeping events and not simply focus on one historical problem embedded within a larger context.

As a result, teachers might engage Yeager and others' first construct, introduction of an historical event and perspectives of the historical actors, by asking students to create a list of categories or themes that will help them begin to organize the event both chronologically and conceptually. For example, students will ask W*hy the Jews*? Their question necessitates an understanding of historical anti-Semitism, not simply the Nazi, or 20th century, response to anti-Semitism.[26] Thus, the question of antecedents plays a pivotal role in terms of depth of understanding. Accordingly, the number 6,000,000, has no real value in terms of student understanding of Jews or Jewish culture without an examination of the nature of Jewish life in Europe before the war; one cannot understand what was lost, if one does not understand what existed in the first place. Likewise, students struggle with the question *Why did Germans hate Jews?*—a question that cannot be answered simply by Hitler's emergence on the historical stage, or great-man theory. Hence, they must dig deeper for their understanding and examine the development of late nineteenth century and early twentieth century German attitudes, or what has been termed by one German intellectual historian as *the youth without Goethe generation*.[27] The relationship between historical antecedents to the topic is paramount in the construction of a robust interpretation.

The importance of context, Yeager and others' second construct, cannot be overstated. According to Stern, "the mastery of context must be the first step in introducing young people to the work of achieving historical understanding."In order for teachers to *teach context*, they must help their students to abandon their impulse to impose current values on past times. In other words, historical understanding does not require, in fact rejects, endorsement or condemnation. For example, when students attempt to evaluate or interpret the motivations of Holocaust rescuers, such as Oscar Schindler, they must take into account the fact that he was at first a war profiteer, someone who took advantage of Jews who had lost their factories and whose labor was purchased from Nazi officials. His change of heart regarding the Jews who worked for him came at a later time, and is still not well understood. Student understanding requires neither endorsement of Schindler's *wartime change of heart* nor condemnation for his earlier profiteering actions. What is required is an attempt to understand 1940s wartime Europe and the possibilities for self-advancement, graft, and corruption faced by men such as Schindler. Accordingly, the challenge for teachers regarding context will be to disentangle it from the current *cult of relativism or presentism*.[28]

As such, teachers play a leading role in what students have an opportunity to learn and understand. Yet too often the natural desire of social studies teachers, to determine what the appropriate or correct interpretation of an event should be, causes them to direct students toward that position, lest they *get it wrong*. However, empathy or the process of historical scholarship requires that one abandon notions of a predetermined outcome in favor of rigorous investigation. This rigorous investigation means that despite a student's own personal lens, she is able to view the actions of the historical actors from the position of context. In her study of *Frauen: German Women Confront the Holocaust*, Stern used empathy as a model for making sense of the experiences of non-Jewish women and their actions during the years of the Third Reich.[29] She wanted to test the difficulty of abandoning personal position—the daughter of a German-Jewish father—in order to understand the motivations of these women to act as they did. She found that the model of empathy under discussion here guided her so that she clearly understood how and why these German women acted as they did, yet still retained her personal view of the Holocaust and its perpetrators. In the final analysis, she understood the motivations of these women to act as they did without endorsement or condemnation of their actions.

Despite Stern's successful application of Yeager's and others' constructs of empathy, one cannot help but wonder if our recent experience with presentism will not color our judgment regarding sources of evidence. In other words, student understanding of the Holocaust or any historical event is dependent upon the evidence a student has the opportunity to analyze. Teachers, therefore, contribute to bias which is inherent in the process of selection, as the entire range of evidence on the Holocaust is beyond the reach of most. One question that remains is to what degree? One way a teacher might unwittingly employ the notion of presentism in the selection of evidence or sources for student examination is to select only those sources that support his or her own position. For example, if teachers only present evidence (excerpts) from *Schindler's Jews* in which they profusely thank him for saving their lives, or newspaper reviews of Steven Spielberg's movie *Schindler's List* which discussed his burial in Israel as a Righteous Gentile, students have little choice but to conclude that Schindler was a noble man, perhaps even raised above the level of ordinary men. However, one only need read the words of Schindler's former wife Emily or other secondary accounts of Schindler's life to understand that he was a complex individual capable of displaying paradoxical behavior.[30] In the case of the recent libel suit, *Irving vs. Lipstadt*, sources of evidence and their interpretations are precisely the issue. Therefore, teachers must assess their own positionality, where they stand in terms of understanding the Holocaust, before they begin the process of selecting evidence.[31]

In a recent issue of *Theory and Research in Social Education*, Blum discussed the special relationship that exists between linguistic forms and historical logic.[32] He asserted that all students possess a preferred "world view" or approach to understanding history. He inferred that regardless of a student's preferred approach, the ability to acquire empathy or historical understanding is largely dependent upon the materials a student is able to examine. In other words, the selection of instructional materials determines to a significant extent the historical understanding a student acquires. Blum's notion supports research on historical empathy that looks at "the analysis of a variety of historical evidence" as one of its four constructs. The theoretical framework of empathy when applied to the Holocaust—discussed in a symposium at the 1997 National Council for the Social Studies meeting in Cincinnati—underscores the symbiotic relationship that exists between sources of knowledge and understanding.[33]

The fourth construct, written narrative of the historical event with conclusions drawn from an analysis of evidentiary data, may actually pose more questions for investigation than render conclusions. The original question *How could something like the Holocaust happen?* opens more doors for investigation rather than narrowing the field. The earlier studies of empathy in which the actions of a key figure were examined will not yield a rich understanding of the Holocaust if one seeks an answer to the unanswerable *How could something like this happen?* For example, if students only examine the actions of Adolf Hitler within the context of his times, they will miss the important centuries-old antecedents to 20th century anti-Semitism that laid the fertile ground for the hatred of Jews. To conclude that Hitler was responsible for the Holocaust is to dismiss the role of other key figures, including Roosevelt and the failure of Evian Conference (July 1938), the constraints of a modern bureaucratic nation, technological advances, and history itself. Therefore, in order to attempt to understand events such as the Holocaust we need to begin with an encompassing question, one that will stir us to build categories for investigation and which will force us to weave together antecedents, historical development, context of the times, and the actions of major figures and communities of actors—victims, bystanders, and perpetrators. The end result of such a process should demonstrate that the individual researcher has considered context, evidence, and the nature of her position in weaving together an explanation of the past. It should also show how the framework of empathy has guided her investigation and enabled her to view the actions of multiple historical actors without endorsement or condemnation and allowed her to render a reasonable interpretation, keeping in mind that sources of evidence not consulted might affect her current interpretation. If we as teachers fail to help our students acquire a useable and useful framework from which they can launch and execute their own investigations, they have little choice but to draw their knowledge from scores of prepared instructional materials which contain the historical interpretations of others, regardless of quality.

The Holocaust and Empathy:
In Search of Historical Understanding

The Holocaust as a topic of study in scores of social studies classrooms has received much attention over the past two decades. With the national Holocaust Memorial Museum only recently completed and the urgency most aging Holocaust survivors feel to remember this historic event, Jewish Federations and Holocaust survivor groups have called upon educators to advance Holocaust studies to the forefront of social education programs. With the idea of fading memory in mind, Seixas points out that "we speak so much of memory because there is so little of it left." He urges us that "exploration of this insight may help us to understand better what is at stake in debates over history curricula."[34] One curricular debate centers on "where to put the Holocaust." The obvious choices for curriculum implementation are secondary social studies stalwarts, world and American history courses. As a consequence, the market for Holocaust-related instructional materials, including videos, CD-ROMS, children's literature, and socials studies curriculum guides and resource books, is large and growing.[35] In fact, one Israeli educator claims that since the 1980s, there has been a "sharp rise of interest in the field [Holocaust] and a veritable explosion in published materials on the subject."[36] However, this growth may offer as many problems as it does solutions as states and their school districts frequently rush to embrace timely topics with new and "untested" instructional materials and methods. This full-speed-ahead approach may result in the adoption of poor instructional products, whose deficiencies range from the omission of important themes to historical inaccuracies, and in the case of some Holocaust curriculum guides, the reinforcement of negative stereotypes either through teacher background information or through poorly-constructed student activities.

This essay, then, offers a critical review of selected curriculum guides and resource texts, within the context of historical empathy. The selected materials are currently in use in states where Holocaust studies are either mandated, recommended, or enjoy wide-spread popularity. This critique will also look at the inclusion or omission of women's and children's voices of the Holocaust, a heretofore neglected area of historical inquiry.[37] It will also consider the content and appropriateness of student activities and teaching strategies. Formal curriculum guides—those with teacher and student objectives, for example— will also be evaluated for their application in classrooms where the teacher is considered either a Holocaust novice or expert. Conversely, resource guides and curricula will be evaluated on the basis of the breadth and depth of Holocaust readings, and the extent to which they can accommodate both the novice and the expert teacher in planning for a robust approach to the topic. Some curriculum guides, for example, are highly prescriptive and may require little formal planning on the part of the classroom teacher, while resource guides or texts clearly allow the individual teacher a good deal of flexibility in planning for a unit of instruction on the Holocaust. Regardless of the quality of prepared curricula, providing students with a useable framework such as historical empathy for investigating and constructing an historical interpretation is superior to offering them a thinned version of an historical event where their only role is that of passive receiver.

Life Unworthy of Life: A Holocaust Curriculum

Few curriculum guides present the Holocaust with such stark reality. From the outset, *Life Unworthy of Life* (1987) offers up its main point contained in the heading of the first lesson: "The Destruction of Families and the Question of Personal Responsibility." In other words, the writers ask readers to understand that 1) a tragedy to humankind occurred, and 2) someone is to blame. The second lesson focuses on the rationale for teaching the Holocaust. Like most Holocaust curriculum efforts of the 1980s, the writers of this guide are motivated by an inoculation rationale for teaching about genocide and the Holocaust:

> By examining the behavior of civilized people, this study takes a painful look at how fragile morality, democracy and the sanctity of human life itself can be. The unit is designed to make us all more aware of our responsibilities to ourselves and others, so that, as one Holocaust survivor noted, no such event will happen again, and the future will be safe for our children—for all children.[38]

Without these lessons, humankind is doomed to repeat the past, so goes the rationale. In support of that idea, the writers point to a set of logical consequences for future generations if the message is ignored, such as a growing tolerance of persecution, the ability to dehumanize those who are different, and a willingness to avoid personal responsibility for the fate of others.[39] The noble aims of the writers notwithstanding, this curriculum guide on the Holocaust, like others, focuses on consequences for the present and fails to create ways in which students might grapple with the complexities of the Holocaust as an historical event. Unlike the framework of historical empathy which contains four key constructs for organizing and interpreting past events, based upon a wide selection of evidence and set within historical context, *Life Unworthy of Life* narrowly selects primary evidence and then interprets it for students.

For example, the section entitled "Brief History of Anti-Semitism" begins with a discussion on the separation of the Christian sect from its Jewish roots from the time of Paul, and concludes with the effect of myths and stereotyping of Jews, over the course of a thousand years, on the European mind. This brief overview is supposed to convey in four pages the essential understandings of the history of European anti-Semitism, contained in one entire text, *Antisemitism Through the Ages*.[40] The essence of these understandings is how anti-Semitism was transformed from a religious-based hatred of Jews, especially in the Middle Ages, to one of racial hatred in the 19th century. Wegner described the history of anti-Semitism as "one of the most sensitive and controversial aspects of Holocaust education" largely owing to the history of Christian/Jewish relations.[41] The answer to the dilemma of how to bridge the historical past with the sensitivities of the present is not an easy one. Controversy can be a great silencer. However, rather than omit or ignore issues, critical pedagogy and historical method seek interpretation to dilemmas by investigating sources of information and looking at issues of reliability and validity.[42] Yet, the brief treatment of the history of anti-Semitism found in countless curriculum guides does not require sustained analysis, only acceptance of a predetermined position.

Despite the curriculum guide's inadequacies, the authors' use of excerpted primary evidence is one of its better features. *However, the use of excerpts from Holocaust documents can be just as reckless as the introduction of excerpts from any other source; without context, they can mislead.* Other evidence from the historical past offered by the writers includes oral testimony, a kind of eyewitness account to the Holocaust. *Life Unworthy of Life* attempts to come to grips with the reality of the Holocaust through the use of these powerful excerpts. For example, one reading, taken from the trial transcript during the Nuremberg war crimes trials, entitled "The Medical Case," seemingly exposes a certain callous disregard for human life by German medical professionals who embraced Nazi ideology:

> PROSECUTOR: Let me draw your attention to Exhibit A, the Registration Form—the questionnaire you mentioned. Why was it necessary to include a category for 'Race'? DR. SCHULTZ: The Euthanasia Program was for the good of the *Volksgemeinschaft*, the German people. We had to know the race and nationality of each subject. Non-Aryans were potential threats to the purity and health of German blood and had to be removed, like an infection or a cancer.[43]

The excerpted response of Dr. Schultz is problematic. Within the framework or methodology of empathy, one would seek to understand under what conditions and for what reasons Schultz answered as he did, much like Stern's test to see if she could understand the actions of the women in *Frauen*, despite the fact that she possesses strong personal feelings about the Holocaust. However, the political nature of the Holocaust has created a climate in which students of history may find it politically incorrect to examine the motives of the perpetrators. In other words, one does not need to understand the motivations of the bad guys of the Holocaust, except to understand that they must have been motivated by evil. However, this is a simplistic and incomplete picture at best. One must study the intellectual historical record to know how individuals of Schultz's generation came to hold such ideas. Hence, the role of evidence is critical to understanding the complete picture.

Chronology is the lifeblood of history curriculum guides and textbooks. As such, *Life Unworthy of Life*—the title was borrowed from a Nazi medical classification—does a fairly good job of covering the developmental historical sequence (necessary themes) of the Holocaust, contained in topics such as Introduction/Overview; the antecedents to the Holocaust in "The Aftermath of World War I"; Hitler and the Nazi Party; Toward the Final Solution; Planet Auschwitz; The Rescuers; Resistance and Survival; Sounds of Silence: World Responses; and Aftermath: Consequences and Implication. Yet, the imposition of these themes relieves students from the experience of building their own categories of inquiry. Despite this problem, teachers who use this curriculum guide can help students by teaching the importance of chronology as a component or construct of empathy. For example, students should consider the relationship of chronology to understanding. One theme or avenue of inquiry is often necessary for an understanding of the next, and combined, they lead the historical investigator to an understanding of the whole. For example, without knowledge of the roots of anti-Semitism, students may believe that the Holocaust is a 20th century phenomenon and something that could have occurred only as a result of 20th century circumstances and attitudes.

While this curriculum guide does a better job than most in addressing the theme of anti-Semitism, it only alludes to Jewish life before the war—a second category or avenue of inquiry—through a series of family photographs which accompany some of the chapters. A correction of this serious neglect would give meaning to the now-recognized number of 6 million. After all, how can students understand what was lost if they do not understand what existed? Also, the dualistic approach most children take toward history prevents them from easily understanding degrees or levels; for example, to many students, all Germans were Nazis. Therefore, in examining the Holocaust, more emphasis needs to be placed on the collective and individual nature of action, choice, and response.

As for student activities contained in *Life Unworthy of Life*, they are generally more meaningful than those found is most curriculum guides dealing with the Holocaust, although few in number. The "Juror's Ballot," for example, asks students to decide if Dr. Schultz was guilty of crimes against humanity.[44] They are asked to base their evaluation on three principles: the Oath of Hippocrates, established moral principles or accepted standards of right and wrong, and German law. However, this activity is perhaps the only one which calls upon students to synthesize information and construct meaning. Conversely, the activity in which students are required to make a list of their daily activities and caloric intake is a simple listing task which does not call for students to offer any interpretation. One might argue that students will be able to connect the obvious—they consume far more calories than were given to camp prisoners, and they are free to move about while prisoners were confined. However, the authors fail to impart why this knowledge is important to the student's over-all understanding of the Holocaust. One objection to textbook or curriculum guide interpretations of historical events is that tasks—student activities—are viewed as reinforcement endeavors for predetermined interpretations. Whereas historical empathy as a process of investigation *is the task* and the interpretation not predetermined, but constructed based upon examined evidence.

While this guide, like most dealing with the Holocaust, underrepresents the fate of the Roma during the Holocaust, it at least does mention in a lengthy definition how Gypsies were defined by the Nazi government, and offers a brief explanation of how they were viewed by the German Criminal Police and the SS. The failure to adequately address the Gypsy experience during the Holocaust is common among Holocaust curricula, and is the source of much criticism leveled by individuals concerned with Gypsy representation in Holocaust studies, such as Professor Ian Hancock, a prominent spokesman for the World Gypsy organization.[45] These types of omissions are common in textbooks and curriculum guides. As such, they convey the message that the persecution of non-Jewish groups by Nazi Germany holds only a minor place within the overall historical record, or an unstated belief that actual numbers rather than percentages indicate substantial loss. What is more disturbing is the notion that quantity is a sort of official determiner of degree of suffering or pain.

Perhaps what can be said about *Life Unworthy of Life* is that it provides a starting place for both the novice teacher and the student who wish to engage in a study of the Holocaust. No curriculum guide is perfect. All have their weaknesses. What this guide offers more than most is the opportunity to understand the Holocaust to a limited extent from multiple perspectives: the perpetrators, the victims, and to a lesser degree, the by-stander or observer. Despite this point, this curriculum guide fails to inspire one to ask questions that require breadth, depth, or sustained study. Rather, one is lulled into a certain comfort that the right questions have been asked and answered and that all that is required is to execute a few activities so that the correct interpretation is reinforced. Historical empathy as a framework for inquiry stands in sharp contrast to this largely one-dimensional account. As such, its constructs define the rigor of historical study. Moreover, textbooks and curriculum guides are no substitute for the experience of analysis. One final consideration for *Life Unworthy of Life* is the extent to which its authors convey the importance of teaching the Holocaust. They, like others, seem to believe that the mere teaching of the topic is enough to bring about the social change they believe is needed so that *something like the Holocaust doesn't happen again*. As for this history-as-social-therapy approach, knowledge of the historical past alone has rarely served as a bulwark against government-sanctioned terror and oppression.

The Holocaust: Prejudice Unleashed

Social studies teachers, particularly history teachers, often resonate to a social criticism approach to teaching history.[46] Social criticism fits easily into the affective domain as it explores individual and collective attitudes, values, and beliefs. However, the problem with working in the affective domain is that teachers often use history to inculcate compassion or other similar feelings within students rather than offer them a useful framework with which they can conduct individual inquiry. Most inquirers into the Holocaust cannot leave their study without feelings of compassion for the victims; however, the primary purpose of investigating the Holocaust should not begin with the aim of feeling the pain of others. Inquiry begins by formulating questions (problems) that necessitate study. When one fails to use the tools of the discipline to understand the Holocaust and instead substitutes how they feel for what they have found out, historical actors or groups of actors, such as European Jewry, often become either romanticized or relegated to victimhood. These perspectives serve as places in the mind from which those who have been romanticized or relegated to victimhood may never escape—the more familiar "all Germans were bad, while all Jews were pure" approach. Consequently, efforts to teach concepts or topics such as "European Jewry Before the War" often become a journey into nostalgia rather than an exploration of the historic moment with real men, women, and children, when the evidence teachers present only represents a view of eastern European Jewish village life as quaint.

In *The Holocaust: Prejudice Unleashed*, writers offer teachers and students first-hand accounts of Jewish village life with reprinted detailed maps from Martin Gilbert's *Atlas of the Holocaust*.[47] Their selected reading, "Bilke, My Hometown—Zichrona Livracha: A Memorial Tribute," describes a journey of the soul taken by a few of the town's remaining Jewish inhabitants as a "sacred duty to record the glory and wonders of our once living heritage."[48] Although richly excerpted, students will only be able to glimpse another way of life, far removed in both distance and time, through vignettes such as this. If student knowledge about eastern European Jewish life were allowed to be shaped by such a limited vision, then perspective would necessarily be distorted. All communities experience periods of stress, uncertainty, and angst. To include only nostalgic accounts of Jewish life in eastern Europe disposes students to accept European Jewish life as quaint and somehow different from any community life they themselves may have experienced.

In order to help students understand the concept that Jews in Europe had different historical experiences—all Jews were not the same—the writers have taken care to compare and contrast, in column form, eastern European Jewry to the western European Jewish experience. This encapsulates for both the teacher and the student the major differences between eastern and western European Jewry. Added to this, the subtopic "The Jews in Interwar Europe 1919-1939" covers the various theories regarding anti-Semitism, such as the economic theory which suggests that Jews were hated because of their economic success, to the intrinsic theory of anti-Semitism, which supports the notion that because Jews were hated in a number of European countries, they must have done something to bring this hatred about. However, students once again are merely the receivers and not the participants in the construction of meaning. Thus, teaching the Holocaust and teaching students how to learn about the Holocaust are two different endeavors. The latter will sustain them whatever the topic they choose to investigate. The former is a one-shot deal which requires the teacher to be an expert on every topic.

In their interpretation, the authors make two questionable claims: 1) that the Holocaust was the result of a carefully drawn genocidal plan of the legally established government of Germany, and 2) that apathy characterized the pre-Holocaust setting in Germany, and the rest of the western world. This apathy, then, naturally led to feelings or attitudes of indifference, which resulted in a critical mass of bystanders. First, the notion of a carefully drawn genocidal plan has been challenged by such historians as Saul Friedlander and Yehuda Bauer, former chair of Holocaust studies at Hebrew University.[49] In Friedlander's recent account of the Holocaust, the author claims that Nazi policies regarding German Jews were often ambiguous and contradictory, while the decision to exterminate the Jews came only after Germany's attack on the Soviet Union.[50] Likewise, Bauer found little to no evidence to support the claim of a well-drawn plan of genocide. Instead, he asserts that the "final aim" alluded to in the now-famous *Schnellbrief* (memo) penned by Heydrich indicated a plan of expulsion, not extermination. The death camps, he added, "were a much later development."[51] According to Bauer, "the Nazis wanted the Jews to leave Germany, but they were not quite sure how to achieve their goal."[52]

Second, what the authors have mistaken for apathy was more likely the result of more than 100 years of growing nationalism, which found a natural complement in the racial theories of the late 19th century. Consider the following: both Italy and Germany were late to unify—Germany did not unify until 1871 under Bismarck. The forces which shaped these unifications included wide-spread aspirations toward nationalism. As an ideology, nationalism embraces sameness or likeness and rebukes foreignness, which it seeks to expel. The unification of Italy which preceded that of Germany, for example, rallied around the idea of expelling Germanic people from provinces in present-day Northern Italy. Consequently, the presence of Jews, always considered a foreign element, represented a certain disequilibrium following a century of growing nationalism whose effect was enhanced by racial theories toward the end of the century. Moreover, Germany was in the best position to absorb these complementary ideas as its people were among the most literate. The use of apathy as an explanation for the role of the bystander completely ignores the possibility that Europeans, Germans and others, were influenced to a greater extent by nationalistic motives and impulses. What these curriculum developers might want to look at are the effects of nationalism and racial theories as justifications for a lack of action—a lessons-well-learned-approach. Likewise, reducing the Holocaust to a carefully-drawn plan misses the mark through its failure to acknowledge conflicting interpretations of one of the most crucial topics of the Holocaust: the effect of German anti-Semitism. However, these insights are not gained without careful study. Therefore, teachers and students will find the shortest route to understanding the Holocaust to be the carefully-drawn-genocidal-plan route, rather than the tortuous path which requires evaluating Nazi policies that worked and those that failed and why.[53] The former is simplistic and requires little more than reading textbook accounts, the latter often leads to contradiction and ambiguity, both of which characterize the Holocaust and other historical events.

What the authors do provide for student examination are a set of laws aimed at excluding Jews from mainstream German life from early 1933, to those affecting Jews in occupied territories, passed by the Nazi German government in the middle of 1940. While the inclusion of documents such as these are noteworthy, and fulfill one of the much-discussed National History Standards which call for students to acquire experience with primary evidence, two problems remain: biased selection and problematic student questions. Again, the act of selecting what students have an opportunity to examine automatically creates bias. However, bias can also occur within questions framed by authors. Rabinsky and Danks ask the following: "Why were these laws passed and enforced with little or no opposition from any source?" Their background section contains little to no information which would allow students to answer such a question. Students could likely construct an answer as to why these laws were passed based upon the wording of the laws themselves, but there is scant background information pertaining to enforcement or opposition. Additionally, the authors have largely ignored historical accounts of opposition to Nazi policies, such as non-Jewish women in Berlin who protested the arrest of their Jewish husbands, or the protests of American Jews, along with protests by Germany's own economic advisors prior to the Nazi boycott of Jewish-owned stores.[54] Thus, posing this question for students to answer without proper background knowledge implies a certain built-in validity, or a we-want-you-to-understand-the-Holocaust-this-way-because-it-is-true approach.

One of the best examples of leading students in a predetermined direction is found in chapter 4 and merits a brief discussion. The problem is with the activity guide for the *Wannsee Conference*, a docudrama which depicts the conference in Wannsee—a district on the outskirts of Berlin—where plans for the Final Solution were discussed on January 20, 1942. Following the movie, teachers are supposed to engage students in a discussion using the question guide developed by the authors.[55] However, some questions on the discussion list are trivial and ill considered. For example, question #9 asks the following: "How would you feel about eating lunch after a discussion such as the one held at the Wannsee Conference?" The question is both silly and meaningless. What does the notion of eating lunch have to do with understanding and responding to issues of cruelty, brutality, immoral or unethical conduct? The politically correct response is one which reassures the teacher that the student is sufficiently upset by what he or she has heard, yet if such a reply occurred, it would likely be little more than a perfunctory remark. High schoolers of the 1990s in the United States were not Germans of the 1940s. Rather than asking students to imagine how they would feel about eating lunch after witnessing such a discussion, teachers should guide students to investigate the actions and motives of the perpetrators in addition to accounts of the victims, and interpret for themselves the meaning of places such as Auschwitz or meetings such as the one at Wannsee. This suggestion is rooted in the theoretical framework of historical empathy, a model whose premise is that students should thoroughly examine the subject and use the tools of the discipline (history) to construct an interpretation.

Facing History and Ourselves

Few educators will argue with the noble purpose of the latest edition of this resource text: to teach that "history is largely the result of human decisions, that prevention is possible, and education must have a moral component if it is to make a difference."[56] Facing History and Ourselves (FHAO) is one of the most well-known organizations in Holocaust education circles and one that produces a popular curriculum resource guide of the same name—*Facing History and Ourselves*. According to one of its founders, Margot Strom, the approach taken by FHAO organizers is to instruct teachers in workshop settings on how to use the tools of the humanities—inquiry, analysis, and interpretation. Following these workshops, teachers are expected to return to their classrooms as social educators, charged with the responsibility of shaping the moral fiber of their students. Moreover, FHAO is clear about its program's aims: commitment to content that furthers democratic values and beliefs.[57] Like other curriculum efforts we have examined, *Facing History* takes an inoculation or prevention approach to this historical event, albeit most historians would likely grimace at the thought of "history as therapy."

FHAO's concern about current social problems prevents it from engaging teachers and students in seeking historical understanding. Its stated and implied goals are to help shape a society whose ultimate goal is to eliminate social inequity by shaping a morally responsive individual. The quest of FHAO is to "build a community of thinkers."[58] The primary endeavor of the program is to help teachers and their students to formulate moral principles. As such, moral education is the goal and purpose of Facing History and can be accomplished only through discourse. More than anything else, FHAO is a forum for teaching the skills of decision making and not the skills of history making. While *Facing History and Ourselves* may find advocates in sociology or psychology classrooms, it may not appeal to teachers of history. The FHAO approach is clearly a sociological one and not an historical one. Hence, little pretense about historical thinking is offered by the writers. While the social education approach to the teaching of history—teaching students how to examine and solve social problems—may appeal to some, most secondary history teachers would likely admit that they are largely confined to teaching the state-mandated curriculum, which often is framed in a political history format. Secondary world and American history programs usually focus on leaders, discoveries, and important dates. Few make room in the history curriculum for overhauling the thinking patterns of students in order to create sensitive and tolerant individuals.

Moreover, without guidance, most teachers would be unable to effectively use the *Facing History* text for the purpose of inquiry. The scope of the Holocaust is vast and requires sustained study. Despite its 500 plus pages, teachers must wade through pages of text that have little to do with the actual events of the Holocaust. For example, centuries of anti-Semitic behavior which laid the groundwork for European attitudes regarding Jews are dealt with in only four pages, while some forty pages contain readings on the individual's relationship to society. While the writers fail to use non-fictional accounts from the historical actors of the Holocaust in the discussion on the "individual and society," they introduce others whose historical experiences have nothing to do with the Holocaust. For example, following the reading entitled "Harrison Bergeron,"[59] the authors ask students to read "First Encounters in North America," which describes European explorers and how they understood the peoples of the New World with whom they came into contact. This reading has no direct bearing on the Holocaust. Hence, this curriculum product takes the approach that one historical understanding or moment will apply to others, regardless of time, context, or circumstance. The writers follow this reading with one on slavery in colonial and early America. Why slavery if the Holocaust is the historical event under discussion? Do the authors regard slavery in the same sense they regard the Holocaust? The employment of comparative pain leads the student to confuse historical events and simply lump them all together as holocausts.

Perhaps most illuminating is the resource text's lack of depth concerning the identity of the victims. For example, Jewish life in Europe before the war is sorely neglected. The victims, Jews, Roma, religious dissenters, the infirm, and others, have little voice. We have little idea of who they were or what their worlds were like. Their stories only appear as support for the writers overarching concept of being different, and not for understanding them or their historic moment. Thus, the number *six million* fails to connect real men, women, and children to the study of the Holocaust. This lack of connection goes back to the goal and purpose of FHAO, which is to use the Holocaust as a platform for teaching moral behavior and shaping attitudes, rather than to help students acquire an understanding of the Holocaust as an historical event in its own right. Even the questions at the end of each chapter direct students to consider how the reading applies to their world today, not to the past.

By the end of the text, the Holocaust becomes diffused into a web of human rights issues and messages. Under the theme "Bystanders and Rescuers" (chapter

8), the authors discuss Holocaust rescuers such as Raoul Wallenberg,[60] a Swedish diplomat credited with protecting more than 70,000 Jews, along with other well-known rescuers. However, woven into the topic of rescue are excerpts from a teacher and his students from Bosnia who make a plea to the world to stop war and hate. Their plea is followed by an excerpt from Liv Ullman's autobiography in which she speaks of traveling to Somalia and encountering children who have no choices in life. Reading #18 concludes with the following questions: "What are ways individuals can help to bring more choices to children in places like Somalia and Bosnia?" and "What roles in particular can American students play in this process?"[61] The implications of this chapter are clear: students will not understand the nature of altruism in the face of war and terror during World War II. Instead, the FHAO approach to the theme of altruism seems to be a certain "we can instill the altruistic spirit in American youth today if we put them in touch with stories of rescuers of the Holocaust." Yet, teaching American students how they can act in an altruistic way will not ensure that they will transfer that learning and understand the role of rescuers during World War II.

What *Facing History* does, like other instructional materials with particular agendas, is discount the importance of words in the construction of understanding. For example, the authors pose two questions about the definition of genocide. One, "How important is a precise definition?" Two, "Can such a definition get in the way of our ability to identify and acknowledge inhumanity and suffering?" They follow these questions with an observation that "others" place their own meaning on the word genocide, which includes:

> the destruction of the native American population by various European colonial powers and later the United States; the enslavement of Africans in the United States; Iraq's treatment of the Kurds after the Gulf War; Serbia's policy of ethnic cleansing in what was once Yugoslavia; the anarchy in Somalia that has led to mass starvation.[62]

FHAO's inclusion of these definitions implies approval for understanding the meaning of genocide driven by relativism, despite its opening remarks that "Facing History is not a program that is mired in relativism."[63] Moreover, its persistent use of present-day analogies seems an added contradiction to their disclaimer.

The final two chapters, "Historical Legacies" and "Choosing to Participate" press at the heart of FHAO's implied and stated goal: moral education for American youth. No fewer than twelve readings are excerpts concerning the plight of African Americans and their struggle for acceptance, while numerous others are devoted to events such as the atrocities perpetrated by the Khmer Rouge in Cambodia, violence in urban America, and the Asian struggle for acceptance. Accordingly, most would agree that FHAO succeeds in its mission of sensitizing students to domestic issues of racial intolerance, violence, and the perceived spiraling effects of personal and emotional detachment in a post-modern world. Yet, one might rightly question the notion of history as therapy. This philosophy might serve psychology and sociology programs well, but what about the history classroom? For some, doing history will require little more than memorizing a shopping list of names, dates, and assorted facts. This collection without analysis or sustained study leaves the student unconnected to the historical record and creates a distance between the past and present which is difficult to bridge. For others, doing history means viewing the themes or outcomes of historical events for the purpose of righting present-day wrongs. However, for social studies teachers charged with the responsibility of guiding students to higher levels of understanding or critical thinking, they must first help students to acquire the tools of the discipline. These tools or constructs of empathy include teaching context, selecting sources or evidence for examination, presenting multiple perspectives, and helping students to construct a reasonable explanation of a particular historical event. Hence, the outcome of this latter approach, an understanding of the event gleaned through sustained study, stands in sharp contrast to the use of history as a curative for social ills which conflicts in a fundamental fashion with the investigation and interpretation of historical events.

Conclusion

To engage students in a study of the Holocaust is to open the floodgates of seemingly endless inquiry. Its paths and interpretations are many, while clear-cut answers are few or elusive. What muddies the waters surrounding the Holocaust are opposing groups who claim ownership of the event and as such are determined that their perspective of it is rendered the *official* interpretation. Often these groups sponsor curricula which entitles them to offer students a predetermined outcome. Perhaps the most riveting event in terms of historical scholarship is the current libel suit between David Irving and Deborah Lipstadt. Its challenge to the sanctity of historical interpretation is chilling. What is clear about the Holocaust and teaching is that the interest in this historical event is large and growing, and that a symbiotic relationship exists between what students have the opportunity to explore and their understanding of this encompassing historical moment. Therefore, a number of considerations face teachers as they decide on approaches to this historical event. One will almost certainly be whether or not to use prepared curriculum materials. Yet, as Wineburg points out, textbook accounts of an historical event employ "the notion that the way things are told are simply the way things were." Therefore, student understanding has already been largely predetermined. This notion is true of most Holocaust curricula which are often written for purposes other than understanding the event itself. Thus, if one believes that understanding is dependent upon sources examined, teachers must first be able to look beyond the packaging of an individual curriculum product and evaluate its efficacy regarding historical understanding.

Yet no curriculum guide can replace solid teacher knowledge of the subject and responsible curriculum decision making in terms of purpose, appropriate strategy, and quality of student activities. For these reasons we must seek ways of organizing large historical events so that the end result or outcome rests upon an informed mind. This essay has looked to the body of research on historical empathy, in particular the model articulated by Yeager and others, as a way to help students understand the Holocaust. The four constructs of empathy in the model outlined by Yeager and others comprises the essential steps embedded in historical methodology. Yet, an added dimension of this model is the notion of empathy as a way of understanding, and outgrowth of sustained investigation. Therefore, it provides students with a framework for examining an event with the result that they will have acquired an understanding of the motives and actions of the historical actors without endorsement or condemnation.

However, while most studies on empathy looked at how student understanding was deepened following an investigation of the actions of key individuals within the context of their times versus textbook accounts with predetermined interpretations, this essay suggests that in order to understand sweeping historical events, we must expand the definition of empathy to include multiple actors. We must apply this empathetical model to sweeping historical events. In other words, an understanding of Hitler's aims and objectives, what he knew or didn't know about European attitudes toward Jews or other groups antagonistic to the dominant group, will not help us to understand how those in other nations such as Poland and Hungary readily complied with Nazi policy regarding Nazi deportation and extermination policies. Without broadening the scope of the empathetical construct that deals with the actions of an historical figure, answers to the obvious question when it comes to the Holocaust, *How was something like this possible?* will largely remain out of our grasp. Therefore, a logical starting place for understanding the Holocaust might be with the obvious question, *Why were Jews targeted for extermination?* This question leads us then to building categories for investigation. Moreover, social studies or history teachers generally develop instructional units based upon large events such as the American Revolution or the Civil War, whose subtopics can be understood as categories of inquiry.

One such category is the role that anti-Semitism has played historically. Other categories or paths of inquiry might be the effect of 19th century German nationalism on early 20th century attitudes, or the Versailles Treaty of 1919 and its destabilizing effect on Germany's social structure and economy in the early 1920s. The number of paths of inquiry regarding the Holocaust is daunting. Yet without sustained investigation, we are left with simplistic explanations: all Germans were evil, all Jews were saintly, or only one man, Hitler, was responsible. Thus, the introduction of such a riveting event should begin by category building. Once teachers have helped students to select avenues of inquiry, the next step is to select sources for examination or analysis. As Totten pointed out, the Holocaust has become a large media industry. Therefore, the question of bias, which is inherent in the selection process, becomes a major consideration.

Teachers who select what materials students have an opportunity to examine must first understand their own positionality or world view. They must be clear on their purpose for introducing the topic of the Holocaust. For example, are they drawn to the Holocaust because they believe that it contains moral lessons for today? or because it offers a multitude of primary and secondary sources for examination? Is their classroom first and foremost a forum for shaping the moral fiber of students or for strengthening their ability to deal with complex historical events so that they understand the event without endorsing or condemning its historical actors? I do not suggest that the two cannot mutually exist in a single classroom, but rather that the steps to learning how to do and understand history do not become subsumed under the umbrella of social criticism. The art of learning how to do history speaks to an acquisition of skills, tools, or dispositions of the discipline of history with a measure of objectivity and understanding as outcomes. Social criticism on the other hand is usually grounded in ideology and agenda building. To mistake social criticism for history results in students who feel or hold certain attitudes about an historical event without understanding the sources of these beliefs or the event itself.

The role of context then should ground the topic under study rather than serve as a springboard to unrelated historical events. In building context, this paper takes an opposite approach to that of the model articulated by Yeager and others. While the latter emanates from the actions or decisions of a key figure, which arguably could spiral outward until all categories of inquiry are identified, the former suggests that context building begins with an identification of paths of inquiry or categories after which an investigation into each can be launched. The reason for taking this approach lies within the types of things most students want to know about the Holocaust. Again, the most common question students ask is *How could something like the Holocaust happen?* Theories abound. To point to this or that as cause is too simplistic. To single out one historical actor or even a group of actors will not enable students to find the answer to their question. However, through a sustained or robust study of the Holocaust, students will likely come to understand that no clear answer to their question exists. Their search only yields more questions. Yet it is this very process that enables them to build any real understanding. The end result of such a process should demonstrate that the individual researcher has considered context, evidence, and the nature of her position in weaving together an explanation of the past. It should also show how the framework of empathy has guided her investigation and enabled her to view the actions of multiple historical actors without endorsement or condemnation and allowed her to render a reasonable interpretation, keeping in mind that sources of evidence not consulted might affect her current interpretation.

If we as teachers fail to help our students acquire a useable and useful framework from which they can launch and execute their own investigations, they have little choice but to draw their knowledge from scores of prepared instructional materials which contain the historical interpretations of others. Regardless of the quality of prepared curricula, providing students with a useable framework, such as historical empathy for investigating and constructing an historical interpretation, is superior to offering them a thinned version of an historical event where their only role is that of believer.

Notes

1. G. Lerner, *Why History Matters* (New York: Oxford University Press, 1997), 123.

2. Lerner, *Why History Matters*, 123.

3. L. Levstik, "Negotiating the History Landscape," *Theory and Research in Social Education* 24 (Fall 1996): 393-7.

4. For an in-depth treatment of the topics, historical empathy, and historical empathy and the Holocaust, see S. J. Foster and E. A. Yeager, "The Role of Empathy in the Development of Historical Understanding," *International Journal of Social Education* 13 (Spring/Summer 1998): 1-24; K. L. Riley, "Historical Empathy and the Holocaust: Theory into Practice," *International Journal of Social Education* 13 (Spring/Summer 1998): 32-42; B. Stern, "Addressing the Concept of Historical Empathy with *Frauen: German Women Confront the Holocaust," International Journal of Social Education* 13 (Spring/Summer 1998): 43-8.

5. K. D. Vinson, "The Traditions Revisited: Instructional Approach and High School Social Studies Teachers," *Theory and Research in Social Education* 26 (Winter 1996): 50-82.

6. See M. T. Downey, "Perspective Taking and Historical Thinking: Doing History in a Fifth-Grade Classroom" (paper presented at the annual meeting of the American Educational Research Association, San Francisco, 1995), for a brief discussion on the relationship between historical thinking and affective learning.

7. D. D. Guttenplan, "The Holocaust on Trial," *Atlantic Monthly* (February 2000): 45-66. The trial between Irving and Lipstadt has now been settled in favor of Lipstadt.

8. The particularists refer to those who believe that the Holocaust was an event in Jewish history first and foremost, while the universalists believe that themes of the Holocaust must be applied to current social problems in order to seek understanding and solutions; the intentionalists insist that the Final Solution of the Jews was a planned event, while functionalists assert that the Final Solution was an outcome of the trials and errors of Nazi policy and bureaucracy.

9. For a brief discussion on the "inherent wickedness of the German people," see the state of Florida curriculum guide, *The Holocaust, Can it Happen to Me?* Library of the Holocaust Memorial Resource and Education Center, 851 N. Maitland Ave., Maitland, Florida.

10. D. J. Goldhagen, *Hitler's Willing Executioners: Ordinary Germans and the Holocaust* (New York: Knopf 1997).

11. For an account of the trial and opposing positions of historians, see, D. D. Guttenplan, "The Holocaust on Trial," 45-66.

12. Guttenplan, "The Holocaust on Trial," 62.

13. S. Wineburg, "Historical Thinking and Other Unnatural Acts," *Phi Delta Kappan* 80 (March 1999): 488-500.

14. K. L. Riley, "The Politically Correct Curriculum in Progressive Education," *Insights* 30 (1994): 18-9.

15. M. T. Glynn, G. Bock, and K. C. Cohn, *American Youth and the Holocaust* (New York: National Jewish Resource Center, 1982), xix.

16. Glynn et al., *American Youth and the Holocaust*, xxiv.

17. M. M. Downey, "Toward a Synthesis in History Education. Research, Instruction, and Public Education." *Theory & Research in Social Education* 24 (Fall 1996): 397-402; K. Barton, "Everybody Knows What History Is," *Theory and Research in Social Education* 24 (Fall 1996): 402-4; E. A. Yeager, S. J. Foster, S. D. Maley, T. Anderson, J. W. Morris, and O. L. Davis Jr., "The Role of Empathy in the Development of Historical Understanding," (paper presented at the Annual Meeting of the National Council for the Social Studies, Washington, D.C., November 1996).

18. Glynn et al., *American Youth and the Holocaust*, xxiv.

19. See the Showtime Original Movie, *The Rescuers*, a B. Streisand Production (Spring 1998); also, see K. L. Riley, *The Rescuers*, a curriculum guide prepared for Kidsnet Television, Washington, D.C. (Spring 1998).

20. E. A. Yeager, Foster, Maley, Anderson, Morris, and Davis, "The Role of Empathy in the Development of Historical Understanding"; S. J. Foster, "Using Historical Empathy to Excite Students About the Study of History: Can you Empathize with Neville Chamberlain?" *Social Studies* 90 (Jan/Feb 1999):18-25.

21. S. Stern, "Beyond the Rhetoric: An Historian's View of the National Standards for United States History," *Journal of Education* 176 (1994): 61-71.

22. E. A. Yeager and S. J. Foster, "The Role of *Empathy* in the Development of *Historical* Understanding" (paper presented at the College and University Faculty Assembly, Washington, D.C., 1996); Yeager, Foster, Maley, Anderson, Morris, and Davis, "The Role of Empathy in the Development of Historical Understanding," 3.

23. For a discussion on historical thinking and perspective taking see, R. Ashby and P. Lee, "Children's Concepts of Empathy and Understanding in History," in C. Portal, ed., *The History Curriculum for Teachers* (London: Falmer Press 1987): 62-88; Portal, "Empathy as an objective for history teaching," in Portal, ed., *The History Curriculum for Teachers* 89-99; P. Rogers, "History: Why, What and How?" *Teaching of History Series* 60 (1990); and D. Shemilt, "Adolescent Ideas About Evidence and Methodology in History," in Portal ed., *The History Curriculum for Teachers*, 39-61.

24. E. A. Yeager and S. J. Foster, "The Role of *Empathy* in the Development of *Historical* Understanding."

25. See note 24.

26. For multiple theories of anti-Semitism, see S. S. Almog, ed., *Antisemitism Through the Ages,* translated by N. H. Reisner (Oxford: Pergamon, 1988).

27. H. Kohn, *The Mind of Germany: The Education of a Nation* (New York: Scribner, 1960).

28. See T. Keneally, *Schindler's List*, (New York: Simon and Schuster, 1993); for a lengthy review of *Schindler's List* visit the *Boston Globe's* website at http://bostonreview.mit.edu/BR19.3/stone.html.

29. For Stern's treatment of *Frauen* within the context of the constructs of empathy defined by Yeager and others, see "Addressing the Concept of Historical Empathy with *Frauen: German Women Confront the Holocaust*," *International Journal of Social Education* 13 (Spring/Summer 1998): 43-8; also, see A. Owings, *Frauen: German Women Recall the Third Reich* (New Brunswick, New Jersey: Rutgers University Press, 1993).

30. T. Cole, *Selling the Holocaust: From Auschwitz to Schindler, How History Is Bought, Packaged and Sold* (New York: Routledge, 1999); according to the History Channel recommended website for *The Holocaust Online Magazine*, at http://www.ios.com/~kimel19/schindler.html, the wife of O. Schindler has written her memoirs entitled "Emily Schindler's Memoirs," in which Schindler is characterized as "a greedy man whose main interest in saving Polish Jews from Adolph Hitler's death camps was to have cheap labor to keep his china factory going."

31. For discussions on "positionality," see B. A. VanSledright, "The Nature and Role of Positionality in Historical Thinking and Understanding" (paper presented at the Annual Meeting of the American Educational Research Association, Montreal, Canada, April 1999); and K. C. Barton, "'Best not to forget them': Positionality and Students' Ideas About Historical Significance in Northern Ireland" (paper presented at the Annual Meeting of the American Educational Research Association, Montreal, Canada, April 1999).

32. M. E. Blum, "Continuity and Discontinuity, Change and Duration: Hobbes' Riddle of the Theseus and the Diversity of Historical Logics," *Theory and Research in Social Education* 24 (Fall 1996): 360-90.

33. O. L. Davis Jr., K. L. Riley, E. A. Yeager, B. S. Stern. "Historical Empathy and the Holocaust: Theory into Practice" *Symposium, Annual Meeting of the National Council for the Social Studies*, Cincinnati, Ohio (November 1997).

34. P. Seixas, "Our Place in the Cottage Industry of Collective Memory," in "Symposium, Research, Instruction," and Public Policy in the History Curriculum," *Theory and Research in Social Education* 24 (Fall, 1996): 406-14.

35. S. S. Totten, "A Holocaust Curriculum Evaluation Instrument: Admirable Aim, Poor Result," *Journal of Curriculum and Supervision* 13 (1998): 148-66.

36. E. Dlin, "New Paradigms for Holocaust Education?" (paper presented at the World Congress of Jewish Studies, August 1997).

37. T. L. Epstein, "Sociocultural Approaches to Young People's Historical Understanding," *Social Education* 61 (1997): 28-31.

38. S. M. Bolkosky, B. R. Ellias, and D. Harris, *Life Unworthy of Life* (Farmington Hills, Michigan: Center for the Study of the Child, 1987).

39. Bolkosky, Ellias, and Harris, *Life Unworthy of Life*, 175-76.

40. For numerous theories on anti-Semitism see Almog, ed., *Antisemitism Through the Ages*.

41. See G. Wegner, "The Historical Roots of Antisemitism: Implications for the Classroom" (paper presented at the College and University Faculty Assembly of the National Council for the Social Studies, Cincinnati, Ohio, November 1997).

42. S. J. Foster and R. Rosch, "Teaching World War I from Multiple Perspectives," *Social Education* 61 (1997): 434.

43. Bolkosky, Ellias, and Harris, *Life Unworthy of Life*, 111.

44. For the "Juror's Ballot," see *Life Unworthy of Life,* 18.

45. I. Hancock, "Jewish Responses to the Porrajmos (The Romani Holocaust)," (paper presented at Remembering for the Future International Conference on the Holocaust, Berlin, Germany, March 1994).

46. K. D. Vinson, "The 'Traditions' Revisited: Instructional Approach and High School Social Studies Teachers," *Theory and Research in Social Education* 26 (Winter 1996): 50-82.

47. L. Rabinsky and C. Danks, eds., *The Holocaust: Prejudice Unleashed* (a curriculum guide sponsored by the Ohio Council on Holocaust Education: Columbus, Ohio, 1989); 14-5.

48. See Reisman, in Rabinsky and Danks, *The Holocaust*, chapters 4 and 7.

49. See S. Friedlander, *Nazi Germany and the Jews* (New York, 1997); and, Y. Bauer, *A History of the Holocaust* (New York, 1982).

50. Friedlander, *Nazi Germany and the Jews*, 4.

51. Bauer, *A History of the Holocaust*, 151.

52. Bauer, *A History of the Holocaust*, 101.

53. K. A. Schleunes, *The Twisted Road to Auschwitz: Nazi Policy toward German Jews, 1933-1939* (Illinois, 1990).

54. For a discussion on protests against Nazi policy, see M. R. Marrus, *The Holocaust in History* (*NAL*, 1989); Bauer, *A History of the Holocaust,* and Schleunes, *The Twisted Road to Auschwitz.*

55. Rabinsky and Danks, eds. *The Holocaust*, chapters 4 and 21.

56. *Facing History and Ourselves*, (a Holocaust resource text sponsored by the Facing History and Ourselves Foundation, Brookline, Massachusetts, 1994): xvi.

57. *Facing History*, xxi.

58. *Facing History*, xxii.

59. *Facing History*, 58-64.

60. *Facing History*, 408-9.

61. *Facing History*, 411.

62. *Facing History*, 461.

63. See the preface of *Facing History*, xxi.

Chapter 9

Historical Empathy in Theory and Practice: Some Final Thoughts

Stuart J. Foster

The purpose of this concluding chapter is two-fold. First, it aims to clarify and to amplify some of the key theoretical components of historical empathy variously acknowledged both by authors associated with this book and by other scholars in the field. Second, it briefly explores how empathy's various theoretical constructs may be translated into practice in history classrooms.

Before tackling these two important issues, recognition must first be given to the fact that empathy remains a problematic and contested term. As Lee and Ashby note in chapter 3, any absolute definition of empathy typically remains subject to dispute. According to Knight, although the origins of the word "empathy" may be traced back to the ancient Greeks (it was used, for example, in Aristotle's *Rhetoric*), its modern use locates it in the parlance of late nineteenth century Germany. Knight claims that the term is "implicated in the hazy notion of *verstehen*" and that it always has been ambiguous.[1] Despite its lack of precision, the term "empathy" has been widely used in, for example, the caring professions and in psychological studies. Indeed, empathy's most common form of expression appears to derive from the field of psychology, but even here its meaning is unclear: for example, Goldstein and Michaels cite seventeen separate definitions of the term.[2] References to psychological works produce myriad meanings: role taking, involvement, identification, sympathetic cognition, feeling with another, and so on. No universal definition emerges.

One may argue that the semantic problems experienced by psychologists are not pertinent to the context within which the historian works. The essential difference is that the historian is concerned with understanding the past and as a consequence is not able, as the psychologist is, to confer with individuals in the present. Knight refers to the psychologist's ability to establish a "reciprocal context" for a "contemporary relationship," whereas the historian is concerned with the distance between the past and present.[3] Shemilt sees this characteristic as unique to the historian: "It is this conceptual difference, this dislocation in the world view of past and present, that the empathizing historian seeks to remedy."[4] Cooper concurs, stating that the psychologist's meanings of empathy are of limited use in the study of history.[5] Clearly, a fundamental difference in the use of empathy in the two fields lies in the availability of hindsight as a way of understanding and interpreting the past in a meaningful way.

Despite these differences, however, confusion over meanings of historical empathy similarly exists. For example, Knight cites a 1986 English survey of 81 history teachers who defined the term as everything from "sympathy" to "understanding of others" to "seeing things as if in another's position." For Knight, the evidence against using empathy in the teaching of history is overwhelming; he asserts that it is a "profoundly unhelpful term in history."[6] Other critics of the term would agree, questioning the logic of planning, assessing, and teaching a concept which cannot be defined. Undeniably, therefore, empathy in history requires greater clarity and more adequate understanding.

In addition to empathy's definitional problems, empathy in history consistently has evoked ideological dispute. For example, the 1980s debate over the implementation of the General Certificate of Secondary Education (GCSE) and the National Curriculum History in England revealed deep divisions over the meaning of the concept of empathy. In England, conservative critics of education, who advocated a traditional content-based approach to history teaching, claimed that the concept was ahistorical, even politically dangerous, because history teachers apparently would be able to "manipulate students by depriving them of essential knowledge—that is indoctrination . . . and this is the essential purpose of the empathy exercise."[7] Prime Minister Margaret Thatcher concurred, fiercely declaring that "New History," "with its emphasis on concepts rather than chronology and empathy rather than facts, was at the root of much that was going wrong."[8] Significantly, when the Conservative government set out its National Curriculum programs of study for history a few years later, the word "empathy" was expunged from the final mandates. Without question the ideological parallels between the controversy in England and the uproar over the UCLA National History Standards Project in the United States are strikingly apparent.[9]

Attacks on empathy, however, have not only been the preserve of the political right. Jenkins, for example, has offered a sharp and provocative postmodernist stab at the concept.[10] Fundamental to Jenkins's argument is that any and all understanding of the past may be constructed from only the distant, and thereby necessarily flawed, perspective of the present. For Jenkins the ability to project oneself into the past and to know and to understand it from the perspective of that era proves exceedingly dubious. As Jenkins affirms, "the possibility of the historian being able to slough off his present to reach someone else's past on their terms looks remote."[11] Ultimately, Jenkins's concerns remain less with issues of definition and more with empathy's impractical nature and dubious ideological function.

As these brief examples illustrate, argument over the meaning, purpose, and practicality of historical empathy remains, ambiguous, controversial, and problematic. In an attempt to clarify and address some of the issues, a careful re-evaluation of the concept based on many of the considerations offered in this book is warranted. Specifically, most of the contributing authors (and other scholars in the field) appear to associate historical empathy with the following six characteristics or components.

Historical Empathy Primarily Does Not Involve Imagination, Identification, or Sympathy

To reiterate and to further develop a point raised in chapter one, closer understanding of historical empathy may be derived from an appreciation of what it is *not*. To begin with, empathy should not be viewed solely as a process in which students of history "get behind the eyeballs" of people in the past and "identify" with historical characters.[12] No historian or student of history has the ability to embrace the persona of another from a different place in time. Moreover, identification with people in the past may prove an undesirable goal. As Gard and Lee provocatively inquire, "Do we really want children to identify with Hitler . . . or become emotionally involved with him?"[13] The question may, therefore, not be one of possibility but of desirability. Perhaps the greatest argument against the idea that empathy is mere "identification" derives from its incompatibility with the study of history; that is, it ignores the perspective of hindsight and is alien to the principle that historians are contemporary interpreters of past events.

Furthermore, historical empathy should not be confused with imagination. Textbook assignments commonly require students to imagine they were present in a bygone age (e.g., imagine you were on the Mayflower; imagine you were on the Oregon Trail). That view of historical empathy, however, leads to an irresponsible and erroneous understanding of our past. True history depends on cautious inquiry and close examination of available evidence. As P. J. Rogers argues, "History is 'no fancy free—let's imagine—let's pretend' exercise in 'making it up.'"[14] Inference and speculation play a role in helping historians explain gaps in the historical record, but empathy is not a process steeped in imagination.[15]

Finally, historical empathy is not directly related to the concept of sympathy or "feeling." For, although sympathy toward some historical characters (e.g., Holocaust victims, plantation slaves) is perhaps welcome in the history classroom, it is not the central purpose of history. Historical study, wherever possible, depends on a process of disciplined reasoning based upon available historical evidence. Unexamined emotional involvement with historical characters potentially endangers these important considerations. At its core historical inquiry remains primarily a cognitive, not an affective, act and one that is chiefly dependent upon knowledge, not feeling or imagination.[16]

Historical Empathy Involves Understanding People's Actions in the Past

A selected review of authors who have contributed to this book suggests a high degree of agreement of what historical empathy is and what historical empathy involves:

"Its [historical empathy's] achievement promises to allow us to assemble accounts of the past that get us as close as we might ever get to what life might have been 'back then.' It makes possible the reconstructions of past events in ways that helps us appreciate the significant differences between the present world and the world being described, while simultaneously bringing that word, theoretically, at least, much closer to us."

VanSledright, chapter 4

". . . [T]the ability to recognize some of the socio-cultural and politcal forces that shape human behavior, now and in the past . . . understanding why people acted the way they did in the past, not just *how* they acted"

Levstik, chapter 5

"Historians need to understand the way in which people in the past saw their world, at various times and places. They also need to understand why people took the actions they did . . . In the UK, understandings of this kind acquired the label 'empathy.'"

Lee and Ashby, chapter 3

Historical empathy, therefore, necessarily involves having students appreciate that the past was a very different place from the present and that careful attention to historical evidence and historical context offers students the possibility of understanding and appreciating why people in the past acted as they did. Employing Yeager and Doppen's focus on Harry Truman as a model, students in this example were not required to "get behind the eyeballs" of the president, nor were they asked to sympathize with his dilemma, or imagine they were the commander-in-chief. Rather, students were required to understand the events and circumstances that shaped his decision, appreciate the context in which he worked, and have knowledge of the consequences of his actions. Above all, students were required, using an assortment of historical evidence, to understand, explain, and evaluate why Truman decided to bomb Hiroshima and Nagasaki. Consequently, the student in chapter five who, after examining Truman's decision, concluded that her position had changed from "completely disliking the decision to disliking but understanding it" may be said to have achieved a degree of empathetic understanding.

As a stimulus to thoughtful empathetic inquiry some educators have argued the desirability of confronting students with a historical scenario which is puzzling or paradoxical to students living in today's world.[17] Chamberlain's decision to appease Hitler, or the Saxon use of "trial by ordeal" are good examples of situations which require students to explain and rationalize actions that might appear unnatural, irrational, or ill-considered to members of contemporary society. Without question, as Davis reminds us in chapter one of this book, children find the act of understanding the actions of people in a bygone era a very difficult proposition. Typically students, particularly, at a younger age, view our predecessors as morally, intellectually, and scientifically inferior and dismiss their actions as stupid or idiotic.[18] Further muddying the waters, Keith Jenkins asserts that any empathy exercise which asks students to commune with the past is futile. As a consequence, he easily dismisses the practice.[19]

Claims that historical empathy is unachievable, or at the very least extraordinarily difficult, for school age children warrants closer examination. To begin with, as Lee and Ashby note in chapter 3 a basic flaw in Jenkins's argument is that he views history as an all-or-nothing enterprise.[20] That is, historians either can absolutely embrace all the mores, values, perspectives, and ideas of a bygone age to fully appreciate and understand actions in the past, or they cannot. For Jenkins no middle ground exists. This narrow position surely is untenable. Clearly, some explanations of why people in the past acted as they did prove more defensible than others. Indeed, even though we may concede that knowing the past in an absolute sense perhaps is impossible, a chief objective for any historian is to examine, interpret, and utilize the available evidence to construct an explanatory paradigm. Unquestionably some historians are better able to do this than others. Accordingly, as Lee and Ashby assert, "As with all interesting or important knowledge claims, we often have better reason for accepting one story than another."[21]

The same is true for children engaged in empathy activities in the classroom. For, although many children do find empathetic inquiry difficult, a wealth of evidence also exists to show that significant numbers of students are indeed able to construct valid explanations of human actions in the past.[22] Furthermore, in chapter 7 Field adds greater richness to the debate by illustrating how many educators consistently have demonstrated the importance of engaging younger students in exercises calling for perspective taking, both in the present and in the past, and on many conceptual levels.

The important challenge for teachers of history undoubtedly is to provide learning environments in which students continually are encouraged to examine historical context and evidence in order to formulate defensible reasons for past actions and motives. To reiterate Shemilt, ultimately "empathetic construction of action and meaning amounts to the reduction of a puzzle, to the rendering of the strange and unintelligible down to the recognizable and comprehensible."[23] It is this ability that teachers of history should encourage and develop in their classrooms.

Historical Empathy Involves a Thorough Appreciation of Historical Context

All advocates of historical empathy agree that in order for students or historians to say anything meaningful about past events or actions a broad understanding of historical context is essential. For example, it would be unreasonable to ask students to reflect on Truman's decision to drop the atomic bomb without first inviting them to consider the timing of the event in relationship to the broader development of World War II, or without considering the perspectives of, and relationships with, the Soviet Union or Great Britain, or to the development of the Manhattan Project, or to Truman's recent ascendancy to the presidency, or to events at Potsdam, and so on. Riley's chapter on the use of empathy in Holocaust studies concurs. In chapter 8 Riley argues that teachers must guard against using the study of the Holocaust as a vehicle for social therapy, propaganda, or indoctrination by assuring that all students have a solid knowledge base on which to build new understandings.

Rogers refers to the development of sound contextual understandings as "enabling knowledge."[24] Central to this very important notion is the belief that students find extremely difficult the ability to appreciate and understand past actions without first (or simultaneously) developing a solid knowledge base of past events. Undoubtedly students who acquire relevant contextual understandings are better placed to understand why people in the past acted as they did. Moreover, these students will be better able to understand how someone in the past might interpret documents, reports, or information relevant to their age.[25]

In addition to developing an appreciation of historical context, students must also utilize the benefit of hindsight. As members of contemporary society we have, to some degree at least, the luxury of knowing the consequences of events (e.g., the decision to drop the atomic bomb). Indeed, Chaffer and Taylor argue that one of the primary purposes of historical study is "to understand people in the past better than they understood themselves."[26] In other words, historians should not try to escape their position in the present in an attempt to acquire the intellectual and social perspectives of the past. Rather, historians and students of history should use their unique contemporary perspective (and all the information available to them) to better understand past actions and events.

A final assertion also appears appropriate here. The requirement that students develop a solid basis in historical knowledge flies in the face of conservative critics who claim that tasks associated with historical empathy lack rigor and intellectual merit. To the contrary, as the authors in this book consistently have demonstrated, sophisticated historical empathy can only be accomplished through a thorough understanding of context, consequence, and historical evidence. Exercises in historical empathy should never be reduced to some fanciful excursion of imagination and pretense. Instead, historical empathy demands intellectual rigor, careful thought and analysis, and studious attention to human thoughts and actions that initially may appear incomprehensible and perplexing.

Historical Empathy Requires Multiple Forms of Evidence and Perspective

The success of any classroom exercise in historical empathy often is dependent upon the nature and quality of the sources that students encounter. Yeager and Doppen's chapter 6 bears striking testimony to this point. Essentially, they note how students who used only narrow textbook interpretations to understand Truman's decision often arrived at shallow and ill-informed conclusions. In contrast, when students were presented with multiple forms of evidence their reasoning became more sophisticated, more considered, and more astute. Riley's extensive attention to the quality and variety of historical evidence associated with teaching the Holocaust also is centered on the belief that "the selection of instructional material [historical evidence] determines to a significant extent the historical understandings a student acquires."[27]

Ideally, students should be encouraged to use a rich variety of sources drawn from different vantage points (e.g., the memoirs of the historical actor, critiques of historians, eye-witness accounts, primary documentation). In addition, the evidence also should include competing accounts and different perspectives on the reasons for human action. Historical empathy requires students to sort through evidence and to entertain some complex thinking in order to arrive at logical and defensible reasons for past actions. Historical empathy becomes problematic when students are offered only limited and/or narrow perspectives. For example, in chapter 4 VanSledright points out an essential difficulty that Lynn encounters in her reading of Howard Zinn's account of Indian removal in the 1830s: that is, she lacks multiple perspectives on the event. Lynn makes no attempt, for example, to understand Jackson's viewpoint and considers no other explanation of the events than Zinn's historical interpretation. Moreover, by her own admission, Lynn lacks sufficient understanding of the period and is therefore devoid of the type of contextual knowledge required to appreciate events in any meaningful sense. Lynn's understanding of Indian removal (though not necessarily her opinion of the event) undoubtedly would prove more complete had she considered the socio-cultural context of the age and entertained sources from alternative perspectives. The challenge for history teachers, therefore, is to encourage students to examine multiple and diverse perspectives before arriving at firm conclusions.

Historical Empathy Requires Students to Examine Their Own Perspectives

The contributions of Levstik (chapter 5) and VanSledright (chapter 4) are important for making us aware that all human beings are both products and victims of their own received culture. Levstik's attention to the viewpoints of children in schools in New Zealand is particularly powerful in that it demonstrates how individuals from different cultures typically acquire socio-cultural perspectives derived from their location (geographic or otherwise) in the world. VanSledright extends the argument by emphasizing that individual human judgments are constructed out of one's temporal and cultural "positionality."

The implications for engaging students in exercises of historical empathy obviously are profound. Most notably, the challenge for teachers is to have students appreciate that their view of the past (or present) is determined by many factors, including their national perspective, their education, their access to knowledge, their upbringing, their language, and their belief systems. VanSledright properly urges students to consider and examine (with other students) the assumptions that they make about historical evidence or actions before jumping to ill-conceived conclusions. Indeed, the very idea that history provides a powerful vehicle through which one's beliefs may be examined proves a particularly strong justification for teaching and learning history in schools.

By extension, students also must be aware that one's opinions and perspectives often are fashioned by the twist that historians give to events and to actions in the past. As E. H. Carr rightly argues, historians are not neutral beings and historical "facts" are subject to interpretation and manipulation:

> The facts are really not at all like fish on a fishmonger's slab. They are like fish swimming about in a vast and sometimes inaccessible ocean; and what the historian catches will depend, partly on chance, but mainly on what part of the ocean he chooses to fish in and what tackle he chooses to use—the two factors being, of course, determined by the kind of fish that he wants to catch. By and large, the historian will get the kind of facts he wants.[28]

Taking Carr's assertion seriously demands that students be encouraged to examine historical evidence critically and skeptically. Certainly, young people should learn not to accept historical evidence at face value but rather to ask questions of sources, process that requires not only an understanding of one's own positionality but also, as VanSledright suggests, the positionalities of those who author historical sources.

Historical Empathy Encourages Well-Grounded But Tentative Conclusions

Although students should be encouraged to use historical evidence to construct rational explanations for human actions, they should also be aware that history is not a scientific process. No absolute rules govern the actions of humans in the past. Different individuals, given very similar circumstances, might act in very different ways. For example, Winston Churchill's policy toward Hitler in 1938 likely would have been very different from that followed by Prime Minister Neville Chamberlain. Students must understand that the complexity of any individual's personality, background, circumstance, character, and beliefs seriously affect how that person might act.

Developed understandings of historical empathy also encourage students to appreciate that any claims to past knowledge may be, at best, only tentative. A promising aspect of the students in Yeager and Doppen's study (chapter 6) was that they increasingly understood the fragile nature of historical evidence and the tentativeness of conclusions. As one perceptive teenager wrote, "the *truth* is what people allow themselves to see."

In the final analysis, historical empathy lies at the core of historical inquiry. Essentially it requires students to examine, appreciate, and understand the perspectives of people in the past and to render them intelligible to contemporary minds. Consequently, empathy requires a firm understanding of historical context, evidence, and hindsight. Furthermore, it demands an element of self-examination, introspection, skepticism, and doubt. Ultimately, to paraphrase E. H. Carr, historical empathy demands a continuous interaction between the student and his evidence, an unending dialogue between the past and present.[29]

Historical Empathy in Practice

Translating historical empathy into meaningful classroom practice involves a variety of issues. Outlined here are some of the major considerations that we urge teachers of history to attend to in order to stimulate empathic understandings in the classroom.

First, empathy exercises work well when focused on a puzzling or paradoxical situation in the past. This type of focus serves both the purpose of distinguishing the period from the present and initiating curiosity among students. For example, as I have written elsewhere, most US history textbooks consider Chamberlain's policy of "appeasement" toward Hitler to be one of abject failure.[30] Understandably, therefore, students often are quick to ask how the prime minister could have followed such a seemingly foolish policy. A useful practice is for teachers to frame the central issue in terms of a question and to display the question prominently in the classroom, thus providing a permanent focus of inquiry (e.g., Why did Chamberlain "appease" Hitler? Why did Truman decide to drop the atomic bomb? Why did Martin Luther King adopt a policy of nonviolent protest?). Once this question is decided upon, it is then helpful to have students write down and share their initial opinions and suppositions. In this way not only are students' initial biases and assumptions aired, but also the comments provide a useful point of comparison at the end of the historical inquiry exercise.

Second, students must acquire some knowledge of historical context and chronology before comprehensively delving into the chosen issue. Naturally, students' prior knowledge will vary from class to class and teachers will obviously take this into consideration. To consider Chamberlain's policy, for example, students will need to acquire a basic appreciation of the main social, political, and economic effects of World War I, the terms of the Treaty of Versailles and international reactions to it, the key events in Hitler's rise to power, Hitler's foreign policy in the 1930s, the reasons why many of the world's powers pursued a policy of isolation or a search for peace in the 1920s and 1930s, and a rudimentary understanding of Chamberlain's character, background, and beliefs. Students should also reap the benefit of hindsight and appreciate the historical consequences of Chamberlain's actions. Teachers must be aware, however, that swamping students with too much information at this initial stage might prove counter-productive.[31] Indeed, throughout the inquiry process (not just at the beginning) students should continually be encouraged to build upon, and ask questions of, their initial contextual understandings. Finally, essential to the success of the process is that teachers avoid conveying contextual information solely in a didactic manner. Breaking students into research teams to focus on a particular element of context and requiring them to report back to the whole class (e.g., group one produces an annotated time line of Hitler's foreign policy, group two produces a one-page biography of Neville Chamberlain, and so on) often proves an effective way of actively engaging students in building a suitable context.

Third, students should be introduced to a wide range of primary and secondary sources. How many sources naturally will depend on the maturity, reading age, and ability of students. In secondary classrooms, however, students typically are able to build initial understandings from two to three dozen sources. The extent to which teachers should provide sources and even edit sources is subject to debate. Certainly, teachers are advised to provide several historical sources as a point of departure. Furthermore, if treated with a sensitivity toward the original meanings, teachers might edit sources and provide glossaries to advance students' understandings (this is especially true of texts written a long time ago). Nevertheless, with so much historical information now available on the World Wide Web, on CD-ROMs, in libraries, and in school media centers, students should be encouraged to search for evidence on their own.

Fourth, students continuously must be encouraged to ask critical questions of sources. Importantly, students of all ages should understand the risks of taking any source at face value. They should be aware that sources have authors and that these authors typically have agendas. Basic historical questions such as, Who wrote the source? When? Why? Is it corroborated by other sources? What was the perspective of the author? and so on should be encouraged in all classroom deliberations.

Fifth, teachers should scaffold and develop students' learning so that they learn to ask more complex and thought-provoking questions as the inquiry progresses. Once some contextual information is acquired, teachers can begin with simple assignments. For example, students may be required to examine in small groups a selection of sources and decide (a) which sources support Chamberlain's policy, (b) which sources are critical of it, and (c) which sources are inconclusive or difficult to categorize. Leading a whole class discussion, teachers might then discuss with students why groups made their selections. Close attention should be paid to the reliability of sources, the extent to which sources corroborate one another, and the reasons behind competing viewpoints. The next stage might be to ask students to look for more sources or search independently for additional evidence to explain Chamberlain's decision. Again, after each stage of student inquiry the essential importance of a plenary session in which teachers probe initial understandings and invite students to share and defend their thoughts and findings cannot be overstated.

Students also should be encouraged to ask questions of themselves when examining historical documents. Fundamentally, students should ask what assumptions or biases influence their understanding of a particular source or action. For example, most students have not experienced first-hand the horrors of war. Chamberlain, however, did indeed experience these horrors; thus, an abiding desire of the prime minister was to avoid another war at all costs. The extent to which students can appreciate Chamberlain's passionate desire from their contemporary perspective is subject to debate. Certainly, this issue, and other similar issues, warrant careful deliberation in the history classroom.

Sixth, students should be encouraged to identify and to explain which sources are most useful in helping contemporaries understand why Chamberlain followed a policy of appeasement. That accomplished, teachers should require students to use this evidence to produce a narrative account of why Chamberlain "appeased" Hitler in the fall of 1938. Requiring each student to write a narrative account is an important, if difficult, final assignment for young people. Fundamentally, this requires students to marshal available evidence in order to construct an explanatory account out of past action—the ultimate task of any historian.

Engagement with such a task demands that students appreciate the role that language and interpretation play in historical narratives. Moreover, it educates students on the importance of accurate referencing and evidence corroboration. Admittedly, some students will find this task problematic without guidance. A way to make the task more accessible is to have students work in small groups to discuss and select, say, the five most useful pieces of evidence which help to explain Chamberlain's policy. Individual students could then take each piece of evidence separately and look for associations with other sources before building a more comprehensive account. Furthermore, in keeping with the assignment that Yeager and Doppen describe in chapter 6, small groups might also create presentations or displays for whole class discussion. Ultimately, however, more powerful understandings are reached if students work individually on their narrative accounts.

Seventh, students always should be aware that final conclusions are at best only tentative, and that historians (and classroom peers) will disagree on their interpretation of the past. Healthy discussions should follow which address why this is the case. Central to this discussion should be deliberations about the availability and reliability of evidence, how contemporary perspectives and "presentism" may distort understandings of the past, and how new and emerging evidence might influence previous assertions about the past.

Finally, as seasoned teachers will recognize, engaging students in meaningful empathy inquiry requires considerable classroom time, energy, and resources. Teachers have to arrive at the difficult balance between providing students with structure and resources while at the same time allowing time for independent thought and group deliberation. The role of the teacher in selecting appropriate materials, asking probing questions, stimulating thoughtful investigation, leading whole-class discussion, and maintaining the momentum of inquiry is undoubtedly central to the success of any classroom assignment involving historical empathy.[32]

In the final analysis, engaging students in inquiries which require them to understand the actions of people in the past offers the potential for extremely powerful classroom learning opportunities. Indeed, sensitive introduction of historical empathy ensures that active participation, critical inquiry, and considered self-reflection remain at the heart of good classroom practice. Moreover, by developing students' capacity to appreciate perspectives and entertain opinions very different from their own, invaluable experiences are provided to young people that are particularly beneficial for living in pluralistic contemporary societies. Many compelling reasons, therefore, warrant the introduction of historical empathy in school settings. Our ultimate hope is that this book goes some way toward clarifying the challenges and issues involved in the teaching of historical empathy, and that it encourages more teachers and students to take their first steps on what assuredly will be an exciting and worthwhile journey.

Notes

1. P. Knight, "Empathy: Concept, Confusion, and Consequences in a National Curriculum," *Oxford Review of Education* 15 (1989): 43.

2. A. P. Goldstein and C. Michaels, *Empathy: Developmental Training and Consequences* (Hillsdale N. J.: Lawrence Erlbaum Associates, 1985).

3. P. Knight, "Empathy: Concept, Confusion, and Consequences in a National Curriculum," 44.

4. D. Shemilt, "Adolescent Ideas about Evidence and Methodology in History," in C. Portal, ed., *The History Curriculum for Teachers* (London: Falmer Press, 1987), 44.

5. H. Cooper, *The Teaching of History: Studies in Primary Education* (London: David Fulton Publishers).

6. P. Knight, "Empathy: Concept, Confusion, and Consequences in a National Curriculum," 46.

7. R. Skidelsky cited in K. Jenkins, "The Empathy Exercise," *Times Educational Supplement*, May 13, 1988: A24.

8. M. Thatcher, *The Downing Street Years* (New York: HarperCollins, 1993), 596. For a detailed discussion of empathy and politics in England during the 1980, see R. Phillips, *History Teaching, Nationhood and the State: A Study in Educational Politics* (London: Cassell, 1998) 20-21, 38-52. For an extended conceptual discussion of empathy, see D. Shemilt, "Beauty and the Philosopher: Empathy in History and Classroom," in A. Dickinson, P. Lee, and P. J. Rogers, eds., *Learning History* (London: Heinemann, 1984).

9. See, for example, L. V. Cheney, "The End of History," *The Historian* 51 (1995): 454-456; R. E. Dunn, "On World History Standards," *The Historian* 51 (1995): 459-464; S. J. Foster, "Politics, Parallels, and Perennial Curriculum Questions: The Battle Over School History in England and the United States," *The Curriculum Journal* 9 (1998): 153-165; G. B. Nash, "On U. S. History Standards," *The Historian* 51 (1995): 457-459; D. W. Saxe, "The National History Standards: Time for Common Sense," *Social Education* 60 (1996): 44-48.

10. K. Jenkins, *Re-thinking History* (London: Routledge, 1991).

11. K. Jenkins, *Re-thinking History*, 40.

12. E. W. Reed, "For Better Elementary Teaching: Methods Old and New," in P. Gagnon, ed., *Historical Literacy: The Case for History in American Education* (Boston: Houghton Mifflin, 1991), 305.

13. A. Gard and P. Lee, "Educational Objectives for the Study of History Reconsidered," in A. Dickinson and P. Lee, eds., *History Teaching and Historical Understanding* (London: Heinemann, 1978), 32.

14. P. J. Rogers, "History: Why? What? and How?" *Teaching of History Series* 60 (London: Historical Association, 1991), 35.

15. C. Portal "Empathy as an Objective for History Teaching," in C. Portal, ed., *The History Curriculum for Teachers*, 87; P. Seixas, "Conceptualizing the Growth of Historical Understanding," in D. R. Olson and N. Torrance, *The Handbook of Education and Human Development* (Cambridge, Mass.: Blackwell, 1996), 774.

16. P. J. Rogers, "History: Why? What? and How?" 35.

17. S. J. Foster, "Using Historical Empathy to Excite Students About the Study of History: Can You Empathize with Neville Chamberlain?" *The Social Studies* 90 (1998): 18; C. Portal, "Empathy as an Objective for History Teaching," 93.

18. See for example, R. Ashby and P. Lee, "Children's Concepts of Empathy and Understanding in History," in C. Portal, ed., *The History Curriculum for Teachers*, 62-89; K. Barton, "Narrative Simplifications in Elementary Students' Historical Thinking," in J. Brophy, ed., *Advances in Research on Teaching Volume 6: Teaching and Learning History* (Greenwich: JAI Press, 1996), 51-83; S. J. Foster, J. D. Hoge, and R. H. Rosch, "Thinking Aloud About History: Children's and Adolescents' Responses to Historical Photographs" *Theory and Research in Social Education* 27 (1999): 179-214.

19. K. Jenkins, *Re-thinking History*, 39-47.

20. See also, P. Seixas, "Conceptualizing the Growth of Historical Understanding," 775.

21. R. Ashby and P. Lee, chapter 3.

22. See for example, R. Ashby and P. Lee, "Children's Concepts of Empathy and Understanding in History," 62-89; H. Cooper, "Children's Learning, Key Stage 2: Recent Findings," in M. Booth, H. Moniot, and K. Pellens, eds., *Communications of the International Society for Didactics* 16 (1995), 55; H. Cooper, "The Teaching of History"; M. Booth, "Students' Historical Thinking and the National History Curriculum in England," *Theory and Research in Social Education* 21 (1993): 105-127; M. Booth, "A Modern World History Course and the Thinking of Adolescent Pupils," *Educational Review* 32 (1980): 245-257; A. Dickinson and P. Lee, "Investigating Progression in Children's Ideas About History," in M. Booth, H. Moniot, and K. Pellens, eds., *Communications of the International Society for Didactics* 16 (1995), 37-47; A. Dickinson, P. Lee, and P. J. Rogers, eds., *Learning History*; D. Shemilt, *Schools Council History 13-16 Project: Evaluation Study* (Edinburgh: Holmes, McDougall, 1980); P. Knight, "A Study of Teaching and Children's Understanding of People in the Past," *Research in Education* 44 (1990): 39-53; R. Ashby and P. Lee, "Children's Concepts of Empathy and Understanding in History," 80-85.

23. D. Shemilt, "Adolescent Ideas about Evidence and Methodology in History," in C. Portal, ed., *The History Curriculum for Teachers*, 44.

24. P. J. Rogers, "History: Why? What? and How?" 34-38.

25. D. Shemilt, "Adolescent Ideas about Evidence and Methodology in History," in C. Portal, ed., *The History Curriculum for Teachers*, 59.

26. J. Chaffer and L. Taylor, *History and the History Teacher* (London: Unwin, 1977), 37.

27. K. Riley, chapter 8.

28. E. H. Carr, *What is History?* (London: Penguin Books, 1976), 23.

29. E. H. Carr, *What is History?* 30.

30. S. J. Foster, "Using Historical Empathy to Excite Students About the Study of History," 18-24.

31. D. Shemilt, "Adolescent Ideas about Evidence and Methodology in History," in C. Portal, ed., *The History Curriculum for Teachers*, 60.

32. See for example, E. A. Yeager, S. J. Foster, S. D. Maley, T. Anderson, J. W. Morris, "Why People in the Past Acted As They Did: An Exploratory Study in Historical Empathy," *The International Journal of Social Education* 13 (1998): 8-25; K. L. Riley, "Historical Empathy and the Holocaust: Theory Into Practice," *The International Journal of Social*

Education 13 (1998): 32-43; M. Booth et al., *Empathy in History: From Definition to Assessment* (Eastleigh, UK: Southern Regional Examination Board, 1986); R. Ashby and P. Lee, "Children's Concepts of Empathy and Understanding in History," 62-89; C. Sansom, "Concepts, Skills and Content: A Developmental Approach to the History Syllabus," in C. Portal, ed., *The History Curriculum for Teachers*, 116-142; J. Brophy and B. VanSledright, *Teaching and Learning History in Elementary Schools* (New York: Teachers College Press, 1997); L. Levstik and K. Barton, *Doing History: Investigating With Children in Elementary and Middle Schools* (Mahwah, N.J.: Lawrence Erlbaum, 1997).

Index

About the Contributors

Rosalyn Ashby is course tutor for the MA and PGCE courses in History in Education in the Curriculum Studies Group, University of London Institute of Education. Her research interests include assessment in history and students' understanding of history. Currently, she is completing her Ph.D. degree on children's understanding of evidence in history. She has strong academic links with researchers in the United States and Canada, Europe, and Taiwan. Rosalyn has worked as a teacher, an LEA adviser and Project Officer for the Cambridge History Project, and later was Research Officer for Project CHATA. Previous publications include "Children's Concepts of Empathy and Understanding" (with P. J. Lee), in C. Portal (ed.), *History in the Curriculum* (1987).

O. L. Davis Jr., Catherine Mae Parker Centennial Professor of Education and professor of curriculum and instruction, the University of Texas at Austin, has served as president of the Association for Supervision and Curriculum Development; Kappa Delta Pi, international honor society in education; Society for the Study of Curriculum History; and the American Association for Teaching and Curriculum; and was vice-president (for Division B: Curriculum Studies), American Educational Research Association. He received the first Citation for Exemplary Research in Social Studies Education awarded by the National Council for the Social Studies (NCSS), was named a Laureate by Kappa Delta Pi, and received the Distinguished Career Research Award from NCSS and the Lifetime Achievement Award for Outstanding Contributions to Curriculum Studies from the American Educational Research Association. Author or co-author of numerous research reports, essays, and books, his most recent book, *Bending the Future to Their Will: Civic Women, Social Education, and Democracy* (1999), was co-edited with Margaret Crocco. He currently edits the *Journal of Curriculum and Supervision*.

Frans H. Doppen is assistant professor and teaches history at the P. K. Yonge Development Research School, College of Education, University of Florida. He has sixteen years of experience in Florida public schools and has taught a variety of social studies courses. Currently, he is pursuing a Ph.D. degree in social studies education at the University of Florida.

Sherry L. Field is associate professor of social science education at the University of Georgia. She is editor of *Social Studies & the Young Learner*, a member of the Executive Board of the College and University Faculty Assembly of the National Council for the Social Studies, and past chair of the American Educational Research Association's Research in Social Studies Special Interest Group (SIG) and Text and Textbooks SIG. She is past president of the Society for the Study of Curriculum History and serves on the Publications Committees of Kappa Delta Pi and National Council for the Social Studies. Advisory board memberships include the Harvard Children's Democracy Project and the American Promise curriculum project. Her research interests include foundations and history of social studies, and elementary social studies teaching, learning, and curriculum.

Stuart J. Foster is associate professor of social science education, the University of Georgia. After ten years as a teacher and department head in UK secondary schools, he completed his Ph.D. degree in curriculum and instruction at the University of Texas at Austin. His research interests include the teaching and learning of history in public schools, curriculum and educational history, and comparative education. Research studies on the teaching and learning of history have appeared in journals including *Theory and Research in Social Education, Journal of Curriculum and Supervision, International Journal of Social Education, The Educational Forum, Education and Culture, The Social Studies,* and *Social Education.* His most recent book, *Red Alert! Educators Confront the Red Scare in American Public Schools, 1947-1954* (2000), examines the impact of the "McCarthy era" on American public education.

Peter Lee is professor of education at the University of London Institute of Education. He also has responsibility for research in the Institute's History Education Unit. His interests include the philosophy of history and research into students' understanding of history. He has directed both curriculum development and research projects (the Cambridge History Project and Project CHATA) and was UK national coordinator for the Youth and History Project. His research activities continue and involve links with Taiwan and in Europe as well as with the United States and Canada. His publications include *History Teaching and Historical Understanding* and *Learning History* as well as numerous research papers. He is a founder-editor of the *International Review of History Education.*

Linda S. Levstik is professor of social studies and humanities education at the University of Kentucky. Her research focuses on the development of historical reasoning in children and adolescents in national and cross-national contexts. She is coauthor of *Doing History: Investigating with Children in Elementary and Middle School* (with Keith C. Barton) and *An Integrated Language Perspective in the Elementary School* (with Christine Pappas and Barbara Kiefer); she is currently working on *Committing Acts of History* (with Keith C. Barton). Her work has appeared in numerous journals, including *AERJ, Teachers College Record, Theory* and *Research in Social Education, Social Education,* and the *Journal of Curriculum Studies,* and as book chapters in volumes on research in social education, gender in social education, and narrative/literature and social studies. Her most recent work includes research on New Zealand adolescents' construction of historical significance and adolescents' construction of the historical significance of women. She chaired the NCSS Task Force that responded to the U.S. History Standards and currently chairs the NAEP U.S. History Assessment Committee.

Karen L. Riley is assistant professor of education at Auburn University at Montgomery. She teaches courses in philosophical and historical foundations of American education, curriculum theory, and social studies education. She has published articles in *The Educational Forum, Education and Culture, Journal of the Midwest History of Education Society,* and *Insights.* Currently, she serves on three editorial boards, chairs the NCSS research committee, is a member of the Board of Directors of the American Association for Teaching and Curriculum, and is vice-president of the Midwest History of Education Society. She recently completed two curriculum guides for Kidsnet Television. Her first book, a history of three schools established within a U.S. World War II internment camp for children of enemy aliens, is forthcoming.

Bruce A. VanSledright is associate professor of curriculum and instruction, University of Maryland, College Park. He has served as a middle and high school history teacher and, for the past ten years, has conducted research on how children learn and teachers teach history. His work has appeared in numerous educational research journals and in the *Newsletter of the Organization of American Historians.* He is co-author (with Jere Brophy) of *Teaching and Learning History in Elementary Schools.* Recently, he spent a semester teaching American history to fifth graders in Maryland and currently is completing a book about the results of that experience.

Elizabeth Anne Yeager is associate professor of social studies education, University of Florida. During her doctoral studies at the University of Texas at Austin, she completed her dissertation on the life and work of Alice Miel while holding an AERA/Spencer Foundation doctoral fellowship. She received the Outstanding Dissertation Award in the area of curriculum from the Association for Supervision and Curriculum Development, AERA's Division B (Curriculum Studies), and the Society for the Study of Curriculum History; also, she was a finalist for the NCSS Outstanding Dissertation Award. Reports of her research have been published in several journals including *Theory and Research in Social Education, Journal of Curriculum and Supervision, International Journal of Social Education*, and *Social Education*.